Reading and Writing about Literature

A Portable Guide

Reading and Writing about Literature

A Portable Guide

Third Edition

JANET E. GARDNER

Bedford/St. Martin's BOSTON ◆ NEW YORK

For Bedford/St. Martin's

Executive Editor: Stephen A. Scipione
Developmental Editor: Deja Earley
Production Editor: Kendra LeFleur
Production Supervisor: Samuel Jones
Marketing Manager: Stacey Propps
Editorial Assistant: Regina Tavani
Production Assistant: Elise Keller
Copy Editor: Linda McLatchie
Indexer: Jake Kawatski
Permissions Manager: Kalina K. Ingham
Senior Art Director: Anna Palchik
Text Design: Sandra Rigney and Janis Owens
Cover Design: Donna Lee Dennison
Cover Photo: Rural France — The Lot © Ocean/Corbis
Composition: Jouve
Printing and Binding: RR Donnelley and Sons

President, Bedford/St. Martin's: Denise B. Wydra
Presidents, Macmillan Higher Education: Joan E. Feinberg and Tom Scotty
Editor in Chief: Karen S. Henry
Director of Marketing: Karen R. Soeltz
Director of Production: Susan W. Brown
Associate Director, Editorial Production: Elise S. Kaiser
Managing Editor: Elizabeth M. Schaaf

Library of Congress Control Number: 2012932570

Manufactured in the United States of America.

7   6   5   4   3   2
f   e   d   c   b   a

For information, write: Bedford/St. Martin's, 75 Arlington Street, Boston, MA 02116 (617-399-4000)

ISBN 978-1-4576-0649-6

Acknowledgments

Preface

Reading and Writing about Literature: A Portable Guide is designed to help students in literature classes master the sometimes daunting task of writing effective critical papers. Its flexible format makes it an ideal book to be used alongside individual literary texts or any anthology lacking substantial writing instruction. It grows out of my years in the classroom working with students from diverse backgrounds and with a variety of skill levels. The text is brief and accessible enough for students to read on their own, without taking too much vital time from the central task of reading and exploring literature. It presents reading, writing, research, and critical thinking as interrelated and mutually supporting skills.

The opening chapter introduces students to the value of reading literature and the unique "culture" of the literature classroom. The second chapter, on the role of good reading, shows students how to move beyond the basics of decoding and initial comprehension by emphasizing the interpretive nature of critical reading. Students are directed, through concrete examples and specific instructions, to take a more active approach to reading than many of them have taken in the past. The chapter encourages textual annotation, note taking, journal keeping, and, above all, the crucial practice of asking questions and approaching the act of reading literature as a collaborative process between author and reader. Students should come away from this chapter more confident that their ideas and responses are a valid and necessary part of understanding literature.

The subsequent chapters devoted specifically to writing instruction further integrate critical reading strategies as they cover the entire writing process from topic choice through proofreading and finalizing manuscript format. Substantial attention is paid to developing an original thesis and supporting that thesis with specific evidence from the primary text as well as other sources. Separate chapters address specific issues related to thinking and writing about short fiction, poetry, and drama, and students are also introduced to some of the most common sorts of writing assignments and several critical theories most useful to their examination of literary texts.

Throughout the book, critical thinking plays a central role, and nowhere is this more apparent than in Chapter 8, devoted to research. Here, the nuts and bolts of library research and MLA documentation are presented in the context of true research—the sort of critical search and synthesis that allows us to satisfy our own curiosity while contributing to the understanding of our readers. To help make these lessons more concrete to students, the book also includes a sampling of literary texts for analysis and several student papers modeling a variety of approaches and styles. Terms commonly used in literature classes appear in **boldface** throughout the text and are indexed and included in the glossary for ease of reference at the back of the book. My hope is that this brief guide will help students increase their understanding of literature and more fully appreciate the intellectual challenges and personal rewards inherent in taking responsibility for their own responses to their reading, in their literature class and beyond.

NEW TO THE THIRD EDITION

The third edition includes more brief examples of literature and specific responses to those examples. Several models of critical reading and writing have been added. For example, Chapter 2 now includes Emily Dickinson's "Because I could not stop for Death" and a student's annotations of the poem that raise questions about the text and point to possible writing topics. Chapter 4 now includes three new poems and features two new samples of student writing—a sample midterm essay exam that responds to the poems and a response paper on Jamaica Kincaid's "Girl." Also, the coverage of elements in each genre has been augmented, as has the treatment of revising and quoting. Chapter 8 has been updated to be more technologically relevant, and the discussion of each type of literary criticism in Chapter 9 is now punctuated with appropriate examples from relevant literary texts that appear in these pages.

ACKNOWLEDGMENTS

For their helpful responses to a questionnaire about their experiences using previous editions of the book, I am grateful to Stephen Adams, Westfield State University; Michael Bibby, Shippensburg University; Patricia Buchanan, Salem State University; Katherine Collin, Vanier College; Roberta Clipper, Rider University; Christina Nation Corriveau, California Lutheran University; Richard Erable, Franklin College; Rob

Franciosi, Grand Valley State University; Hank Galmish, Green River Community College; Kathryn Henkins, Mount San Antonio College; Tommie Jackson, St. Cloud State University; Michael Mahin, National University; Shannon Mrkich, West Chester University of Pennsylvania; Ryan Naughton, Ohio University; Deborah Schlacks, University of Wisconsin–Superior; and Meryl Siegal, Laney College.

I am, of course, deeply grateful to the many people who were instrumental in helping me with the creation of this book. Among the people at Bedford/St. Martin's who deserve special thanks are Joan Feinberg, Denise Wydra, Karen Henry, and Steve Scipione. Developmental editor Deja Earley helped shape this volume into the best pedagogical tool it could be, and editorial assistant Regina Tavani efficiently conducted the review program and kept things moving along. Production editor Kendra LeFleur kept the project running smoothly, coordinating a myriad of details. Joanne Diaz made indispensable contributions to the book. Special thanks to Sarah Curow, a fine writer and a precious friend, to Pat McCorkle for his editorial acumen and good humor, and above all to Dan Tritle for his unflagging support.

Janet E. Gardner

YOU GET MORE RESOURCES FOR *READING AND WRITING ABOUT LITERATURE*.

Reading and Writing about Literature doesn't stop with a book. Online, you'll find both free and affordable premium resources to help students get even more out of the book and your course. You'll also find convenient instructor resources and a nationwide community of teachers. To learn more about or order any of the products below, contact your Bedford/St. Martin's sales representative, e-mail sales support (sales_support@bfwpub.com), or visit the Web site at **bedfordstmartins .com/writingaboutlit/catalog**.

Reading and Writing about Literature now comes with videos.

Invite today's best writers into your classroom with *VideoCentral: Literature,* our growing library of more than fifty video interviews with today's writers, including Ha Jin on how he uses humor, Chitra Banerjee Divakaruni on how she writes from experience, and T. Coraghessan Boyle on how he works with language and style. Biographical notes and questions make each video an assignable module. See **bedfordstmartins .com/videolit/catalog** for a preview.

This resource can be packaged at a discount with new student editions of this book. An activation code is required and must be purchased. To order *VideoCentral: Literature* with this print text, use ISBN 978-1-4576-4137-4.

Visit *Re:Writing for Literature* bedfordstmartins.com/rewritinglit

Supplement your print text with our free and open resources for literature (no codes required) and flexible premium content.

Get free online help for your students. *Re:Writing for Literature* provides close reading help, reference materials, and support for working with sources.

- *VirtuaLit Tutorials* for close reading (fiction, poetry, and drama)
- *AuthorLinks* and biographies for 800 authors
- Glossary of literary terms
- MLA-style student papers
- Help for finding and citing sources, including access to Diana Hacker's *Research and Documentation Online*

Get teaching ideas you can use today.

Are you looking for professional resources for teaching literature and writing? How about some help with planning classroom activities?

TeachingCentral. We've gathered all of our print and online professional resources in one place. You'll find landmark reference works, sourcebooks on pedagogical issues, award-winning collections, and practical advice for the classroom—all free for instructors and available at **bedfordstmartins.com/teachingcentral**.

LitBits *Blog: Ideas for Teaching Literature and Creative Writing.* Our new *LitBits* blog—hosted by a growing team of instructors, poets, novelists, and scholars—offers a fresh, regularly updated collection of ideas and assignments. You'll find simple ways to teach with new media, excite your students with activities, and join an ongoing conversation about teaching. Go to **bedfordstmartins.com/litbits/catalog** and **bedfordstmartins.com/litbits**.

Brief Contents

Preface   v

1. Introduction to Reading and Writing about Literature   1
2. The Role of Good Reading   6
3. The Writing Process   21
4. Common Writing Assignments   51
5. Writing about Stories   72
6. Writing about Poems   96
7. Writing about Plays   111
8. Writing a Literary Research Paper   130
9. Literary Criticism and Literary Theory   166

Index of Terms   207

Contents

Preface   v

1. INTRODUCTION TO READING AND WRITING ABOUT LITERATURE   1

Why Read Literature?   2

Why Write about Literature?   3

What to Expect in a Literature Class   3

Literature and Enjoyment   5

2. THE ROLE OF GOOD READING   6

The Value of Rereading   6

Critical Reading   7

The Myth of "Hidden Meaning"   7

Active Reading   8

  Annotating   *8*

    EMILY DICKINSON, "Because I could not stop for Death"
    (Annotated Poem)   *10*

  Note Taking   *11*

  Journal Keeping   *12*

  Using Reference Materials   *13*

Asking Critical Questions of Literature   14

  Questions about the Text   *14*

    BEN JONSON, "On My First Son" (Annotated Poem)   *15*

  Questions about the Author   *15*

  Questions about the Cultural Context   *16*

  Questions about the Reader   *17*

  Checklist for Good Reading   **19**

3. THE WRITING PROCESS — 21

Prewriting — 21
Choosing a Topic — 21
Developing an Argument — 22
The Thesis — 23
Gathering Support for Your Thesis — 26
Organizing Your Paper — 27

Drafting the Paper — 29
Introductions, Conclusions, and Transitions — 29

Revising and Editing — 32
Global Revision — 32
Global Revision Checklist — 33
Local Revision — 34
Local Revision Checklist — 35
Final Editing and Proofreading — 35
Final Editing Checklist — 36

Peer Editing and Workshops — 38

Tips for Writing about Literature — 40

Using Quotations Effectively — 42
Adding to or Altering a Quotation — 43
Omitting Words from a Quotation — 44
Quotations within Quotations — 44
Quotation Marks with Other Punctuation — 44
Quoting from Stories — 45
Quoting from Poems — 46
Quoting from Plays — 47

Manuscript Form — 49

4. COMMON WRITING ASSIGNMENTS — 51

Summary — 51

Response — 53
JAMAICA KINCAID, *"Girl"* — 53
Tom Lyons, *"A Boy's View of 'Girl'"* — 55

Explication   56

   ROBERT HERRICK, "Upon Julia's Clothes"   57

     Jessica Barnes, "Poetry in Motion: Herrick's 'Upon Julia's Clothes'"   58

Analysis   59

   ROBERT BROWNING, "My Last Duchess"   60

     *Adam Walker, "Possessed by the Need for Possession: Browning's
'My Last Duchess'"*   62

Comparison and Contrast   63

   CHRISTINA ROSSETTI, "After Death"   64

     *Todd Bowen, "Speakers for the Dead: Narrators in 'My Last Duchess'
and 'After Death'"*   65

Essay Exams   66

   WILLIAM SHAKESPEARE, Sonnet 73   69

   ROBERT HERRICK, "To the Virgins, to Make Much of Time"   69

     Midterm Essay   71

5. WRITING ABOUT STORIES   72

Elements of Fiction   72

   Plot   72

   Character   72

   Point of View   73

   Setting   73

   Theme   74

   Symbolism   74

   Style   74

Stories for Analysis   75

   CHARLOTTE PERKINS GILMAN, "The Yellow Wallpaper"   75

   KATE CHOPIN, "The Story of an Hour" (Annotated Story)   89

   Questions on the Stories   92

   SAMPLE PAPER: An Essay That Compares and Contrasts   92

     Melanie Smith, "Good Husbands in Bad Marriages"   93

6. WRITING ABOUT POEMS 96

Elements of Poetry 96
The Speaker 96
The Listener 97
Imagery 97
Sound and Sense 98

Two Poems for Analysis 100
WILLIAM SHAKESPEARE, "Sonnet 116" (Annotated Poem) 101
Questions on the Poem 102
T. S. ELIOT, "The Love Song of J. Alfred Prufrock" (Annotated Poem) 102
Questions on the Poem 107
SAMPLE PAPER: An Explication 107
Patrick McCorkle, "Shakespeare Defines Love" 108

7. WRITING ABOUT PLAYS 111

Elements of Drama 111
Plot, Character, and Theme 111
Diction 111
Melody and Spectacle 112
Setting 112

How to Read a Play 113
Director's Questions for Play Analysis 114
SUSAN GLASPELL, "Trifles" 115
SAMPLE PAPER: An Analysis 126
Sarah Johnson, "Moral Ambiguity and Character Development in Trifles" 127

8. WRITING A LITERARY RESEARCH PAPER 130

Finding Sources 130
Online Indexes 131
Periodicals 133
Books 134
Interlibrary Loan 134
The Internet 134

Evaluating Sources   135

Working with Sources   136
   Quotations   *137*
   Paraphrases and Summaries   *137*
   Commentaries   *138*
   Keeping Track of Your Sources   *138*

Writing the Paper   139
   Refine Your Thesis   *139*
   Organize Your Evidence   *139*
   Start Your Draft   *139*
   Revise   *140*
   Edit and Proofread   *140*

Understanding and Avoiding Plagiarism   140

What to Document and What *Not* to Document   143

Documenting Sources: MLA Format   143
   In-Text Citations   *146*
   Preparing Your Works Cited List   *149*
   SAMPLE RESEARCH PAPER   *160*
      Jarrad S. Nunes, "Emily Dickinson's 'Because I could not stop
      for Death': Challenging Readers' Expectations"   *161*

9. LITERARY CRITICISM AND LITERARY THEORY   166
   Formalism and New Criticism   167

   Feminist and Gender Criticism   168

   Queer Theory   169

   Marxist Criticism   169

   Cultural Studies   170

   Postcolonial Criticism   171

   Historical Criticism and New Historicism   172

   Psychological Theories   173

Reader-Response Theories   174

Structuralism   176

Poststructuralism and Deconstruction   177

Glossary of Critical and Literary Terms   179

Index of Terms   207

CHAPTER 1

Introduction to Reading and Writing about Literature

"Nobody reads anymore."

"People don't know how to write."

"We're becoming a nation of illiterates."

Maybe you've heard laments like these. They have sounded through our culture for several years now, indeed for at least several decades. Proclamations on the sad lack of literacy in modern life have been widely reported, as in January 2008, when Apple Computer cofounder Steve Jobs predicted that Amazon's Kindle e-book reader was doomed to failure because "people don't read anymore." (Perhaps ironically, he said this in a room full of reporters and must have known that these writers were going to quote these words in print and that millions of people would read them.) If we take these warnings seriously, it would seem that modern culture and modern education are in big trouble.

But news of the death of literacy is premature. In fact, one can make a good case that reading and writing occupy a more central place in our day-to-day life than they have at any other point in history. We are bombarded all day long with written messages. Billboards, product packaging, Web sites, blogs, flyers, wikis, advertisements, restaurant menus, e-mails, text messages, social media updates—the list goes on and on. Even while watching TV, arguably the least literary of media, we are often given a reading task: think of the "crawl" of updates that appears at the bottom of the screen during newscasts, the captions that identify interview subjects, even the station logos in the corner of the screen. The average North American in the early twenty-first century encounters literally hundreds of written messages every day, and most of us have no particular problem reading these messages. Often we don't even notice that we are doing so.

In a similar vein, most of us spend more time writing than people have at any earlier point in history. The vast majority of jobs these days require some amount of writing. Sometimes this requirement is extensive, as when engineers write sophisticated reports on their projects, while some work-related writing is as simple as a daily e-mail to communicate with others on the job. Students, of course, take notes, complete home-work assignments, and write papers. Even in our leisure time, we are likely to update our social media, comment on a friend's blog post, send a text message, or write a note to a family member or friend.

If you were to keep a list of every single thing you read and wrote in a day (a list that would, of course, have to include an entry for the list you were writing), you might be surprised at how extensive that list was by the end of the day.

So, if literacy is alive and well in the modern world, why is a book like this one necessary? Why do colleges and universities offer, or even re-quire, literature classes? Don't we already know enough about reading and writing? Do we really need to learn how to read and write about lit-erature? The answer as to why people *do* need to learn these skills is that imaginative literature is different from most of the other writing we read every day, and reading and writing about literature requires, and builds, a very different set of skills than those we bring to a Wikipedia article or a Facebook posting.

WHY READ LITERATURE?

Let's take a moment to reflect on why we read literature. Of course, there is no single or simple answer. People read to be informed, to be enter-tained, to be exposed to new ideas, or to have familiar concepts re-inforced. Often, people read just to enjoy a good story or to get a glimpse of how other people think and feel. But literature does much more than give us a compelling plot or a look into an author's thoughts and emo-tions—although at its best it does these things as well. Literature ex-plores the larger world and the ways in which people interact with that world and with one another. So even when what we read is entirely fic-tional, we nevertheless learn about real life. And, indeed, by affecting our thoughts and feelings, literature can indirectly affect our actions as well. Thus literature not only reflects but even helps to shape our world.

Literature, then, is not merely informational, like so much of the read-ing we do in our everyday lives. It does not stand up well to haste, dis-tractions, or multitasking. It is not meant to be browsed, skimmed, or linked away from as we search for particular facts or knowledge as effi-ciently as possible. Instead, it is designed for sustained reading, meaning that to do it justice we need to read it from beginning to end and pay it our full attention for all that time. What is most important in literature is rarely highlighted for us. Rather, we must use our intelligence to figure out the significance the literature holds for us, and we must realize that this significance may be different for a different reader. Because of this, reading literature helps us develop the skills of introspection, sustained attention, and deep analysis, skills that can help us in other areas of our lives as well.

WHY WRITE ABOUT LITERATURE?

Even students who enjoy reading poems, stories, or plays do not always enjoy writing about them. Some claim that having to analyze literature kills the fun they find in a good story. For others, the task of writing about literature can seem intimidating, frustrating, or just plain dull. If you share any of these prejudices, try to put them aside while we consider the value of writing about literature.

Writing about literature requires a special set of knowledge and skills. When you write about a story, a poem, or a play, you need to be particularly attentive to language, the medium of literature. This hones both analytical ability and creativity. In this sort of writing, you also need to pay close attention to your own use of language—just as you must pay attention to the language of the story, poem, or play—and doing so may have ripple effects that improve all your writing. Writing about literature, then, can help make you more thoughtful and articulate, better able to make yourself heard and understood, and obviously those are qualities that can improve your life well beyond the bounds of your literature classroom. And, far from killing the enjoyment of reading, writing about literature can increase that enjoyment and provide a sense of accomplishment as you look at the well-crafted paper you've written.

Writing about literature also has real-world usefulness. By forcing us to organize our thoughts and state clearly what we think, writing an essay helps us clarify what we know and believe. It gives us a chance to affect the thinking of our readers. Even more important, we actually learn as we write. In the process of writing, we often make new discoveries and forge new connections between ideas. We find and work through contradictions in our thinking, and we create whole new lines of thought as we work to make linear sense out of an often chaotic jumble of impressions. So, while *reading* literature can teach us much about the world, *writing* about literature often teaches us about ourselves.

WHAT TO EXPECT IN A LITERATURE CLASS

Every classroom, like every group of people in any setting, is its own unique world, with its own set of expectations and social interactions. However, there are certain features common to most literature classes, what might be considered the culture of a college or university literature class.

Unlike some other classes on campus, a literature class is not the sort of class where attendance is optional as long as you master the material and are able to pass the tests. Though your class may have a lecture component, it will almost certainly have a large discussion component as well, a give-and-take between students and instructor regarding the stories, poems, and plays you have read. In some ways, these discussions are the most important part of a literature class, and no amount of extra study on your own or sharing notes with a classmate can make up for having missed class. To follow these discussions, let alone to participate, you obviously will have to complete the reading. Whether or not your class has a stated attendance policy, to do well you need to be there and to be caught up with all reading and writing assignments. Participation is important.

Discussions in literature classes are usually interesting, because no two people come away from a particular literary text with exactly the same impressions. You may dislike a particular story and be surprised to discover that most of your fellow students loved it. A poem may leave you smiling while it makes one of your classmates cry. A character's motivation might seem obvious to you but baffle someone else. These differences arise because each reader is distinctive. Because you have lived a unique life, you have a knowledge of the world that is slightly different from any other reader's. You bring this personal history and knowledge to your reading, along with your own mind and temperament, your own likes and dislikes, and even all the knowledge gained from your past reading. Differing opinions are valid in literature classes, and each reader is in a position to enrich the conversation by speaking up in class.

Just as speaking up is part of participating, so too is attentive listening. While it is fair to regard your take on a piece of literature as valid, that doesn't mean you need only consider your own opinions. Listening to what your instructor and classmates have to say is equally important, especially when they disagree with you. If your position has value, so do theirs. Perhaps they have seen something you missed, or perhaps they consider crucial something that you had dismissed as unimportant. You may find your first impressions shifting during these discussions, or you may find them solidifying. Either of these outcomes is a good sign that you're learning. The most important thing you bring to a literary discussion is a willingness to share your own perspectives while remaining open to the possibility of learning from others.

Attentive listeners tend to make the best note takers, and having good class notes will prove incredibly helpful when you sit down to write your papers. This important skill will be covered in the next chapter.

LITERATURE AND ENJOYMENT

You may have noticed that little has been said so far about the idea that reading and writing about literature can also be fun. Some students really enjoy reading imaginative literature and writing papers about it. If you're in that group, you're lucky; your literature class will be fun and interesting for you, and—not incidentally—you'll probably do good work in the course. If you've never been fond of reading and writing about literature, though, you might spend a little time thinking about why some of your classmates enjoy this sort of work as well as what you might do to increase your own enjoyment of literature and investment in the writing process. You'll be happier and write better papers if you can put aside any previous negative experiences with literature and writing you may have had and approach your task with a positive mind-set. As you are introduced to new authors, new characters and settings, and new ideas, your literature class may surprise you. It could even end up being a favorite.

CHAPTER 2

The Role of Good Reading

Writing about literature begins, of course, with reading, so it stands to reason that good reading is the first step toward successful writing. But what exactly is "good reading"? Good reading is, generally speaking, not fast reading. In fact, often the best advice a student can receive about reading is to *slow down*. Reading well is all about paying attention, and you can't pay attention if you're text-messaging a friend as you read or racing to get through an assignment and move on to "more important" things. If you make a point of giving yourself plenty of time and minimizing your distractions, you'll get more out of your reading and probably enjoy it more as well.

THE VALUE OF REREADING

The best reading is often rereading, and the best readers are those who are willing to go back and reread a piece of literature again and again. It is not uncommon for professional literary critics—who are, after all, some of the most skilled readers—to read a particular poem, story, or play literally dozens of times before they feel equipped to write about it. And well-written literature rewards this willingness to reread, allowing readers to continue seeing new things with each reading. If you have a favorite book you return to over and over, or a favorite song you like to listen to again and again, you intuitively understand this truth. Realistically, of course, you will not have the time to read every assigned piece many times before discussing it in class or preparing to write about it, but you should not give up or feel frustrated if you fail to "get" a piece of literature on the first reading. Be prepared to go back and reread key sections, or even a whole work, if doing so could help with your understanding.

CRITICAL READING

The sort of reading that works best with imaginative literature—or any other complex writing—is sometimes called "active reading" or "critical reading," though *critical* here implies not fault-finding but rather thoughtful consideration. Much of the reading we do in everyday life is passive and noncritical. We glance at street signs to see where we are; we check a sports Web site to find out how our favorite team is doing; we read packages for information about the products we use. And in general, we take in all this information passively, without questioning it or looking for deeper meaning. For many kinds of reading, this is perfectly appropriate. It would hardly make sense to ask, *"Why* is this Pine Street?" or "What do they *mean* when they say there are twelve ounces of soda in this can?" There is, however, another type of reading, one that involves asking critical questions and probing more deeply into the meaning of what we read, and this is the kind of reading most appropriate to imaginative literature (especially if we intend to discuss or write about that literature later).

THE MYTH OF "HIDDEN MEANING"

There is a persistent myth in literature classes that the purpose of reading is to scour a text for "hidden meaning." Do not be taken in by this myth. In fact, many instructors dislike the phrase *hidden meaning*, which has unpleasant and inaccurate connotations. First, it suggests a sort of willful subterfuge on the part of the author, a deliberate attempt to make his or her work difficult to understand or to exclude the reader. Second, it makes the process of reading sound like digging for buried treasure rather than a systematic intellectual process. Finally, the phrase implies that a text has a single, true meaning and that communication and understanding move in one direction only: from the crafty author to the searching reader.

In truth, the meanings in literary texts are not hidden, and your job as a reader is not to root around for them. Rather, if a text is not immediately accessible to you, it is because you need to read more actively, and meaning will then emerge in a collaborative effort as you work *with* the text to create a consistent interpretation. (This is the basis of reader-response criticism, which is explained on pages 174–175.) Obviously, active reading requires effort. If you find this sort of reading hard, take that as a good sign. It means you're paying the sort of attention that a well-crafted poem, story, or play requires of a reader. You also should not assume that English teachers have a key that allows them to unlock the one secret truth of a text. If, as is often the case, your instructor sees more or different meanings in a piece of literature than you do, this is because he or she is trained to read actively and has probably spent much more time than you have with literature in general and more time with the particular text assigned to you.

ACTIVE READING

Annotating

If the first suggestions for active reading are to slow down and to know that a second (or even a third) reading is in order, the next suggestion is to read with a pen or pencil in hand in order to annotate your text and take notes. If you look inside a literature textbook belonging to your instructor or to an advanced literature student, chances are you'll see something of a mess—words and passages circled or underlined, comments and questions scrawled in the margins (technically called *marginalia*) or even between the lines (called *interlinear* notes), and unexplained punctuation marks or other symbols decorating the pages. You should not interpret this as disrespect for the text or author or as a sign of a disordered mind. Indeed, it is quite the opposite of both these things. It is simply textual annotation, and it means that someone has been engaged in active reading. Perhaps an extreme example is the poet and critic Samuel Taylor Coleridge, who was famous for annotating not only his own books but also those he borrowed from friends—a habit unlikely to secure a friendship—and his marginalia actually make up one entire volume of his collected works.

If you are not accustomed to textual annotation, it may be hard to know where to begin. There is no single, widely used system of annotation, and you will almost certainly begin to develop your own techniques as you practice active reading. Here, however, are a few tips to get you started:

- **Underline, circle, or otherwise highlight passages that strike you as particularly important.** These may be anything from single words to whole paragraphs—but stick to those points in the text that really stand out, the briefer and more specific, the better. Don't worry that you need to find *the* most crucial parts of a poem, play, or story. Everyone sees things a little differently, so just note what makes an impression on *you*.
- **Make notes in the margins as to *why* certain points strike you.** Don't just underline; jot down at least a word or two in the margin to remind yourself what you were thinking when you chose to

highlight a particular point. It may seem obvious to you at the moment, but when you return to the text in two weeks to write your paper, you may not remember.

- **Ask questions of the text.** Perhaps the most important aspect of active reading is the practice of asking critical questions of a text. Nobody—not even the most experienced literary critic—understands everything about a literary text immediately, and noting where you are confused or doubtful is an important first step toward resolving any confusion. Types of questions are discussed a little later in this chapter, but for now just remember that any point of confusion is fair game, from character **motivation** (*"Why would she do that?"*), to cultural or historical references (*"Where is Xanadu?"*), to the definitions of individual words (*"Meaning?"*). Most likely, you will eventually want to propose some possible answers, but on a first reading of the text it's enough to note that you have questions.

- **Talk back to the text.** Occasionally, something in a literary text may strike you as suspicious, offensive, or just plain wrong. Just because a story, poem, or play appears in a textbook does not make its author above criticism. Try to keep an open mind and realize that there may be an explanation that would satisfy your criticism, but if you think an author has made a misstep, don't be afraid to make note of your opinion.

- **Look for unusual features of language.** In creating a mood and making a point, literary works rely much more heavily than do purely informational texts on features of language such as **style** and **imagery**. As a reader of literature, then, you need to heighten your awareness of style. Look for patterns of images, repeated words or phrases, and any other unusual stylistic features—right down to idiosyncratic grammar or punctuation—and make note of them in your marginalia.

- **Develop your own system of shorthand.** Annotating a text, while it obviously takes time, shouldn't become a burden or slow your reading too much, so keep your notes and questions short and to the point. Sometimes all you need is an exclamation point to indicate an important passage. An underlined term combined with a question mark in the margin can remind you that you didn't immediately understand what a word meant. Be creative, but try also to be consistent, so you'll know later what you meant by a particular symbol or comment.

Student Jarrad Nunes was assigned to read Emily Dickinson's poem "Because I could not stop for Death." Here are some of the annotations he made as he read the poem:

EMILY DICKINSON   [1830–1886]

Because I could not stop for Death

Because I could not stop for Death—
He kindly stopped for me—
The Carriage held but just Ourselves—
And Immortality.

Death personified:
kind; not the grim reaper.

We slowly drove—He knew no haste
And I had put away
My labor and my leisure too,
For His Civility—

Strange punctuation,
esp. all the dashes.

We passed the School, where Children strove
At Recess—in the Ring—
We passed the Fields of Gazing Grain—
We passed the Setting Sun—

Most nouns capitalized. Why?

How does grain "gaze"?

Or rather—He passed Us—
The Dews drew quivering and chill—
For only Gossamer, my Gown—
My Tippet—only Tulle—

Who is "he"? The Sun?

Repeated sounds—
dews/drew, etc.

We paused before a House that seemed
A Swelling of the Ground—
The Roof was scarcely visible—
The Cornice—in the Ground—

This "house" seems like a grave.

cornice = horizontal projection
from a wall (Dictionary.com)

Since then—'tis Centuries—and yet
Feels shorter than the Day
I first surmised the Horses' Heads
Were toward Eternity—

Eternity and Immortality,
but no reference to God or religion.

Ends with a dash, not a period. Not a final ending?

[*c. 1863;* 1890]

Jarrad's annotations cover everything from major points of content, like the personification of the character Death and the absence of overt religiosity, to small notations on style. He asks lots of questions and sometimes provides tentative answers. Having annotated the poem in this way, he was ready to participate in discussions both in the classroom and online, and later he had some good starting notes when he decided to write a paper on the poem.

Note Taking

It's a good idea, especially if you are reading a difficult text or one about which you expect to be writing, to keep a notebook handy as you read, a place to make notes that would be too long or complex to fit in the margins. What should these notes contain? Essentially, they should be more extensive versions of your marginalia. Note any unusual repetitions or juxtapositions, as well as anything that surprises you or frustrates your expectations as you read. Note passages that seem particularly crucial, or particularly confusing (using page numbers, and perhaps placing an asterisk or other symbol in the margins), and write a few sentences explaining why these stood out for you. Ask plenty of questions, as explained later in this chapter.

You might want to use the same notebook that you keep with you in class so that you can make reference to your class notes while reading at home and bring the insights from your reading to your class discussions. In class, write down any information your instructor writes on the board or projects using PowerPoint or other presentation software. If he or she thought it was important enough to write down, you probably should too. Your class notes should include new terminology or vocabulary, as well as any point the instructor repeats more than once or twice. Also take note of comments by your classmates that seem especially salient to your evolving understanding of the literature, particularly points you disagree with or would not have thought of on your own. Just be sure to distinguish which ideas in your notes are yours and which you read or heard from someone else. It may be obvious to you now, but can you guarantee that a month from now, when you're writing a paper, you'll remember who produced that gem of insight?

Remember that the best note takers are not necessarily those who have amassed the most pages of notes at the end of the term. Good notes need not be well-reasoned paragraphs or even complete sentences. In fact, they seldom are. The key to taking good notes is to take them quickly, with minimal interruption to your reading or participation in a discussion. As with annotating texts, try to develop your own shorthand for note taking. Just be sure that you write enough to jog your memory when you return to the notes days, weeks, or even months later. Try to be consistent in what and how you abbreviate. One specific piece of advice, though: it's a good idea to jot down page numbers in your notes, referring to the specific lines or passages under discussion. That way, you'll have no problem matching up the notes with the texts to which they refer.

Journal Keeping

You may be assigned to keep a reading journal for your class. Of course, you should follow your instructor's guidelines, but if you aren't sure what to write in a reading journal, think of it as a place to go a step further than you do in your annotations and notes. Try out possible answers, preferably several different ones, to the questions you have raised. Expand your ideas from single phrases and sentences into entire paragraphs, and see how they hold up under this deeper probing. Although a reading journal is substantially different from a personal journal or diary, it can at times contain reflections on any connections you make between a piece of literature and your own life and ideas. Some instructors ask students to respond to their readings with Web resources, including discussion boards, e-mail messages, or blog entries. These platforms allow you to build an archive of your responses so that you can easily return to them when you begin writing a draft of your paper; in addition, you can respond to other students as they develop their ideas. Here is an example of a Blackboard discussion board response to "Because I could not stop for Death":

Forum: Because I could not stop for Death
Date: Mon 10 Feb 2010 22:15
Author: Nunes, Jarrad
Subject: Hymn Meter

We read some Emily Dickinson poems in high school, and I remember my teacher saying that Emily Dickinson wrote all her poems in "hymnal stanzas," which are the typical meter used in hymns. My teacher used "Amazing Grace" as an example of a hymn in this style. "Because I could not stop for Death" follows this meter exactly, except in the first two lines of stanza 4, which reverses the scheme. According to Britannica Online, Dickinson was raised in a religious family, but she herself had a lot of questions and doubts about Christianity. It's notable that in this poem she never mentions God or associates death with heaven the way you might expect from a Christian. Is this maybe a sign of her religious doubts? She must have grown up singing hymns and associating that particular rhythm with church. I wonder why someone who was skeptical about religion would write her poems in a form that is so strongly associated with the church.

In this brief response, the student explores questions about both form and content. He connects his reading of the poem with insights gleaned from both previous experience in high school and some online research.

This kind of response will serve Jarrad well when it's time to generate a thesis for his paper on the subject. Even if your instructor doesn't require online forum participation or a journal for your class, many students find keeping a journal a useful tool for getting more out of their reading, not to mention a wealth of material to draw from when they sit down to write a paper.

Using Reference Materials

Many students are reluctant to use the dictionary or encyclopedia while reading, thinking they should be able to figure out the meanings of words from their context and not wanting to interrupt their reading. But the simple truth is that not all words are definable from context alone, and you'll get much more out of your reading if you are willing to make the small effort involved in looking up unfamiliar words. If you are reading John Donne's "A Valediction: Forbidding Mourning" and you don't know what the word *valediction* means, you obviously start at a big disadvantage. A quick look in a dictionary would tell you that a valediction is a speech given at a time of parting (like the one a *valedictorian* gives at a graduation ceremony). Armed with that simple piece of information, you begin your reading of Donne's poem already knowing that it is about leaving someone or something, and understanding the poem becomes much simpler. Notice that the annotations for the Dickinson poem earlier in the chapter include a definition of *cornice*.

An encyclopedia like *Britannica Online* (an online subscription service available at most university libraries) can also be a useful tool. If, as you're reading Dickinson's poem, you want to read her biography, *Britannica Online* can provide biographical and cultural context for her life and work. Or, if you want to learn more about the meter of the poem, you could look up "hymnal stanza" to develop an understanding of its use, or "personification" to understand how the poet makes characters out of Death and Immortality. *Britannica Online* often provides a bibliography for further reading, so it can be a good place to start your research.

ASKING CRITICAL QUESTIONS OF LITERATURE

As mentioned, one important part of active, critical reading is asking questions. If you are reading well, your textual annotations and notes will probably be full of questions. Some of these might be simple inquiries of fact, the sort of thing that can be answered by asking your instructor or by doing some quick research. But ideally, many of your questions will be more complex and meaty than that, the sort of probing queries that may have multiple, complex, or even contradictory answers. These are the questions that will provoke you and your classmates to think still more critically about the literature you read. You need not worry—at least not at first—about finding answers to all of your questions. As you work more with the text, discussing it with your instructor and classmates, writing about it, and reading other related stories, poems, and plays, you will begin to respond to the most important of the issues you've raised. And even if you never form a satisfactory answer to some questions, they will have served their purpose if they have made you think.

Questions about literature fall into one of four categories—questions about the text, about the author, about the cultural context of the work, and about the reader. We'll discuss each of these in the next few pages.

Questions about the Text

Questions about a text focus on issues such as **genre**, **structure**, language, and style. Queries regarding the text can sometimes, though not always, be answered with a deeper examination of the story, poem, or play at hand. You might ask about the presence of certain images—or about their absence, if you have reason to expect them and find that they are not there. Sometimes authors juxtapose images or language in startling or unexpected ways, and you might ask about the purpose and effect of such **juxtaposition**. You might wonder about the meanings of specific words in the context of the work. (This is especially true with older works of literature, as meanings evolve and change over time, and a word you know today might have had a very different definition in the past.) When looking at a poem, you might inquire about the purpose and effect of sound, rhythm, rhyme, and so forth.

Your previous experiences are a big help here, including both your experiences of reading literature and your experiences in everyday life. You know from personal experience how you expect people to think and act in certain situations, and you can compare these expectations to the literature. What might motivate the characters or persons to think and act as they do? Your previous reading has likewise set up expectations for you. How does the text fulfill or frustrate these expectations? What other literature does this remind you of? What images seem arresting or unexpected? Where do the words seem particularly powerful, strange, or otherwise noteworthy?

Notice some of the questions one reader asked in his annotations upon first reading Ben Jonson's "On My First Son."

BEN JONSON   [1572–1637]

On My First Son

Farewell, thou child of my right hand, and joy;
My sin was too much hope of thee, loved boy:
Seven years thou' wert lent to me, and I thee pay,
Exacted by thy fate, on the just day.
O could I lose all father now! for why
Will man lament the state he should envy,
To have so soon 'scaped world's and flesh's rage,
And, if no other misery, yet age?
Rest in soft peace, and asked, say, "Here doth lie
Ben Jonson his best piece of poetry."
For whose sake henceforth all his vows be such
As what he loves may never like too much.

Why is hope for his child a "sin"?

The rhyme in ll. 1-2 aligns "joy" with "boy."

Why does the speaker treat the son like a bank transaction?

The word just has two meanings: exact and fair. Which does the poet mean?

What does he mean by this line? (confusing)

Here the poem works as a kind of epitaph on a tombstone. Is it actually the boy's epitaph?

The questions the student asks of the poem are, for the most part, substantial and difficult, and they will require a good deal of thinking and interpretation to get to an answer. These are the sorts of questions that prompt good discussions and good writing.

Questions about the Author

When thinking about the connection between authors and the works they produce, two contradictory impulses come into play. One is the desire to ignore the biography of the author entirely and focus solely on the work at hand, and the other is to look closely at an author's life to see what might have led him or her to write a particular poem, story, or play. It is easy to understand the first impulse. After all, we are not likely to be able to ask an author what is meant by a certain line in a play or whether an image in a story is supposed to be read symbolically. The work of literature is what we have before us, and it should stand or fall on its own merits. This was, in fact, one of the principal tenets of **New Criticism**, a method of interpretation that dominated literary criticism for much of the twentieth century and is discussed on pages 167–168.

We cannot deny, however, that a writer's life does affect that writer's expression. An author's age, gender, religious beliefs, family structure, and many other factors have an impact on everything from topic choice to word choice. Therefore, it is sometimes appropriate to ask questions about an author as we try to come to a better understanding of a piece of literature. It is crucial, however, that we remember that not everything an author writes is to be taken at surface value. For instance, if the narrator or principal character of a story is beaten or neglected by his parents, we should not jump to the conclusion that the author was an abused child. And if this character then goes on to justify his own actions by pointing to the abuse, we should also not assume that the author endorses this justification. In other words, we must distinguish between narrative voice and the actual author as well as between what is written and what is meant.

This separation of biography and narrative is relatively easy with stories and plays that we know to be fiction; just because a character says something doesn't necessarily mean the author believes it. Poetry is a little trickier, though, because it has the reputation of being straight from the heart. Not all poetry, however, is an accurate representation of the author's thoughts or beliefs. To give just two examples, T. S. Eliot's "The Love Song of J. Alfred Prufrock" (page 102) voices the thoughts of the fictional Prufrock, not of Eliot himself, and many of the poems of Robert Browning are "dramatic monologues," delivered by speakers very different from Browning himself, including murderous noblemen and corrupt clergy. (An example of such a monologue is "My Last Duchess" on page 60.)

Questions about the Cultural Context

We are all creatures of a particular time and place, and nobody, no matter how unique and iconoclastic, is immune to the subtle and pervasive force of social history. Many appropriate questions about literature, then, involve the **cultural context** of the work. What was going on in history at the time a piece of literature was written? Were there wars or other forms of social disruption? What was the standard of living for most people in the author's society? What was day-to-day life like? What were the typical religious beliefs and traditions? How was society organized in terms of power relations, work expectations, and educational possibilities? How about typical family structure? Did extended families live together? What were the expected gender roles inside (and outside) the family? All of these issues, and many more besides, have an impact on how authors see the world and how they respond to it in their writing.

As you read and ask questions of literature, you have another cultural context to be concerned with: your own. How does being a resident of twenty-first-century America affect your reading and understanding? We are every bit as influenced by issues of history, culture, and lifestyle as were authors and readers of the past, but it is harder for us to see this, since the dominant way of living tends to seem "natural" or even "universal." Indeed, one of the great benefits of reading literature is that it teaches us about history and helps us understand and appreciate diverse cultures, not the least of which is our own.

In asking and answering the following questions about Ben Jonson's culture (seventeenth-century England), an attentive reader of "On My First Son" will also note features of our own present-day society, in which childhood death is relatively rare, family roles may be different, and religious attitudes and beliefs are considerably more diverse.

- How common was childhood death in the seventeenth century? What was the life expectancy?
- Typically, how involved were fathers in young children's lives at the time?
- Is the quotation in the poem (lines 9–10) the boy's epitaph?
- How difficult was life then? What exactly does Jonson mean by the "world's and flesh's rage"?
- How common was poetry on this topic? How "original" was Jonson's poem?
- What attitudes about God and heaven were common then? What was the conception of sin?

Questions about the Reader

Except in the case of private diaries, all writing is intended to be read by somebody, and an intended audience can have a big influence on the composition of the writing in question. Think about the differences in tone and structure between a text message you send to a friend and a paper you write for a course, and you'll get some idea of the impact of intended audience on a piece of writing. It is therefore worth considering a work's originally intended readers as you seek to understand a piece more fully. Who were these intended readers? Were they actually the people who read the literature when it was first published? How are readers' expectations fulfilled or disappointed by the structure and content of the literature? How did the original readers react? Was the work widely popular, or did only certain readers enjoy it? Did it have detractors as well? Was there any controversy over the work?

Of course, in addition to the original readers of any work of literature, there are also contemporary readers, including yourself. It is often said that great literature stands the test of time and can cross cultures to speak to many different sorts of people, but your reaction to a work may be very different from that of its original audience, especially if you are far removed from the work by time or culture. In earlier centuries in Europe and America, nearly all educated people were very familiar with the Bible and with stories and myths from Greek and Roman antiquity. Writers, therefore, could assume such knowledge on the part of their readers and make liberal reference in their work to stories and characters from these sources. Today many readers are less familiar with these sources, and we often need the help of footnotes or other study aids to understand such references. So what might have been enjoyable and enlightening for the original readers of a work might sometimes be tedious or frustrating for later readers. If we are to read a work critically, we must keep both past and present audiences in mind.

The first three of the following questions deal with the original audience of "On My First Son," while the final two compare this audience and a contemporary one.

- If childhood death was common in the seventeenth century, how would Jonson's readers have related to the subject of his poem?
- Did Jonson write this for wide circulation, or was it meant just for family and friends?
- Where was the poem first published, and who was likely to read it?
- Do readers with children of their own read the poem differently? Would I?
- Now that childhood death is fairly uncommon, do we take this poem more seriously than past readers? Or less seriously?

Looking over these questions about Jonson's poem—about the text, the author, the cultural context, and the reader—you will note that there are many differences among them. Some can be answered with a simple yes or no (*Is the quotation the boy's epitaph?*), while others require much more complex responses (*What was the conception of sin in Jonson's time?*). Others are matters of conjecture, opinion, or interpretation (*Do contemporary readers take this poem more seriously?*). Some can be answered simply by rereading and considering (*How can a child's death ever be considered fair?*), while others require discussion (*Do readers with children respond to the poem differently?*) or research (*Where was the poem first published?*).

For some inquiries, you may have tentative answers, as did the reader who asked these questions when she proposed both God and fate as potential candidates for who "lent" the child to the father. Others you won't be able to answer at first. If you are genuinely curious about any of them, do a little informal research to begin formulating answers. Some basic information can be found in the brief biographies or notes about authors that appear in most textbooks. There you could learn, for instance, the dates of Jonson's birth and death and some basic facts about his life and family. A quick look at a reputable reference work or Web site could provide still more valuable background information, like the fact that Jonson also lost his first daughter and that he wrote a poem about her death as well.

CHECKLIST FOR GOOD READING

Questions to ask as you read and think about literary texts:

☐ Have you *slowed down* and *reread* complex passages several times?

☐ Are you *looking up difficult words* in the dictionary to see if they have secondary meanings?

☐ Are you *annotating* the text by *underlining* key phrases? Writing questions or concerns in the *margins*?

☐ Are you taking your reading to the next level by asking *how* or *why* these passages are compelling to you?

☐ Are you marking those places in the text that make you feel uncomfortable, or present a worldview that feels strange to you?

☐ After you read, are you *taking notes* so that you can keep track of your ideas?

☐ Have you identified the genre of the text? Have you described its style and **tone**?

☐ Have you checked *Britannica Online* or other reference sources to learn more about the author and his or her cultural context?

☐ Have you reflected on your perspective as a twenty-first-century *reader*, and how that might affect your interpretation of literature from another time period?

Having simply formulated some questions, you've already gone a long way toward understanding and interpreting a poem or other work of literature. If you bring such a list of questions with you to class, you will be more than ready to contribute to the discussion, and when the time comes to write an essay, you will have a rich mine of source material from which to draw.

CHAPTER 3

The Writing Process

Experts often divide the writing process into three major components: prewriting, drafting, and revision (which includes editing). Bear in mind, though, that the process for most people is not as linear as this suggests, and the three components don't always happen in a straightforward fashion. For instance, you might begin revising a partial draft before completing the drafting process. Or you may find yourself stuck at a fairly late point in the draft and decide to revisit your prewriting. Don't think that these three steps need to be completed one at a time. Different projects will likely call for different strategies, and you'll enjoy the process more if you allow yourself to go back and forth between the steps according to the needs of the particular assignment you're trying to complete.

PREWRITING

Prewriting is everything that you do before beginning an actual draft of your paper. It includes annotating and questioning texts, taking notes and participating in class, and discussing the assignment with your instructor and/or classmates. It also includes specific topics covered in this chapter: choosing a topic, developing an argument and a thesis, gathering support, and proposing an organizational strategy for the paper.

Choosing a Topic

Obviously, your choice of a topic for your paper is of key importance, since everything else follows from that first decision. Your instructor may assign a specific topic, or the choice may be left to you. The most important piece of advice for choosing a topic is to write about something that genuinely interests you. If your instructor gives your class a choice, chances are that he or she really wants to see a variety of topics and approaches and expects you to find a topic that works for *you*. You'll write a better paper if your topic is something of genuine interest to you. A bored or uncertain writer usually writes a boring or unconvincing paper. On the other hand, if you care about your topic, your enthusiasm will show in the writing, and the paper will be far more successful.

Even if your instructor assigns a fairly specific topic, you still need to spend a little time thinking about and working with it. You want your paper to stand out from the rest, and you should do whatever you can to make the assignment your own. When you receive an assignment, give some thought as to how it might relate to your own interests and how you might call upon your background and knowledge to approach the topic in fresh and interesting ways.

Finally, if you've put in some thought and effort but still don't know what to write about, remember that you do not need to go it alone. Seek out guidance and help. Talk with other students in your class and see what they have decided to write about; although of course you don't want simply to copy someone else's topic, hearing what others think can often spark a fresh idea. And don't forget your instructor. Most teachers are more than happy to spend a little time helping you come up with a topic and an approach that will help you write a good paper.

Developing an Argument

With the possible exception of a *summary* (a brief recap of a text's most important points), all writing about literature is to some degree a form of argument. Before proceeding, though, let's dispel some of the negative connotations of the word *argument*. In everyday usage, this term can connote a heated verbal fight, and it suggests two (or more) people growing angry and, often, becoming less articulate and more abusive as time passes. It suggests combat and implies that the other party in the process is an opponent. In this sort of argument, there are winners and losers.

Clearly this is not what we have in mind when we say you will be writing argumentatively about literature. Used in a different, more traditional sense, argument refers to a writer's or speaker's attempt to establish the validity of a given position. In other words, when you write a paper, you work to convince your reader that what you are saying is valid and persuasive. The reader is not the enemy, not someone whose ideas are to be crushed and refuted, but rather a person whose thoughts and feelings you have a chance to affect. You are not arguing *against* your reader; rather, you are using your argumentative abilities to *help* your reader see the logic and value of your position.

The Thesis

To begin writing a literary argument, then, you must take a position and have a point to make. This principal point will be the *thesis* of your paper. It is important to distinguish between a topic and a thesis: your topic is the issue or area upon which you will focus your attention, and your thesis is a statement *about* this topic.

Here is an example of a topic for Emily Dickinson's "Because I could not stop for Death" from a student journal:

Topic: I am interested in how Dickinson portrays the character of Death.

Here is an example of a thesis statement for a paper on this topic:

Thesis: "Because I could not stop for Death" challenges preconceptions that Dickinson's contemporaries had about death, and in doing so it makes us challenge ours as well.

It might help to phrase your thesis as a complete sentence in which the topic is the subject, followed by a predicate that makes a firm statement or claim regarding your topic. This is your **thesis statement**, and it will probably appear toward the beginning of your paper. The foremost purpose of a paper, then, is to explain, defend, and ultimately prove the truth of its thesis.

Keep the following guidelines in mind as you think about a tentative thesis for your paper:

- **Your thesis should be both clear and specific.** The purpose of a thesis is to serve as a guide to both the reader and the writer, so it needs to be understandable and to point clearly to the specific aspects of the literature that you will discuss. This does not mean it will stand alone or need no further development or explanation — after all, that's what the rest of the paper is for. But a reader who is familiar with the story, poem, or play you are writing about (and it is fair to assume a basic familiarity) should have a good sense of what your thesis means and how it relates to the literature.

- **Your thesis should be relevant.** The claim you make should not only interest you as a writer but also give your reader a reason to keep reading by sparking his or her interest and desire to know more. Not every paper is going to change lives or minds, of course, but you should at least state your thesis in such a way that your reader won't have the most dreaded of responses: "Who cares?"

- **Your thesis should be debatable.** Since the purpose of an argumentative paper is to convince a reader that your thesis is correct (or at least that it has merit), it cannot simply be an irrefutable fact. A good thesis will be something that a reasonable person, having read the literature, might disagree with or might not have considered at all. It should give you something to prove.

- **Your thesis should be original.** Again, originality does not imply that every thesis you write must be a brilliant gem that nobody but you could have discovered. But it should be something you have thought about independently, and it should avoid clichés, contain something of you, and do more than parrot back something said in your class or written in your textbook.

- **You should be able to state your thesis as a complete sentence.** This sentence, generally referred to as the *thesis statement*, should first identify your topic and then make a claim about it. (Occasionally, especially for longer papers with more complex ideas behind them, you will need more than one sentence to state your thesis clearly. Even in these cases, though, the complete thesis must both identify the topic and make a claim about it.)

- **Your thesis should be stated in strong, unambiguous language.** Avoid thesis statements that begin, "In this paper, I will prove. . . ." If you have a point to prove, just prove it. Keep the reader's attention on the topic, not on your paper. For similar reasons, avoid phrases like "in my opinion . . ." or "I think. . . ." It is assumed that the paper is made up of your thoughts and opinions, and language like this turns the reader's focus to your thought process rather than the topic at hand.

- **Your thesis should be appropriate to the assignment.** This may seem obvious, but as we work with literature, taking notes, asking questions, and beginning to think about topics and theses, it is possible to lose sight of the assignment as it was presented. After you have come up with a tentative thesis, it's a good idea to go back and review the assignment as your instructor gave it, making sure your paper will fulfill its requirements.

Let us take a look at how two students arrived at strong, workable theses for their papers. Jarrad Nunes knew that he wanted to write about how Emily Dickinson dealt with the theme of death in her poetry. His first attempt at a thesis, however, was far too weak and general:

> Emily Dickinson's poems about death are some of the most interesting ever written.

This is not so much a thesis statement as an assertion of personal preference and opinion. All we know from reading it is that Jarrad likes

Dickinson's death poems. He needs a thesis that is both more specific and more controversial:

> Dickinson's poems look at death in unconventional ways.

This version is better because it makes an assertion that can be defended, but it is still far too general. Here is the final version of Jarrad's thesis:

> "Because I could not stop for Death" challenges preconceptions that Dickinson's contemporaries had about death, and in doing so it makes us challenge ours as well.

Here we have a much stronger thesis. It limits the paper's scope by focusing on a single poem, it makes an assertion to defend (that Dickinson challenged nineteenth-century preconceptions about death), and it shows why this point is significant to a reader (because we too might have our preconceptions challenged).

Here is one more example of the process of refining and developing a thesis. When she first decided to write about the male characters in two nineteenth-century stories, Melanie Smith came up with the following:

> The husbands in the stories "The Yellow Wallpaper" by Charlotte Perkins Gilman and "The Story of an Hour" by Kate Chopin are very controlling of their wives.

This is not an adequate thesis because it is simply a statement of fact, something that will be immediately obvious to anyone who has read the stories. It left Melanie with nothing to defend, no point to prove, so she gave it a little more thought and refined her tentative thesis:

> Though the husbands in "The Yellow Wallpaper" and "The Story of an Hour" are controlling, they are not really as bad as they first appear.

At this point, the writer is definitely moving in the right direction. This version shows that she has a particular interpretation and a point to make, one that is not necessarily shared by everyone who reads the stories. However, it still doesn't give a reader much guidance about what to expect in the paper. In the end, Melanie needed two sentences to get her thesis right:

> By modern standards, the husbands of the two protagonists, particularly John in "The Yellow Wallpaper," seem almost unbearably controlling of their wives. From the vantage point of the late nineteenth century, however, their behavior looks quite different.

This version is much clearer and more precise. After reading this thesis, we are much more focused and have a good sense of what to expect in the paper as a whole.

You will note that in this discussion the phrase *tentative thesis* has come up several times. The word *tentative* is important. As you start to gather support and to write your paper, your thesis will help you focus clearly on your task and sort out which of your ideas, observations, and questions are relevant to the project at hand. But you should keep an open mind as well, realizing that your thesis is likely to evolve as you write. You are likely to change the focus in subtle or not so subtle ways, and you might even change your mind completely as you write and therefore need to create a new thesis from scratch. If this happens, don't regard it as a failure. On the contrary, it means you have succeeded in learning something genuine from the experience of writing, and that is what a literature class is all about.

Gathering Support for Your Thesis

Once you have crafted a tentative thesis, it is time to think about the evidence or support you will need to convince your reader of the claim's validity. But what exactly counts as support? What can you include in your paper as evidence that your thesis is true? Essentially, all support comes from one of three sources:

- **The text itself is the most obvious source of support.** It is not enough to *say* that a certain piece of literature says or means a certain thing. You will need to *show* this by summarizing, paraphrasing, or quoting the literature itself.

- **Other people's ideas are a good source of support.** Chances are you will find a lot of useful material for your paper if you pay attention to easily available sources of ideas from other readers. These include the notes and biographical information in your textbooks, research conducted online or in the library, lectures and discussions in class, and even informal conversations about the literature with your friends and classmates.

- **Your own thoughts are your most important source of support.** Remember that although you may want to integrate ideas and information from a variety of sources, your paper is yours and as such should reflect *your* thinking. The most indispensable source of material for your paper is your own mind; your own thoughts and words should always carry the heaviest weight in any paper you write.

One of the best ways to gather supporting ideas for your paper is **brainstorming**. You can brainstorm—alone or with classmates—even before settling on your topic and thesis, to explore the many possible threads that you could follow in your writing. When brainstorming to gather evidence, the idea is to write down, very quickly, every idea that comes to you, every possible idea that might be included in the draft of your paper. Don't censor yourself during this process. Allow yourself to write down everything that interests, puzzles, or delights you. Later you will have ample opportunity to prune your list of repetitions, tangents, or weaker ideas. For the time being, just let the ideas flow, and get as many as you can down on a piece of paper or a word processing document.

At this stage, use every resource available to you to find support for your thesis. What lines in the poem, short story, or play reinforce your claims? Have you looked up words in the dictionary? Have you checked difficult concepts in a respectable encyclopedia or other reference? Have you asked your teacher for further reading suggestions? Have you read articles or book chapters that are appropriate to your topic, and are you formulating your responses to them? Treat ideas from outside sources much as you would your own brainstorming: don't censor too soon. When the time comes to organize and draft your paper, it's far better to have too many ideas and have to eliminate some than to have too few and have to root around for more.

Organizing Your Paper

Once you've determined what evidence to use, it is time to begin sorting and organizing it. The organizing principle for any paper is the sequence of paragraphs, so at this stage you should be thinking at the level of paragraph content. Remember that each paragraph should contain one main idea and sufficient evidence and explanation to support that idea. When added together, these paragraph-level ideas lead a reader to your paper's ultimate point—your thesis. So the first stage of organizing the content of your essay is to cluster together similar ideas in order to begin shaping the substance of individual paragraphs. The second stage is to determine the order in which these paragraphs will appear.

As you write and revise your paper, you may have different ideas about how to structure it. You may want to put the topic sentence somewhere other than at the beginning of a paragraph, or perhaps the topic is so clear that no specific topic sentence is even needed. You may devise a more interesting way to structure your introduction or conclusion. (Some additional, more specific thoughts for those tricky introductory and concluding paragraphs follow.) Unless your instructor has specified the form in which your paper is to be organized, you should feel free to experiment a bit.

For most writers, creating some version of an outline is the best way to approach the task of organizing evidence into a logical sequence for a paper. In the past, you may have been asked to write a formal outline, complete with Roman numerals and capital letters. If this technique has been helpful in organizing your thoughts, by all means continue to use it. For many writers, however, an informal outline works just as well and is less cumbersome. To construct an informal outline, simply jot down a heading that summarizes the topic of each paragraph you intend to write. Then cluster your gathered evidence—quotations or paraphrases from the literature, ideas for analysis, and so on—into groups under the headings.

The following is an example of an informal outline for a paper on Shakespeare's Sonnet 116. (The full paper appears on pages 108–110.) In this outline, the student focuses on the positive and negative language in the poem and how it results in a more interesting definition of love than he had seen in other love poems.

Introduction
>   Two kinds of typical love poems: happy and sad
>   Sonnet 116 is more complex and interesting
>   Tentative thesis: By including both negative and positive images and
>   language, this sonnet gives a complex and realistic definition of
>   love.

Vivid images in poem
>   Positive/expected: "star," "ever-fixèd mark," "rosy lips and cheeks"
>   Negative/unexpected: "sickle" (deathlike), "wandering bark" (lost
>   boat), "tempests"

Negative language
>   Words/phrases: "Let me not," "Love is not," "never," "nor," "no," etc.
>   Abstractions: "alteration," "impediments," "error"

Conclusion
>   Love never changes
>   Shakespeare's definition still works some 400 years later

Obviously, this is not a formal outline. It does, however, group similar items and ideas together, and it gives the writer a basic structure to follow as he moves on to drafting, the next stage of the composing process.

DRAFTING THE PAPER

You have a topic. You have a tentative thesis. You have gathered evidence. You have an outline or tentative structure in mind for this evidence. It is time to begin writing your first draft. Every writer has his or her own slightly different process for getting the words down on paper. Some begin at the beginning of the paper and work straight through to the end in a clear, organized fashion. Others begin with the first body paragraph and save the introduction for later. Still others write bits and pieces of the paper out of order and allow the overall structure to emerge at a later time.

Some writers claim that they work better at the last minute and focus better under the pressure of a looming deadline. This, however, is almost always a justification for sloppy work habits, and procrastination rarely if ever results in a superior paper. When habitual procrastinators change their working methods and give themselves more time on a project, they are frequently surprised to discover that the process is more enjoyable and the final product of their efforts better than what they have produced in the past. Start early and work steadily—it will prove more than worth it.

Try to write your first draft fairly quickly. You don't need to get every sentence just right—that's what the revision phase of writing is for. What you want now is just to get as much good raw material as possible into the mix and see what works. Don't worry too much yet about style, transitions, grammar, and so forth. In fact, you don't even need to start at the beginning or work right through to the end. If you get stuck on one part, move on. You can always come back and fill in the gaps later. Introductions can be especially tricky, particularly since you haven't yet finished the essay and don't really know what it is you're introducing. Some writers find it easier to start with the body of the essay, or to write a short, sloppy introduction as a placeholder. You can go back and work on the real introduction when the draft is complete.

Introductions, Conclusions, and Transitions

Ideally, of course, all of the parts of your paper will be equally compelling and polished, but there are certain points in a paper that most often cause trouble for writers and readers, and these points may require a little additional attention on your part. The most typical trouble spots are introductory and concluding paragraphs and the transitional sentences that connect paragraphs. Although there is no one formula to help you navigate these waters, as each writing situation and each paper are different, we offer some general guidelines that can help you think through the problems that might arise in these areas.

Introductions

Essentially, an introduction accomplishes two things. First, it gives a sense of both your topic and your approach to that topic, which is why it is common to make your thesis statement a part of the introduction. Second, an introduction compels your readers' interest and makes them want to read on and find out what your paper has to say. Some common strategies used in effective introductions are to begin with a probing rhetorical question, a vivid description, or an intriguing quotation. Weak introductions tend to speak in generalities or in philosophical ideas that are only tangentially related to the real topic of your paper. Don't spin your wheels: get specific and get to the point right away.

Consider this introduction from a student essay on Susan Glaspell's *Trifles*:

> What is the relationship between legality and morality? Susan Glaspell's short play *Trifles* asks us to ponder this question, but it provides no clear answers. Part murder mystery, part battle of the sexes, the play makes its readers confront and question many issues about laws, morals, and human relationships. In the person of Mrs. Peters, a sheriff's wife, the play chronicles one woman's moral journey from a certain, unambiguous belief in the law to a more situational view of ethics. Before it is over, this once legally minded woman is even willing to cover up the truth and let someone get away with murder.

The student poses a philosophical question at the very beginning of the paper and then offers a tentative answer. (This paper appears in its entirety on pages 127–129.)

Conclusions

Your conclusion should give your reader something new to think about, a reason not to forget your essay as soon as the reading is done. Some writers like to use the conclusion to return to an idea, a quotation, or an image first raised in the introduction, creating a satisfying feeling of completeness and self-containment.

In this example from the same student paper, note how the student offers a tentative answer in her conclusion to the question that began the essay:

In the end, Mrs. Peters gives in to what she believes to be emotionally right rather than what is legally permissible. She collaborates with Mrs. Hale to cover up evidence of the motive and hide the dead canary. Though very little time has gone by, she has undergone a major transformation. She may be, as the county attorney says, "married to the law," but she is also divorced from her old ideals. When she tries to cover up the evidence, a stage direction says she "goes to pieces," and Mrs. Hale has to help her. By the time she pulls herself together, the new woman she is will be a very different person from the old one. She, along with the reader, is now in a world where the relationship between legality and morality is far more complex than she had ever suspected.

Some writers use the conclusion to show the implications of their claims or the connections between the literature and real life. This is your chance to make a good final impression, so don't waste it with simple summary and restatement.

Transitions

Each paragraph is built around a different idea, and the job of the transitions is to show how these separate ideas are related to one another, to make the juxtaposition of two paragraphs seem as logical to a reader as it is to the writer. When you think a transition isn't working effectively, the first question you should ask yourself is, *why* does one paragraph follow another in this particular order? Would it make more sense to change the placement of some paragraphs, or is this really the best organizational strategy for this portion of the paper? Once you know why your paper is structured as it is, transitions become much easier to write, simply making apparent to your audience the connections you already know to be there. As you begin each new paragraph, give some consideration to the links between it and the previous paragraph, and try to make those links explicit in the opening sentence.

As with any other aspect of your writing, if you've had trouble in the past with introductions, conclusions, or transitions, one of your best sources of help is to be an attentive reader of others' writing. Pay special attention to these potential trouble spots in the writing you admire, whether by a classmate or a professional author, and see how he or she navigates them. Don't stick with the writing methods that have caused you headaches in the past. Be willing to try out different strategies, seeing which ones work best for you. In time you'll find you have a whole array of ways to approach these trouble spots, and you'll be able to find a successful response to each particular writing situation.

REVISING AND EDITING

Once you have a complete, or near-complete, draft, it's time to begin thinking about revision. Try to avoid the common pitfall of thinking of revision as locating and fixing mistakes. Revision is far more than this. Looking at the parts of the word, you can see that *re-vision* means "seeing again," and indeed the revision stage of the writing process is your chance to see your draft anew and make real and substantial improvements to every facet of it, from its organization to its tone to your word choices. Most successful writers will tell you that it is in the revision stage that the real work gets done, where the writing takes shape and begins to emerge in its final form. Most professional writers spend much more time revising than they do writing the first draft. Don't skimp on this part of the process or try to race through it.

It is a good idea not to start a major revision the minute a draft is complete. Take a break. Exercise, have a meal, do something completely different to clear your mind. If possible, put the draft aside for at least a day, so that when you return to it you'll have a fresh perspective and can begin truly re-seeing it. Print out your draft. Attempting serious revision on-screen is generally a bad idea—we see differently, and we usually see more, when we read off a printed page. Read with a pen in your hand and annotate your text just the way you would a piece of literature, looking for the strengths and weaknesses of your argument. The process laid out here consists of three phases: *global revisions*, or large-scale revisions; *local revisions*, or small-scale revisions; and a final *editing and proofreading*. If you haven't done so before, revising your paper three times may seem like a lot of work, but bear in mind that most professional writers revise their work many more times than that. Revision is the real key to writing the best paper you can.

Global Revision

On a first pass at revision—the large-scale, global part of the process—don't worry too much about details like word choice, punctuation, and so forth. Too many students focus so much on these issues that they miss the big picture. The details are important, but you will deal with them in depth later. You wouldn't want to spend your time getting the wording of a sentence just right only to decide later that the paragraph it is in weakens your argument and needs to be deleted. So at first, look at the overall picture—the argument, organization, and tone of the paper as a whole. While there's nothing wrong with making a few small improvements as you read, nothing smaller than a paragraph should concern you at this point. Here are some possibilities for how you might revise your paper globally.

GLOBAL REVISION CHECKLIST

Further develop your focus and thesis.

- ☐ Can your reader immediately identify what the topic of the essay will be—that is, which text(s), and which aspect of the text (for example, character development or the use of particular language features), you will analyze?

- ☐ Have you narrowed the scope of the thesis for your reader? How could it be further narrowed? Remember, it's not enough to say "Women are portrayed differently in X and Y." What do you mean by "differently"? Get as specific as possible.

- ☐ Does your thesis clearly identify a claim that is debatable but valid?

- ☐ Has your thinking about the issues evolved as you have written? If so, how will you change the thesis statement?

- ☐ Have you answered the larger "So what?" question? Do you get your reader thinking beyond your paper to the question of why this argument is important?

Reorganize your paper, if necessary.

- ☐ Does the order of the ideas and paragraphs make immediate sense to you, or does some alternate structure suggest itself?

- ☐ Experiment with different organizing principles, using the cut-and-paste feature of your word processor (or even old-fashioned paper and scissors). You can always put things back if your original organization worked better.

Expand your paper with new paragraphs or with new evidence within existing paragraphs.

- ☐ What textual evidence have you used? Is it sufficiently provocative and persuasive? Or does it veer off into another direction?

- ☐ Have you successfully integrated quotations, summaries, or paraphrases into your own writing, while at the same time acknowledging your source?

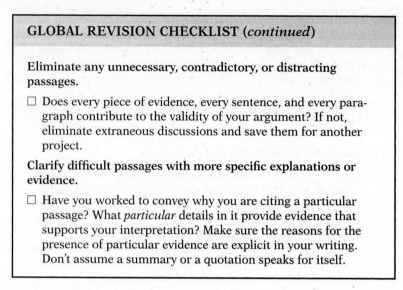

GLOBAL REVISION CHECKLIST (*continued*)

Eliminate any unnecessary, contradictory, or distracting passages.

☐ Does every piece of evidence, every sentence, and every paragraph contribute to the validity of your argument? If not, eliminate extraneous discussions and save them for another project.

Clarify difficult passages with more specific explanations or evidence.

☐ Have you worked to convey why you are citing a particular passage? What *particular* details in it provide evidence that supports your interpretation? Make sure the reasons for the presence of particular evidence are explicit in your writing. Don't assume a summary or a quotation speaks for itself.

Once you have completed your first, large-scale revision, chances are you will feel more confident about the content and structure of your paper. The thesis and focus are strong, the evidence is lined up, and the major points are clear. Print out the new version, take another break if you can, and prepare to move on to the second phase of revision, the one that takes place at the local level of words, phrases, and sentences.

Local Revision

The focus here is on style and clarity. The types of changes you will make in this stage are, essentially, small-scale versions of the changes you made in the first round of revision: adding, cutting, reorganizing, and clarifying. Are you sure about the meanings of any difficult or unusual words you have used? Is there enough variety in sentence style to keep your writing interesting? Do the same words or phrases appear again and again? Are the images vivid? Are the verbs strong? One way to assess the effectiveness of a paper's style is to read it aloud and hear how it sounds. You may feel a little foolish doing this, but many people find it very helpful.

LOCAL REVISION CHECKLIST

Consider your sentences.

☐ Do you keep the writing interesting by using a variety of sentence types and sentences of different lengths?

☐ Have you perhaps used an occasional rhetorical question to get your readers thinking? (This strategy should be used in moderation. Too many questions in a paper become distracting.)

☐ Does each sentence clearly follow from the last one? Or do you need to reorganize the sentences within a particular paragraph to provide clearer transitions between sentences?

☐ Look at the first and last sentences in each paragraph. Do they provide sufficient transitions from one paragraph to the next?

Consider your word choice.

☐ Do you use the same words and phrases again and again? If so, could you vary your word choice a bit?

☐ If you use any special literary terms or other jargon, are you absolutely certain that you are using these terms correctly?

☐ Take a look at the verbs. Are many of them strong and active, or do most sentences rely on dull linking verbs like *is* or *seems*?

Final Editing and Proofreading

Once you have revised your essay a second time and achieved both content and a style that please you, it's time for final editing. This is where you make it "correct."

FINAL EDITING CHECKLIST

Check your spelling.

☐ Have you spelled everything correctly? (Should it be *their* or *there*? *It's* or *its*?)

☐ Do not rely on your computer's spell-check function. This only tells you if the word you typed is a word, not if it's the correct word. When in doubt, look it up.

Check your punctuation.

☐ Look for things that have caused you trouble in the past. Should you use a comma or a semicolon? Again, when in doubt, look it up.

☐ Pay special attention to quotations. Does the question mark go inside or outside of the quotation marks? Have you used both opening and closing quotation marks for each quotation?

Check your formatting.

☐ Is your manuscript format correct? Unless your instructor has provided other instructions, follow the format described on pages 49–50.

☐ Have you italicized or underlined titles of plays and novels (*Othello* or *The Woman Warrior*) and put the titles of short stories and poems in quotation marks ("Love in L.A.," "The Fish")?

☐ Does your works cited list follow MLA format, and do you properly cite your quotations in the body of the text? Nobody expects you to know all the rules on your own, but you should know where to look for them.

☐ If you have questions about citation and formatting, look them up in this book or in a good dictionary, grammar handbook, or other reference. A good online source is Diana Hacker's *Research and Documentation Online*: http://www.dianahacker.com/resdoc/.

Here is a paragraph ready for final editing from a student essay on *Hamlet*. Notice the kinds of corrections that the student will have to make before the paragraph is done.

The supernatural relm affects the revenge tragedy in other ways than the appearance and presence of ghosts. In Hamlet, the religious concern with final absolution both inflames Hamlet's desire for revenge and causes him to hesitate in carrying out revenge. Not only has Hamlet's father been murdered, but he was also Cut off even in the blossoms of [his] sin, / Unhousled, disappointed, unanel'd, / No reck'ning made, but sent to [his] account / With all [his] imperfections on [his] head (1.5.77-80). For Hamlet's father, being murdered is doubly disastrous; not only is his life cut short. But he must burn away "the foul crimes done in [his] days of nature" in purgatory before he can be granted access to heaven (1.5.13). A normal death would have afforded him final absolution, and thus a direct route to heaven. The same concern that makes Hamlet's father's death even more terrible also causes Hamlet to pass on a perfect opportunity to exact revenge on his father's murderer. Hamlet finds Claudius praying, alone. To kill a man in prayer means to kill a man who has had all his sins absolved. Hamlet observes Claudius and reasons: "A villain kills my father, and for that, / I, his sole son, do this same villain send / To heaven." (3.3.76-78) Hamlet's concern for the supernatural afterlife affects his carrying out revenge.

Spelling: "realm"

Italicize "Hamlet."

Remember to add quotation marks around the direct quotation.

This should be a comma joining two sentence fragments.

This period belongs outside the parentheses, after the act, scene, and line number.

One final word of advice as you revise your paper: ask for help. Doing so is neither cheating nor an admission of defeat. In fact, professional writers do it all the time. Despite the persistent image of writers toiling in isolation, most successful writers seek advice at various stages. More important, they are willing to listen to that advice and to rethink what they have written if it seems not to be communicating what they had intended.

PEER EDITING AND WORKSHOPS

Some instructors give class time for draft workshops, sometimes called peer editing, in which you work with your fellow students, trying to help one another improve your work-in-progress. Such workshops can benefit you in two ways. First, your classmates can offer you critiques and advice on what you might have missed in your own rereading. Second, reading and discussing papers other than your own will help you grow as a writer, showing you a variety of ways in which a topic can be approached. If you really like something about a peer's paper—say, a vivid introduction or the effective use of humor—make note of how it works within the paper and consider integrating something similar into a future paper of your own. We are not, of course, advocating copying your classmates; rather, we are pointing out that you can learn a lot from other people's writing.

Some students are uncomfortable with such workshops. They may feel they don't know enough about writing to give valid advice to others, or they may doubt whether advice from their peers is particularly valuable. But you don't need to be a great literary critic, much less an expert on style or grammar, to give genuinely useful advice to a fellow writer. Whatever your skills or limitations as a writer, you have something invaluable to give: the thoughts and impressions of a real reader working through a paper. It is only when we see how a reader responds to what we've written that we know if a paper is communicating its intended message. If you are given an opportunity to engage in peer workshops, make the most of them.

Your instructor may give you guidelines regarding what to look for in others' drafts, or you may be left more or less on your own. In either case, keep these general guidelines in mind:

- **Be respectful of one another's work.** You should, of course, treat your peers' work with the same respect and seriousness that you would want for your own. Keep your criticism constructive and avoid personal attacks, even if you disagree strongly with an opinion. You can help your fellow writers by expressing a contrary opinion in a civilized and thoughtful manner.

- **Be honest.** This means giving real, constructive criticism when it is due. Don't try to spare your workshop partner's feelings by saying "That's great" or "It's fine," when it really isn't. When asked what went badly in a peer workshop, students most commonly respond *not* that their peers were too harsh on their work but that they were not harsh enough. Wouldn't you rather hear about a problem with your work from a peer in a draft workshop than from your professor after you have already handed in the final draft? So would your classmates.

- **Look for the good as well as the bad in a draft.** No paper, no matter how rough or problematic, is completely without merit. And no paper, no matter how clever or well written, couldn't be improved. By pointing out both what works and what doesn't, you will help your classmates grow as writers.

- **Keep an eye on the time.** It's easy to get wrapped up in a discussion of an interesting paper and not allow adequate time for another paper. Say you're given half an hour to work with your draft and that of one classmate. When you reach the fifteen-minute mark, move on, no matter how interesting your discussion is. Fair is fair. On the other hand, don't stop short of the allotted time. If you are reading carefully and thinking hard about one another's drafts, it should be impossible to finish early.

- **Take notes on your draft itself or on a separate sheet.** You may be certain that you will remember what was said in a workshop, but you would be amazed how often people forget the good advice they heard and intended to follow. Better safe than sorry—take careful notes.

- **Ask questions.** Asking questions about portions of a draft you don't understand or find problematic can help its writer see what needs to be clarified, expanded, or reworked. Useful questions can range from the large scale (*What is the purpose of this paragraph?*) to the small (*Is this a quote? Who said it?*).

- **Don't assume that explaining yourself to your workshop partner can replace revision.** Sometimes your workshop partners will ask a question, and when you answer it for them, they will say, "Oh, right, that makes sense," leaving you with the impression that everything is clear now. But remember, your classmates didn't understand it from the writing alone, and you won't be there to explain it to your instructor.

- **Be specific in your comments.** Vague comments like "The introduction is good" or "It's sort of confusing here" are not much help. Aim for something more like "The introduction was funny and really made me want to read on" or "This paragraph confused me because it seems to contradict what you said in the previous one." With comments like these, a writer will have a much better sense of where to focus his or her revision energies.

- **Try to focus on the big picture.** When you are reading a draft, it's tempting to zero in on distracting little mistakes in spelling, punctuation, or word choice. While it's generally fine to point out or circle such surface matters as you go along, a draft workshop is not about correcting mistakes. It's about helping one another to re-see and rethink your papers on a global scale.

- **Push your partners to help you more.** If your workshop partners seem shy or reluctant to criticize, prompt them to say more by letting them know that you really want advice and that you are able to take criticism. Point out to them what you perceive as the trouble spots in the essay, and ask if they have any ideas to help you out. It feels good, of course, to hear that someone likes your paper and cannot imagine how to improve it. But in the long run it is even better to get real, useful advice that will lead to a better paper. If your classmates are not helping you enough, it's your responsibility to ask for more criticism.

Even if your class does not include workshop time, you can still use the many resources available to you on campus. Find one or two other members of your class and conduct your own peer workshop, reading and critiquing one another's drafts. Be sure to arrange such a meeting far enough in advance of the due date so that you will have ample time to implement any good revision advice you receive. Many campuses also have writing or tutoring centers, and the workers in these centers, often advanced students who are skilled writers, can offer a good deal of help. Remember, again, that you should make an appointment to see a tutor well in advance of the paper's due date, and you should *not* expect a tutor or mentor to revise or "fix" your paper for you. That is, ultimately, your job. And, of course, you can also approach your instructor at any phase of the writing process and ask for advice and help.

But remember, no matter where you turn for advice, the final responsibility for your paper is yours. Any advice and help you receive from classmates, tutors, friends—or even your instructor—is just that: advice and help. It is *your* paper, and *you* must be the one to make the decisions about which advice to follow and which to ignore, and how to implement changes to improve your paper. The key is to keep an open mind, seek help from all available sources, and give yourself plenty of time to turn your first draft into a final paper that makes you truly proud.

TIPS FOR WRITING ABOUT LITERATURE

Each genre of literature—fiction, poetry, and drama—poses its own, slightly different set of assumptions, opportunities, and problems for writers, which are covered in more detail in the sections that follow.

However, the following general principles can help you as you write about any form of literature:

- **Don't assume that your readers will remember (or consider important) the same ideas or incidents in the literature that you do.** You should assume that your readers have *read* the literature but not necessarily that they have reacted to it the same way you have. Therefore, whenever possible, use specific examples and evidence in the form of quotations and summaries to back up your claims.

- **Do not retell the plot or text at length.** Some writers are tempted to begin with a plot summary or even to include the text of a short poem at the beginning of a paper. However, this strategy can backfire by delaying the real substance of your paper. Be discriminating when you summarize—keep quotations short and get to the point you want to make as quickly as possible.

- **Do not assume that quotations or summaries are self-sufficient and prove your point automatically.** Summaries and quotations are a starting point; you need to analyze them thoroughly in your own words, explaining why they are important. As a general rule, each quotation or summary should be followed by at least several sentences of analysis.

- **It is customary to use the present tense when writing about literature**, even if the events discussed take place in the distant past. Example:

  When she sees that Romeo is dead, Juliet kills herself with his knife.

- **The first time you mention an author, use his or her full name.** For subsequent references, the last name is sufficient. (Do not use first names only; it sounds as if you know an author personally.)

- **Titles of poems, short stories, and essays should be put in quotation marks. Titles of books, plays, and periodicals (magazines, newspapers, etc.) should be italicized or underlined.** In titles and in all quotations, follow spelling, capitalization, and punctuation exactly as it occurs in the work itself.

- **Give your paper a title.** A title doesn't need to be elaborate or super clever, but it should give some clue as to what the paper is about and begin setting up expectations for your reader. Simply restating the assignment, such as "Essay #2" or "Comparison and Contrast Paper," is of little help to a reader and might even suggest intellectual laziness on the part of the writer. For the same reason, avoid giving your paper the same title as the work of literature you are writing about; unless you're Shakespeare or Hemingway, don't title your paper *Hamlet* or "A Clean, Well-Lighted Place."

- **Above all, use common sense and *be consistent*.**

USING QUOTATIONS EFFECTIVELY

At some point, you will want to quote the literature you are writing about, and you might also want to quote some secondary research sources as well. Quotations ground your paper in the literature you are discussing and prevent your argument from being overly abstract. They also allow the author of the literature a chance to shine through in his or her own words, showing that you respect and appreciate the author's work. Quotations bring emphasis, variety, and specificity to your writing. Be selective, though, in your use of quotations so that the dominant voice of the paper is your own, not a patchwork of the words of others. Here is general advice to help you integrate quotations effectively into your essays.

Try to avoid floating quotations. Sometimes writers simply lift a sentence out of the original, put quotation marks around it, and identify the source (if at all) in a subsequent sentence.

> "I met a traveler from an antique land." This is how Shelley's poem "Ozymandias" begins.

Doing so can create confusion for a reader, who is momentarily left to ponder where the quotation comes from and why have you quoted it. In addition to potentially causing confusion, such quoting can read as awkward and choppy, as there is no transition between another writer's words and yours.

Use at least an attributed quotation; that is, one that names the source *within* the sentence containing the quotation, usually in a lead-in phrase.

> Shelley begins his poem "Ozymandias" with the words "I met a traveler from an antique land."

This way the reader knows right away who originally wrote or said the quoted material and knows (or at least expects) that your commentary will follow. It also provides a smoother transition between your words and the quotation.

Whenever possible, use an integrated quotation. To do this, you make the quotation a part of your own sentence.

> When the narrator of "Ozymandias" begins by saying that he "met a traveler from an antique land," we are immediately thrust into a mysterious world.

This is the hardest sort of quoting to do since it requires that you make the quoted material fit in grammatically with your own sentence, but the payoff in clarity and sharp prose is usually well worth the extra time spent on sentence revision.

Adding to or Altering a Quotation

Sometimes, especially when you are using integrated quotations effectively, you will find that you need to slightly alter the words you are quoting. You should, of course, keep quotations exact whenever possible, but occasionally the disparity between the tense, point of view, or grammar of your sentence and that of the quoted material will necessitate some alterations. Other difficulties can arise when you quote a passage that already contains a quotation or when you need to combine quotation marks with other punctuation marks. When any of these situations arise, the following guidelines should prove useful. The examples of quoted text that follow are all drawn from this original passage from *Hamlet*, in which Hamlet and his friend Horatio are watching a gravedigger unearth old skulls in a cemetery:

> HAMLET: That skull had a tongue in it, and could sing once. How the knave jowls it to the ground, as if 'twere Cain's jaw-bone, that did the first murder! This might be the pate of a politician, which this ass now o'erreaches, one that would circumvent God, might it not?
> HORATIO: It might, my lord.
> HAMLET: Or of a courtier, which could say "Good morrow, sweet lord! How dost thou, sweet lord?" This might be my Lord Such-a-one, that prais'd my Lord Such-a-one's horse when 'a meant to beg it, might it not?

If you ever alter anything in a quotation or add words to it in order to make it clear and grammatically consistent with your own writing, you need to signal to your readers what you have added or changed. This is done by enclosing your words within square brackets in order to distinguish them from those in the source. If, for instance, you feel Hamlet's reference to the gravedigger as "this ass" is unclear, you could clarify it either by substituting your own words, as in the first example here, or by adding the identifying phrase to the original quote, as in the second example:

> Hamlet wonders if it is "the pate of a politician, which [the gravedigger] now o'erreaches."

> Hamlet wonders if it is "the pate of a politician, which this ass [the gravedigger] now o'erreaches."

Omitting Words from a Quotation

To keep a quotation focused and to the point, you will sometimes want to omit words, phrases, or even whole sentences that do not contribute to your point. Any omission is signaled by ellipses, or three spaced periods, with square brackets around them. (The brackets are required to distinguish your own ellipses from any that might occur in the original source.)

> Hamlet wonders if the skull "might be the pate of a politician [. . .] that would circumvent God."

It is usually not necessary to use ellipses at the beginning of a quotation, since a reader assumes you are quoting only a relevant portion of text, but MLA style recommends using ellipses at the end of a quotation if words are dropped at the end of the final quoted sentence.

Quotations within Quotations

If you are quoting material that itself contains a quotation, the internal quotation is set off with single quotation marks rather than the standard double quotation marks that will enclose the entire quotation.

> Hamlet wonders if he might be looking at the skull "of a courtier, which could say 'Good morrow, sweet lord! How dost thou, sweet lord?'"

When the text you're quoting contains *only* material already in quotation marks in the original, the standard double quotation marks are all you need.

> Hamlet wonders if the courtier once said "Good morrow, sweet lord! How dost thou, sweet lord?"

Quotation Marks with Other Punctuation

When a period or a comma comes at the end of a quotation, it should always be placed inside the closing quotation marks, whether or not this punctuation was in the original source. In the first example that follows, note that the period following "horse" is within the quotation marks, even though there is no period there in the original. In the second example, the comma following "once" is also within the quotation marks, even though in Shakespeare's original "once" is followed by a period.

> Hamlet muses that the skull might have belonged to "my Lord Such-a-one, that prais'd my Lord Such-a-one's horse."

> "That skull had a tongue in it, and could sing once," muses Hamlet.

Question marks and exclamation points are placed inside quotation marks if they are part of the original quotation and outside of the marks if they are part of your own sentence but not part of the passage you are quoting. In the first example, the question is Hamlet's, and so the question mark must be placed within the quotation marks; in the second example, the question is the essay writer's, and so the question mark is placed outside of the quotation marks.

> Hamlet asks Horatio if the skull "might be my Lord Such-a-one, that prais'd my Lord Such-a-one's horse when 'a meant to beg it, might it not?"

> Why is Hamlet so disturbed that this skull "might be the pate of a politician"?

These sorts of punctuation details are notoriously hard to remember, so you should not feel discouraged if you begin forgetting such highly specialized rules moments after reading them. At least know where you can look them up, and do so when you proofread your paper. A willingness to attend to detail is what distinguishes serious students and gives writing a polished, professional appearance. Also, the more you work with quotations, the easier it will be to remember the rules.

Quoting from Stories

The guidelines that follow should be used not only when you quote from stories but also when you quote from any prose work, be it fiction or nonfiction.

Short Quotations

For short quotations of four lines or fewer, run the quotation in with your own text, using quotation marks to signal the beginning and end of the quotation.

> Young Goodman Brown notices that the branches touched by his companion "became strangely withered and dried up, as with a week's sunshine."

Long Quotations

When a quotation is longer than four lines in your text, set it off from your essay by beginning a new line and indenting it one inch from the left margin only, as shown here. This is called a block quotation.

> Young Goodman Brown then notices something strange about his companion:
>
> > As they went, he plucked a branch of maple to serve for a walking stick, and began to strip it of the twigs and little boughs, which were wet with evening dew. The moment his fingers touched them they became strangely withered and dried up, as with a week's sunshine. Thus the pair proceeded, . . . until suddenly, . . . Goodman Brown sat himself down on the stump of a tree and refused to go any further.

Note that no quotation marks are used with block quotations. The indentation is sufficient to signal to your readers that this is a quotation.

Quoting from Poems

Short Quotations

For quotations of up to three lines, run the text right into your own, using quotation marks just as you would with a prose quotation. However, since the placement of line endings can be significant in a poem, you need to indicate where they occur. This is done by including a slash mark, with a single space on each side, where the line breaks occur. (Some students find this awkward-looking at first, but you will quickly get used to it. Your instructor will expect you to honor the poet's choices regarding line breaks.)

> In "Sailing to Byzantium," Yeats describes an old man as "a paltry thing, / A tattered coat upon a stick."

Long Quotations

For quotations of four lines or more, "block" the material, setting it off one inch from the left margin, duplicating all line breaks of the original. Do not use quotation marks with block quotations.

> In "Sailing to Byzantium," Yeats describes both the ravages of age and the possibility of renewal in the poem's second stanza:

An aged man is but a paltry thing,
A tattered coat upon a stick, unless
Soul clap its hands and sing, and louder sing
For every tatter in its mortal dress,
Nor is there singing school but studying
Monuments of its own magnificence.

Quoting from Plays

Short Single-Speaker Passages

When you quote a short passage of drama with a single speaker, treat the quoted text just as you would prose fiction:

> Nora's first words in *A Doll House* are "Hide the tree well, Helene. The children mustn't get a glimpse of it till this evening, after it's trimmed."

Longer or More Complex Passages

For a longer quotation, or a quotation of any length involving more than one character, you will need to block off the quotation. Begin each separate piece of dialogue indented one inch from the left margin with the character's name, typed in all capital letters, followed by a period. Subsequent lines of the character's speech should be indented an additional one-quarter inch. (Your word processor's "hanging indent" function is useful for achieving this effect without having to indent each separate line.) As with fiction or poetry, do not use quotation marks for block quotations.

> We see the tension between Nora and her husband in their very first confrontation:
>
> > NORA. Oh, but Torvald, this year we really should let ourselves go a bit.
> >   It's the first Christmas we haven't had to economize.
> > HELMER. But you know we can't go squandering.
> > NORA. Oh yes, Torvald, we can squander a little now. Can't we?

Verse Drama

Many older plays, including classical Greek drama and much of the work of Shakespeare and his contemporaries, are written at least partly in poetic verse. When you quote a verse drama, you must respect the line endings, just as you do in quoting poetry. The first example here shows a short quotation with slash marks that indicate line endings; the second shows a longer, block quotation in verse form.

> Hamlet's most famous soliloquy begins, "To be, or not to be, that is the question: / Whether 'tis nobler in the mind to suffer / The slings and arrows of outrageous fortune."

> Hamlet then begins his most famous soliloquy:
> To be, or not to be, that is the question:
> Whether 'tis nobler in the mind to suffer
> The slings and arrows of outrageous fortune,
> Or to take arms against a sea of troubles,
> And by opposing end them.

Tips for Quoting

- **Double-check the wording, spelling, and punctuation of every quotation you use.** Even if something seems "wrong" in the original source—a nonstandard spelling, a strange mark of punctuation, or even a factual error—resist the urge to correct it. When you put quotation marks around something, you indicate that you are reproducing it exactly as it first appeared. If you feel the need to clarify that an error or inconsistency is not yours, you may follow it by the word *sic* (Latin for *thus*), not italicized, in square brackets. Example: The mother in the anonymous poem "Lord Randal" asks her son "wha [sic] met ye there?"
- **Use the shortest quotation you can while still making your point.** Remember, the focus should always be on your own ideas, and the dominant voice should be yours. Don't quote a paragraph from a source when a single sentence contains the heart of what you need. Don't quote a whole sentence when you can simply integrate a few words into one of your own sentences.
- **Never assume a quotation is self-explanatory.** Each time you include a quotation, analyze it and explain why you have quoted it. Remember that your reader may have a different reaction to the quotation than you did.
- **If you are quoting a *character* in a story, play, or poem, be sure to distinguish that character from the *author*.** Hamlet says "To be or not to be," not Shakespeare, and you should make that distinction clear.

- **Take care not to distort the meaning of a quotation.** It is intellectually dishonest to quote an author or a speaker out of context or to use ellipses or additions in such a way as to change the meaning or integrity of source material. Treat your sources with the same respect you would want if you were to be quoted in a newspaper or magazine.

MANUSCRIPT FORM

If your instructor gives you directions about what your paper should look like, follow them exactly. If not, the following basic guidelines on manuscript form, recommended by the Modern Language Association of America (MLA), will work well in most instances. The most comprehensive guide to MLA style is *MLA Handbook for Writers of Research Papers*, 7th edition (New York: MLA, 2009). For an online guide to MLA style, see Diana Hacker's *Research and Documentation Online*: http://www.dianahacker.com/resdoc/. The guiding principle here is readability—you want the look of your paper to distract as little as possible from the content.

- **Use plain white paper, black ink, and a standard, easy-to-read font.** To make your paper stand out from the masses, it might seem like a nice touch to use visual design elements like colored or decorated paper, fancy fonts, and so forth. However, your instructor has a lot of reading to do, and anything that distracts or slows down that reading is a minus, not a plus, for your paper. For the same reason, avoid illustrations, pictures of authors, and so forth, unless they are needed to clarify a point. Distinguish your paper through content and style, not flashy design.
- **No separate cover page is needed.** Also, don't waste your time and money on report covers or folders unless asked to do so by your instructor. Many instructors, in fact, find covers cumbersome and distracting.
- **Include vital information in the upper left corner of your first page.** This information usually consists of your name, the name of your instructor, the course number of the class, and the date you submit the paper.
- **Center your paper's title.** The title should appear in upper- and lowercase letters, and in the same font as the rest of your paper—not italicized, boldface, or set within quotation marks.

- **Page numbers should appear in the upper right corner of each page.** Do not include the word *page* or the abbreviation *p.* with the page numbers. Use your word processing program's "header" or "running head" feature to include your last name before the page numbers.

See the sample student papers in this book for examples of correct MLA-style formatting. These basic guidelines should carry you through most situations, but if you have any questions regarding format, ask your instructor for his or her preferences.

CHAPTER 4

Common Writing Assignments

Chances are you will encounter a variety of writing assignments in your literature class, possibly ranging from a brief personal response to an extended literary research paper. Each assignment offers you two opportunities. First, writing about a particular piece (or multiple pieces) of literature forces you to think more closely than a simple reading does, so you will end up learning more about the story, poem, or play. Second, writing is your best opportunity to share your thoughts with your instructor, and possibly your classmates, so you can have an impact on someone else's thinking as well. Generally, the assignments in such a class build cumulatively on one another, so that explication and analysis, for instance, are useful techniques in a research paper, and writing a comparison and contrast paper might give you tools to help you answer a question on an essay exam. Each time you get a new assignment, ask yourself, "What did I learn from the last assignment that I might apply to this one?" This chapter outlines some of the assignments you might be given (summary, response, explication, analysis, comparison and contrast, and essay exams), provides examples of each, and demonstrates how each skill might build on the previous skill.

SUMMARY

A **summary** is a brief recap of the most important points—plot, character, and so on—in a work of literature. To demonstrate that you have understood a story or play, for instance, you may be asked to summarize its plot as homework before class discussions. A summary of Nathaniel Hawthorne's "Young Goodman Brown" follows:

> Set in seventeenth-century Salem, Massachusetts, Nathaniel Hawthorne's "Young Goodman Brown" follows the fortunes of the title character when he leaves his young wife, Faith, for a mysterious rendezvous in a forest at night. The character he meets in the forbidding woods is unnamed, but Hawthorne hints that he may be the Devil himself. As they proceed deeper into the forest on their unspecified but presumably unholy errand, Goodman

Brown's misgivings increase, especially when they encounter his fellow townsfolk—people Goodman Brown thought were good Christians—en route to the same meeting. But when they are joined by Faith, Brown recklessly resolves to participate. At the ceremony, the new converts are called forth, but as he and Faith step forward to be anointed in blood, he rebels and urges Faith to resist. Instantly he finds himself alone in the forest, and when he returns to town the next morning, uncertain whether it was all a dream, he finds himself suspicious and wary of his neighbors and his wife. His "Faith" has been corrupted, and to the end of his days he remains a bitter and untrusting man: "his dying hour was gloom."

A summary can be longer or shorter than this example, depending on your purpose. Notice that interpretation is kept to a minimum ("His 'Faith' has been corrupted") and the summary is recounted in the present tense ("he returns to town," "he remains a bitter and untrusting man").

It is rare for a full essay assignment to be based on summary alone. Keep in mind that for most of the papers you write, your readers—your teacher and possibly your classmates—are probably familiar with the literary work you are writing about, and do not need a recap of the entire work. Generally, they need only to be reminded of key points about the text that are most relevant to the argument you are making about it.

While a *summary* is not a kind of writing assignment that you will likely have to produce often in a literature course, *summarizing* is a skill you will need to develop. It is useful to be able to focus on the most important parts of a text, knowing what is most vital. Short summaries, either of a work (or part of a work) of literature or of critical essays about literature, are commonly used as part of the supporting evidence in more complex papers. When you are using secondary sources in a paper about a literary work—as when you write a literary research paper—chances are that your audience has not read the critical essays you have read. Therefore, you may need to summarize for your readers the arguments of those critical essays.

Often such summaries are only a few sentences in length and restate the author's thesis, possibly with a few examples of the kind of evidence the author uses to support the thesis. Just as often, you may want to summarize only part of a critical essay, a part that is pertinent to your paper. For example, if you have read an essay about Hawthorne's use of imagery in "Young Goodman Brown," for the purposes of your paper you may need to summarize only the section that deals with the imagery of light and darkness in the story. Ask yourself, "What do my readers need to know to follow my argument, and what evidence do I need to provide to convince them of my point of view?" Summarize accordingly.

RESPONSE

Though you may state or imply whether or not you liked the literary selection in question when you write a response paper, the main purpose is not to provide a review or a rating. Rather, the goal of such a paper is twofold: to describe your personal response to a particular reading assignment and to explain why you had this reaction. Of course, our reactions to literature are often multiple and complex, so you need to be selective in what you write. Don't try to explain every response and every thought you had while reading. Rather, choose one significant thought you had while reading and explore that in depth.

Response papers in general are somewhat informal and do not necessarily follow the thesis-and-support model common in other types of literature papers. Response papers are often fairly brief, and since you are writing about your personal responses, it's generally okay to use the first-person pronoun I. Remember, though, that this is not simply a personal essay in which you explore your own life and thoughts. Keep the literature as the main focus, and if you call on your own experiences, do so in order to explain and analyze some facet of the story, poem, or play. Since there are no hard-and-fast rules about response papers, be sure to read your instructor's directions carefully and follow them closely. If you have any questions, ask.

After reading Jamaica Kincaid's very short story "Girl," take a moment to consider your own response to it and where that response comes from. Then read and consider the student response paper that follows.

JAMAICA KINCAID   [b. 1949]

Girl

Wash the white clothes on Monday and put them on the stone heap; wash the color clothes on Tuesday and put them on the clothesline to dry; don't walk barehead in the hot sun; cook pumpkin fritters in very hot sweet oil; soak your little cloths right after you take them off; when buying cotton to make yourself a nice blouse, be sure that it doesn't have gum on it, because that way it won't hold up well after a wash; soak salt fish overnight before you cook it; is it true that you sing benna° in Sunday

Benna: Calypso music.

school?; always eat your food in such a way that it won't turn someone else's stomach; on Sundays try to walk like a lady and not like the slut you are so bent on becoming; don't sing benna in Sunday school; you mustn't speak to wharf-rat boys, not even to give directions; don't eat fruits on the street—flies will follow you; *but I don't sing benna on Sundays at all and never in Sunday school*; this is how to sew on a button; this is how to make a button-hole for the button you have just sewed on; this is how to hem a dress when you see the hem coming down and so to prevent yourself from looking like the slut I know you are so bent on becoming; this is how you iron your father's khaki shirt so that it doesn't have a crease; this is how you iron your father's khaki pants so that they don't have a crease; this is how you grow okra—far from the house, because okra tree harbors red ants; when you are growing dasheen,° make sure it gets plenty of water or else it makes your throat itch when you are eating it; this is how you sweep a corner; this is how you sweep a whole house; this is how you sweep a yard; this is how you smile to someone you don't like too much; this is how you smile to someone you don't like at all; this is how you smile to someone you like completely; this is how you set a table for tea; this is how you set a table for dinner; this is how you set a table for dinner with an important guest; this is how you set a table for lunch; this is how you set a table for breakfast; this is how to behave in the presence of men who don't know you very well, and this way they won't recognize immediately the slut I have warned you against becoming; be sure to wash every day, even if it is with your own spit; don't squat down to play marbles—you are not a boy, you know; don't pick people's flowers—you might catch something; don't throw stones at blackbirds, because it might not be a blackbird at all; this is how to make a bread pudding; this is how to make doukona;° this is how to make pepper pot; this is how to make a good medicine for a cold; this is how to make a good medicine to throw away a child before it even becomes a child; this is how to catch a fish; this is how to throw back a fish you don't like, and that way something bad won't fall on you; this is how to bully a man; this is how a man bullies you; this is how to love a man, and if this doesn't work there are other ways, and if they don't work don't feel too bad about giving up; this is how to spit up in the air if you feel like it, and this is how to move quick so that it doesn't fall on you; this is how to make ends meet; always squeeze bread to make sure it's fresh; *but what if the baker won't let me feel the bread?*; you mean to say that after all you are really going to be the kind of woman who the baker won't let near the bread?

[1978]

Dasheen: Taro, an edible starchy plant.
Doukona: A spicy plantain pudding.

Tom Lyons
Professor Tritle
English 112
17 October 2011

A Boy's View of "Girl"

It may sound peculiar for a young man to say this, but I could really relate to the character in Jamaica Kincaid's story "Girl." My father is a very old-fashioned, conservative man, and all through my childhood he constantly instructed my brother and me about proper behavior for a boy. His instructions and corrections were meant to be for our own good, but they put a lot of pressure on us from a very young age. This is similar to the experience of the young girl in Kincaid's story.

I assume the speaker in the story is the girl's mother, or at least some older female relative. She keeps saying "this is how" you do things, as though there is only one right way for every-thing. It's as if the girl can't figure out anything for herself, not even how to smile at someone she likes. I notice that the girl doesn't even have a name, and she has almost no chance to speak for herself. It seems that the mother doesn't particularly care who the girl is as an individual; what matters is just the fact that she is a girl. The mother also makes huge assumptions about what the girl is like. She thinks that the girl sings inappropriate songs in Sunday school and that she is trying to become a "slut." The poor girl never gets a chance to defend herself against these accusations.

Of course, my father was not worried about me becoming a slut, but he was very concerned that my brother and I should grow up to be strong, masculine men. The mother in the story empha-sizes the girl's domestic duties like cooking, cleaning, and sewing. My father always said that men should be good providers and that a man's work was very important. Men should also be responsible for protecting the family. I remember he went on a business trip when I was about twelve years old, and he said, "You need to take care of your mother while I'm gone." That's a big responsibility for a kid. My father thinks that our culture is too permissive and that

Tom's introduc-tion makes clear his focus: the similarities between his own experience and that of the girl in Kincaid's story.

Tom points out particular fea-tures of the story that struck him, all related to the way the girl's mother forces her will on the girl.

Tom uses specifics from the story to demonstrate his point.

When Tom turns to his own childhood experience, he makes direct comparison to "Girl," so the focus is always on the story.

Lyons 2

many boys are not raised to be responsible men. This is similar to the mother in the story, who seems to think the daughter needs to be told constantly how to be a proper woman.

This story hit home for me. It really shows how parents and elders can pass on expectations about gender roles to future generations. Young boys and girls do need advice and strong role models, but parents can sometimes go too far in imposing their own values on the next generation. I hope that as time goes by, both boys and girls are subjected to less of this sort of pressure so that they are free to develop their own unique personalities as people, not just as gender stereotypes.

Tom ends his response paper by explaining the thoughts and feelings the story provoked in him.

EXPLICATION

One common assignment is to perform an **explication** or a close-reading of a poem or short prose passage. As the word implies, an *explication* takes what is implicit or subtle in a work of literature and makes it explicit and clear. Literary language tends to be densely packed with meaning, and your job as you explicate it is to unfold that meaning and lay it out for your reader. The principal technique of explication is close-reading; indeed, explication and close-reading are so closely related that many writers use the words virtually interchangeably. When you write this sort of paper, you will examine a piece of literature very closely, paying special attention to such elements of the language as sentence structure, **style**, **imagery**, **figurative language** (such as **similes** and **metaphors**), word choice, and perhaps even grammar and punctuation. The job of an explication is twofold: to point out particular, salient elements of style and to explain the purpose and effect of these elements within the text.

When assigned an explication or a close-reading, you might be tempted to simply walk through a text line by line, pointing out interesting features of style as they occur. A paper written in this way, though, can devolve into little more than summary or restatement of the literature in more prosaic language. A better idea is to isolate the various features of the literature on which you will focus and then deal separately with the specifics and implications of each.

The paper that follows is an example of a student essay that provides an explication of a literary text. First, take a look at Robert Herrick's "Upon Julia's Clothes," and then read the student's paper.

ROBERT HERRICK   [1591–1674]

Upon Julia's Clothes

Whenas in silks my Julia goes,
Then, then (methinks) how sweetly flows
That liquefaction of her clothes.

Next, when I cast mine eyes, and see
That brave vibration each way free,   5
O how that glittering taketh me!

[1648]

Jessica Barnes
Professor White
English 108
13 March 2008

Poetry in Motion: Herrick's "Upon Julia's Clothes"

In its brief six lines, Robert Herrick's "Upon Julia's Clothes" is a celebration of the physical sensuousness of the speaker's object of desire. The poem is structured like a seashell with two parts. In the first stanza, the speaker makes a seemingly simple observation: when Julia walks past, her silken clothes seem to flow as if they're liquid. In the second stanza, though, he provides a second observation: when Julia's body is "each way free" of the clothing, the speaker is completely overtaken by the beauty of Julia's "brave vibration."

Jessica's introduction lays out clearly the focus and structure of her paper.

Herrick provides several inversions of syntax to place emphasis on certain images. For example, in line 1, Herrick inverts "my Julia goes" with "in silks" to emphasize the importance of "silks" to Julia's sensuality. He creates another inversion in lines 2-3. The sense of the lines is as follows: "Then, then (methinks) that liquefaction of her clothes flows sweetly." Herrick rearranges the sentence to emphasize the sweetness of the flowing and to place the emphasis on "flows" and "clothes" at the ends of the lines.

In this paragraph, Jessica focuses on a specific language feature, syntax, and provides several examples from Herrick's poem.

Herrick also provides several changes in the iambic tetrameter meter to create varied lines within the poem's strict form. In line 2, he repeats "then" two times. In doing so, he forces the reader to pause deeply between each "then" and encourages the reader to meditate on the poet's decision to repeat the word in the first place. In line 6, too, Herrick alternately accelerates and decelerates the tempo of the line. The exclamatory "O" at the beginning of the line suggests that the speaker has been utterly charmed by Julia's beauty. It is a long sound that slows the reader down at the beginning of the line; in addition, it provides a stress on the first syllable of the line, instead of an unstressed syllable followed by a

This paragraph examines a different language feature, poetic meter.

Barnes 2

stressed one (see, for example, "That **brave** vi**bra**tion" in line 5). "Glittering" also disrupts the strict tetrameter of the line. Its three syllables are compressed into two brief syllables ("**glitt**ring") so that the next accent can fall on "**tak**eth me," which emphasizes the fact that the speaker is totally overwhelmed by Julia's naked body.

Jessica begins to tie up her observations about specific language features with some preliminary analysis.

Ultimately, the poem reveals that Julia's beauty is beyond words. We cannot know whether Julia has actually taken her clothes off, or whether she has done so in the imagination of the speaker. Either way, the poem provides many sounds that mirror the "O" of line 6. The end rhyme for all of the lines in the first stanza rhyme with the "O": *goes, flows, clothes*. Each of these words reinforces the importance of Julia's shimmering beauty, and the power of her movements. The "ee" rhymes at the ends of the lines in stanza 2 — *see, free, me* — reinforce the idea that Julia's freedom in her nakedness also frees the poet's pleasure in imagining, or seeing, the "brave vibration" of her body.

The final language feature the paper examines is the repetition of vowel sounds.

ANALYSIS

To analyze, by definition, is to take something apart and examine how the individual parts relate to one another and function within the whole. Engineers frequently analyze complex machinery, looking for ways to improve efficiency or performance. In a similar way, you can take apart a piece of literature to study how a particular part of it functions and what that part contributes to the whole. Typical candidates for literary analysis include **plot development**, **characterization**, **tone**, **irony**, and **symbols**.

Here is an example of a student essay that provides an analysis. First, take a look at Robert Browning's "My Last Duchess"; then read the student's paper.

ROBERT BROWNING [1812–1889]

My Last Duchess

Ferrara°

That's my last Duchess° painted on the wall,
Looking as if she were alive. I call
That piece a wonder, now: Frà Pandolf's° hands
Worked busily a day, and there she stands.
Will't please you sit and look at her? I said   5
"Frà Pandolf" by design, for never read
Strangers like you that pictured countenance,
The depth and passion of its earnest glance,
But to myself they turned (since none puts by
The curtain I have drawn for you, but I)   10
And seemed as they would ask me, if they durst,
How such a glance came there; so, not the first
Are you to turn and ask thus. Sir, 'twas not
Her husband's presence only, called that spot
Of joy into the Duchess' cheek: perhaps   15
Frà Pandolf chanced to say "Her mantle laps
Over my lady's wrist too much," or "Paint
Must never hope to reproduce the faint
Half-flush that dies along her throat": such stuff
Was courtesy, she thought, and cause enough   20
For calling up that spot of joy. She had
A heart—how shall I say?—too soon made glad,
Too easily impressed; she liked whate'er
She looked on, and her looks went everywhere.
Sir, 'twas all one! My favor at her breast,   25
The dropping of the daylight in the West,
The bough of cherries some officious fool
Broke in the orchard for her, the white mule

Ferrara: The poem is based on events that occurred in the life of Alfonso II,
duke of Ferrara in Italy, in the sixteenth century.
1. last Duchess: Ferrara's first wife, Lucrezia, died in 1561 at age seventeen after
three years of marriage.
3. Frà Pandolf: Brother Pandolf, a fictional painter.

She rode with round the terrace—all and each
Would draw from her alike the approving speech,   30
Or blush, at least. She thanked men,—good! but thanked
Somehow—I know not how—as if she ranked
My gift of a nine-hundred-years-old name
With anybody's gift. Who'd stoop to blame
This sort of trifling? Even had you skill   35
In speech—(which I have not)—to make your will
Quite clear to such an one, and say, "Just this
Or that in you disgusts me; here you miss,
Or there exceed the mark"—and if she let
Herself be lessoned so, nor plainly set   40
Her wits to yours, forsooth, and made excuse,
—E'en then would be some stooping; and I choose
Never to stoop. Oh sir, she smiled, no doubt,
Whene'er I passed her; but who passed without
Much the same smile? This grew; I gave commands;   45
Then all smiles stopped together. There she stands
As if alive. Will't please you rise? We'll meet
The company below, then. I repeat,
The Count your master's known munificence
Is ample warrant that no just pretence   50
Of mine for dowry will be disallowed;
Though his fair daughter's self, as I avowed
At starting, is my object. Nay, we'll go
Together down, sir. Notice Neptune, though,
Taming a sea-horse, thought a rarity,   55
Which Claus of Innsbruck° cast in bronze for me!

                                                          [1842]

56. Claus of Innsbruck: A fictional sculptor.

Adam Walker
Professor Blitefield
English 203
22 February 2008

Possessed by the Need for Possession:
Browning's "My Last Duchess"

In "My Last Duchess," Robert Browning's duke reveals his feelings of jealousy and betrayal as he discusses the duchess's portrait. In his dramatic monologue, the duke's public persona as an aristocratic gentleman is shattered by the revelations of his actual feelings about his dead duchess. The duke reveals what upsets him most: his late wife's liberal smiles and attentions to others besides himself. With this focus on the duchess's attentions, Browning creates a compelling portrait of a gentleman who could not exert complete control over his former wife, and may fail to control his future wife as well.

The introduction names the poem to be analyzed and clearly explains that the focus of the paper will be the duke's jealous nature.

The duke repeatedly calls attention to what he sees as the duchess's misinterpretations. The duke imagines the duchess as she sat for Fra Pandolf: "such stuff / Was courtesy, she thought, and cause enough / For calling up that spot of joy" (lines 19-21). According to the duke, the duchess mistook the painter's attentions as courtesies. Her blush, or "spot of joy" (21) on her cheeks, was too indiscriminate for the duke. The duke admits that the duchess blushed at his own advances, but she also blushed at the painter, the "dropping of the daylight in the West" (26), a bough of cherries, and a white mule. The duchess's gaze is an indiscriminate one: she appreciates whatever pleases her, whether it be human, animal, or organic. This infuriates the duke, who thinks that his "nine-hundred-years-old name" (33) ought to make him more valuable in the eyes of the duchess.

Adam quotes specific lines from the poem in order to demonstrate his point. In each case, he integrates the quotation cleanly into his own prose.

The quotation is immediately followed by an explanation of its purpose in the paper.

Eventually, the duke restricts the duchess's blushes with commands: "This grew; I gave commands; / Then all smiles stopped together. There she stands / As if alive" (45-47). These lines are concise and quick compared with the rhetoric of the other

Walker 2

lines in the poem. Even so, they are in some ways the most important. What made the smiles stop? Was the duchess silenced in life? Or was it her death that stopped the smiling? And why does the duke need this portrait that resembles the duchess when she was alive?

Adam uses rhetorical questions to provide stylistic variety and to get the reader thinking.

Ultimately, the showing of the portrait is a way for the duke to show his possessions — and his command of his possessions — to the envoy of the Count. As the duke invites the envoy to come downstairs, he already characterizes his future bride as a kind of possession:

> I repeat,
> The Count your master's known munificence
> Is ample warrant that no just pretence
> Of mine for dowry will be disallowed;
> Though his fair daughter's self, as I avowed
> At starting, is my object. (48-53)

Note that the long quotation is blocked (indented from the left margin) and does not use quotation marks.

After alluding to the generous dowry that he will receive, the duke checks himself by saying that it is "his [the Count's] fair daughter's self" that he has found so compelling. Even so, the duke has started to limit and control the status of his future bride, suggesting that he will exert the same controls on her that he exerted on his late wife. In the end, she runs the same risk of becoming a sea horse that requires Neptune's taming.

Adam's concluding sentence alludes to the final lines of the poem.

COMPARISON AND CONTRAST

Another common paper assignment is the **comparison and contrast** essay. You might be asked to draw comparisons and contrasts within a single work of literature—say, between two characters in a story or play. Even more common is an assignment that asks you to compare and contrast a particular element—characters, setting, style, tone, and so on—in two or more stories, poems, or plays. A *comparison* emphasizes the similarities between two or more items, while a *contrast* highlights their differences. Though some papers do both, it is typical for an essay to emphasize one or the other.

If you are allowed to choose the works of literature for a comparison and contrast paper, take care to select works that have enough in common to make such a comparison interesting and valid. Even if Henrik Ibsen's *A Doll House* and Shirley Jackson's "The Lottery" are your favorites, it is difficult to imagine a well-focused paper comparing these two, as they share virtually nothing in terms of authorship, history, theme, or style, having been written in different genres, in different centuries, and on different continents. It would make far more sense to select two seventeenth-century poems or two love stories.

The paper that follows compares Robert Browning's "My Last Duchess" and Christina Rossetti's "After Death." First, read Rossetti's poem; then read the student paper.

CHRISTINA ROSSETTI   [1830–1894]

After Death

The curtains were half drawn, the floor was swept
  And strewn with rushes, rosemary and may°
Lay thick upon the bed on which I lay,
Where through the lattice ivy-shadows crept.
He leaned above me, thinking that I slept   5
  And could not hear him; but I heard him say,
  "Poor child, poor child": and as he turned away
Came a deep silence, and I knew he wept.
He did not touch the shroud, or raise the fold
  That hid my face, or take my hand in his,   10
    Or ruffle the smooth pillows for my head:
    He did not love me living; but once dead
  He pitied me; and very sweet it is
To know he still is warm though I am cold.

[1849]

May: green or flowering branches used for May Day celebrations.

Bowen 1

Todd Bowen
Professor Harrison
English 215
12 May 2008

Speakers for the Dead:
Narrators in "My Last Duchess"
and "After Death"

In "My Last Duchess," Robert Browning creates a duke whose tight control over his wife — and his preoccupation with his own noble rank — reveal a misogynistic character. Browning's dramatic monologue stands in stark contrast to Christina Rossetti's "After Death," a sonnet in which the speaker comes back from the dead to reveal what she observes about her lover. When paired together, these poems speak to each other in a time period that seemed to have a gothic obsession with the death of young women.

In the poems' style and structure, Browning and Rossetti create completely different portraits of women after death. In "My Last Duchess," the duke uses the actual portrait of his dead wife to create a portrait in words of a woman who smiled too liberally at men who fawned over her. The duke says, "She had / A heart — how shall I say? — too soon made glad, / Too easily impressed; she liked whate'er / She looked on, and her looks went everywhere" (lines 21-24). Throughout his long dramatic monologue, the duke meditates on several moments when the duchess betrays him by smiling at others; however, we as readers never get to hear the duchess's side of the story.

In Rossetti's "After Death," however, the tables are turned: the dead woman gets to speak back to the man who performs his grief over her death. In doing so, she carefully observes the behavior of her lover, who thinks that she is merely a lifeless corpse. In each line of the small sonnet, the speaker observes the man as he leans above her, says "Poor child, poor child" (7), and then turns away without actually touching her body. Even so, the woman suggests that this is an improvement from when she was

Todd's concise introduction names the authors and poems that will be the subject of his comparison, as well as the paper's focus on certain shared features of the poems.

The first two body paragraphs each focus on one of the poems, providing a combination of specific evidence — mostly in the form of quotations — and analysis of this evidence.

Bowen 2

alive: "He did not love me living; but once dead / He pitied me" (ll. 12-13). The speaker's final couplet is especially chilling: "and very sweet it is / To know he still is warm though I am cold" (13-14). The speaker says that it is "sweet" to know that the man has outlived her. She doesn't explain this sweetness, but perhaps it is because she can observe his emotion in a way that she never could have while she was alive.

Note that Todd distinguishes between the poet Rossetti and the speaker of the poem.

When read together, Rossetti's "After Death" and Browning's "My Last Duchess" function as companion pieces, each speaking to the other in a kind of call-and-response. Browning's duke shuts down any speech beyond his own, talking at length in the silence of the portrait and the visitor who looks at it. His story is the only story that he wants to present, even if his speech reveals his own shortcomings. Rossetti's woman provides an alternative perspective of death and mourning as the woman speaks from the dead to reveal the shortcomings of the man who mourns her. Both poems provide chilling perspectives on death, mourning, and marriage in the Victorian period.

The concluding paragraph contains the heart of the actual comparison of the poems.

ESSAY EXAMS

The key to getting through the potentially stressful situation of an essay exam is to be prepared and to know what will be expected of you.

Preparation takes two forms: knowing the material and anticipating the questions. Knowing the material starts with keeping up with all reading and homework assignments throughout the term. You can't possibly read several weeks' or months' worth of material the night before the test and hope to remember it all. The days before the test should be used not for catching up but for review—revisiting the readings, skimming or rereading key passages, and studying your class notes. It's best to break up study sessions into manageable blocks if possible. Reviewing for two hours a night for three nights before the exam will be far more effective than a single six-hour cram session on the eve of the test.

Anticipating the questions that might be on the exam is a bit trickier, but it can be done. What themes and issues have come up again and again in class lectures or discussions? What patterns do you see in your class notes? What points did your instructor stress? These are the topics most likely to appear on the exam. Despite what you might think, it is very rare that an instructor poses intentionally obscure exam questions in an attempt to trip up students or expose their ignorance. Most often, the instructor is providing you with an opportunity to demonstrate what you know, and you should be ready to take that opportunity. You can't, of course, second-guess your instructor perfectly and know for sure what will be on the test, but you can spend some time in advance thinking about what sorts of questions you are likely to encounter and how you would answer them.

Your exam may be open-book or closed-book; find out in advance which it will be, so that you can plan and study accordingly. In an *open-book* test, you are allowed to use your textbook during the exam. This is a big advantage, obviously, as it allows you access to specific evidence, including quotations, to support your points. If you know the exam is going to be open-book, you might also jot down any important notes in the book itself, where you can find them readily if you need them. Use your textbook sparingly, though—just enough to find the evidence you know to be there. Don't waste time browsing the literature hoping to find inspiration or ideas. For a *closed-book* exam, you have to rely on your memory alone. But you should still try to be as specific as possible in your references to the literature, using character names, recalling plot elements, and so forth.

When you sit down to take the exam, you may have the urge to start writing right away, since your time is limited. Suppress that urge and read through the entire exam first, paying special attention to the instruction portion. Often the exam will offer you choices, such as "Answer two of the following three questions" or "Select a single poem as the basis of your answer." If you miss such cues, you may find yourself racing to write three essays and running out of time or discussing several poems shallowly instead of one in depth. Once you are certain what is expected of you, take a few more minutes to plan your answers before you start writing. A few jotted notes or an informal outline may take a moment, but it will likely save you time as you write. If you will be writing more than one essay, take care not to repeat yourself or to write more than one essay about any one piece of literature. The idea is to show your instructor your mastery of the course material, and to do so effectively you should demonstrate breadth of knowledge.

When you do begin writing, bear in mind that instructors have different expectations for exam answers than they do for essays written outside of class. They know that in timed exams you have no time for research or extensive revisions. Clarity and concision are the keys; elegant prose style is not expected (though, of course, it will come as a pleasant surprise if you can manage it). Effective essay answers are often more formulaic than other sorts of effective writing, relying on the schematic of a straightforward introduction, simple body paragraphs, and a brief conclusion.

Your introduction should be simple and to the point. A couple of sentences is generally all that is needed, and these should avoid rhetorical flourishes or digressions. Often the best strategy is to parrot back the instructions as an opening statement. Body paragraphs for essay answers should also be simple and will often, though not always, be briefer than they would be in an essay you worked on at home. They should still be as specific as possible, making reference to and perhaps even quoting the literature to illustrate your points. Just as in a more fully developed essay, try to avoid dwelling in generalities; use specific examples and evidence. Conclusions for essay exams are usually brief, often just a sentence or two of summary.

Finally, take a watch with you on exam day and keep a close eye on the time. Use all the time you are given and budget it carefully. If you have an hour to write two answers, don't spend forty-five minutes on the first. Even though you will likely be pressed for time, save a few minutes at the end to proofread your answers. Make any corrections as neatly and legibly as possible. Watch the time, but try not to watch your classmates' progress. Keep focused on your own process. Just because someone else is using his or her book a lot, you shouldn't feel you need to do the same. If someone finishes early and leaves, don't take this as a sign that you are running behind or that you are less efficient or less smart than that person. Students who don't make full use of the exam time are often underprepared; they tend to write vague and underdeveloped answers and should not be your role models.

An open-book essay exam on poetry gave students several options, including "Select two poems by different poets, each of which deals with the theme of time, and compare how the authors present this theme." A student chose William Shakespeare's Sonnet 73 and Robert Herrick's "To the Virgins, to Make Much of Time." Read the two poems and then the student's essay exam answer.

WILLIAM SHAKESPEARE   [1564–1616]

Sonnet 73

That time of year thou mayst in me behold
When yellow leaves, or none, or few, do hang
Upon those boughs which shake against the cold,
Bare ruined choirs,° where late° the sweet birds sang.   *choir stalls/lately*
In me thou seest the twilight of such day   5
As after sunset fadeth in the west,
Which by and by black night doth take away,
Death's second self, that seals up all in rest.
In me thou seest the glowing of such fire
That on the ashes of his youth doth lie,   10
As the deathbed whereon it must expire,
Consumed with that which it was nourished by.
   This thou perceiv'st, which makes thy love more strong,
   To love that well which thou must leave ere long.

[1609]

ROBERT HERRICK   [1591–1674]

To the Virgins, to Make Much of Time

Gather ye rosebuds while ye may,
   Old time is still a-flying;
And this same flower that smiles today
   Tomorrow will be dying.

The glorious lamp of heaven, the sun,   5
   The higher he's a-getting,
The sooner will his race be run,
   And nearer he's to setting.

That age is best which is the first,
    When youth and blood are warmer;   10
But being spent, the worse, and worst
    Times still succeed the former.

Then be not coy, but use your time,
    And while ye may, go marry;
For having lost but once your prime,   15
    You may forever tarry.

[1648]

Midterm Essay: Option #2

Shakespeare's Sonnet 73 ("That time of year thou mayest in me behold") and Herrick's "To the Virgins, to Make Much of Time" both deal with the theme of time, and particularly the effect that time has on love. Though there are important differences in their focus and style, both poems urge their readers to love well and make the most of the time they have left.

The introductory paragraph is brief and restates the assignment, adding in specifics to begin focusing the essay.

Both poems make their points about time through a series of metaphors, and in fact they use some of the same metaphors. Herrick begins with the image of rosebuds, which bloom and then die quickly. Shakespeare's first metaphor is also drawn from the natural world of plants, in this case a tree losing its leaves in the autumn. In the sonnet, the natural world is even connected to the spiritual world of church when the poet refers to the branches of the tree as "choirs." Both poems also compare life to a single day, with the setting sun symbolizing death. Toward the end of his sonnet, Shakespeare writes of life as a fire that burns brightly in youth and then cools as a person nears death. While Herrick does not refer to fire specifically, he follows a similar line of reasoning when he mentions a time "When youth and blood are warmer" (line 10).

The two body paragraphs are also fairly brief, but they give lots of specific examples from the poems rather than relying on generalizations.

Because this was an open-book exam, the student was even able to incorporate brief quotations in her answer.

The most significant difference between the two poems lies in the characters of the speaker and the implied listener. Herrick offers his advice about the nature of time and its effect on love to "the Virgins" generally. He tells them to "go marry," but he offers no specifics about whom they should be marrying or how they might choose these mates. Shakespeare's poem, on the other hand, seems to be addressed to a single "you" who is in some sort of relationship with the speaker, the "me" who narrates the poem. When he urges the listener "To love that well which thou must leave ere long" (line 14), he is referring to himself as the object of love.

The organization is clear and straightforward, with one body paragraph comparing similarities between the poems and one contrasting a key difference.

In the end, the differences end up overshadowing the superficial similarities of theme and purpose. Herrick's poem, with its relative lack of specificity, comes across as the sort of kindly advice an older person, perhaps an uncle, might give to any young man or woman. Shakespeare's is a more intimate, and ultimately somewhat darker, poem.

The conclusion is also simple in form and purpose; it restates the main points of the body paragraphs in new language and makes the contrast more explicit.

CHAPTER 5

Writing about Stories

Fiction has long been broken down and discussed in terms of specific elements common to all stories, and chances are you will be focusing on one or more of these when you write an essay about a story.

ELEMENTS OF FICTION

The **elements of fiction** most commonly identified are **plot, character, point of view, setting, theme, symbolism,** and **style.** If you find yourself wondering what to write about a story, a good place to begin is isolating these elements and seeing how they work on a reader and how they combine to create the unique artifact that is a particular story.

Plot

While on some level we all read stories to find out what happens next, in truth plot is usually the least interesting of the elements of fiction. Students who have little experience writing about fiction tend to spend too much time retelling the plot. You can avoid this by bearing in mind that your readers will also have read the literature in question and don't need a thorough replay of what happened. In general, readers just need small reminders of the key points of plot about which you will write, and these should not be self-standing but rather should serve as springboards into analysis and discussion. Still, writing about the plot sometimes makes sense, especially when the plot surprises your expectations by, for instance, rearranging the chronology of events or otherwise presenting things in nonrealistic ways. When this happens in a story, the plot may indeed prove fertile ground for analysis and may be the basis of an interesting paper.

Character

Many interesting essays analyze the actions, motivations, and development of individual characters. How does the author reveal a character to the reader? How does a character grow and develop over the course of a story? Readers have to carefully examine what insights the text provides about a character, but sometimes readers have to consider what's left out. What does the reader have to infer about the character that isn't explicitly written? What does the character refrain from saying? What secrets do characters keep from others, or from themselves? These questions can be fertile ground for analysis. Although the most obvious character to write about is usually the **protagonist**, don't let your imagination stop there. Often the **antagonist** or even a minor character can be an interesting object of study. Keep in mind, too, that characters can start out as antagonistic figures and experience a transformation in the eyes of the narrator or other characters, or in the eyes of the reader. Your job in writing a paper is to consider these transformations and try to understand why a text explores these complex character developments. Usually not a lot has been said and written about less prominent characters, so you will be more free to create your own interpretations. (Playwright Tom Stoppard wrote a very successful full-length play entitled *Rosencrantz and Guildenstern Are Dead* about two of the least developed characters in *Hamlet*.)

Point of View

Related to character is the issue of point of view. The perspective from which a story is told can make a big difference in how we perceive it. Sometimes a story is told in the *first person*, from the point of view of one of the characters. Whether this is a major or a minor character, we must always remember that **first-person narrators** can be unreliable, as they do not have access to all vital information, and their own agendas can often skew the way they see events. The **narrator** of Edgar Allan Poe's "The Cask of Amontillado" seeks to gain sympathy for a hideous act of revenge, giving us a glimpse into a deeply disturbed mind. A **third-person narrator** may be **omniscient**, knowing everything pertinent to a story; or limited, knowing, for instance, the thoughts and motives of the protagonist but not of any of the other characters. As you read a story, ask yourself what the point of view contributes and why the author may have chosen to present the story from a particular perspective.

Setting

Sometimes a setting is merely the backdrop for a story, but often place plays an important role in our understanding of a work. John Updike chooses a small, conservative New England town as the setting of his story "A & P." It is the perfect milieu for an exploration of values and class interaction, and the story would have a very different feel and meaning if it had been set, say, in New York City. As you read, ask your-self how significant a setting is and what it adds to the meaning of a story. Remember that setting refers to time as well as place. "A & P" is about three young women walking into a small-town grocery store wear-ing only bathing suits, an action more shocking when the story was writ-ten in 1961 than it would be now (although it would doubtless still raise eyebrows in many places).

Theme

All short stories have at least one theme—an abstract concept such as *love, war, friendship, revenge,* or *art*—brought to life and made real through the plot, characters, and so on. Identifying a theme or themes is one of the first keys to understanding a story, but it is not the end point. Pay some attention to how the theme is developed. Is it blatant or subtle? What actions, events, or symbols make the theme apparent to you? Gen-erally, the driving force of a story is the author's desire to convey some-thing *about* a particular theme, to make readers think and feel in a cer-tain way. First ask yourself what the author seems to be saying about love or war or whatever themes you have noted; second, whether you agree with the author's perceptions; and finally, why or why not.

Symbolism

Some students get frustrated when their instructors or their classmates begin to talk about **symbolism**. How do we know that an author intended a symbolic reading? Maybe that flower is just a real flower, not a stand-in for youth or for life and regeneration as some readers insist. And even if it is a symbol, how do we know we are reading it correctly? While it's true that plenty of flowers *are* simply flowers, and while students should iden-tify symbols with caution, the more prominent an image in a story, the more likely it is meant to be read symbolically. Careful writers choose their words and images for maximum impact, filling them with as much meaning as possible and inviting their readers to interpret them. When John Steinbeck entitles his story "The Chrysanthemums," we would do well to ask if the flowers are really just plants or if we are being asked to look for a greater significance.

Style

The final element of fiction isolated here is style, sometimes spoken of under the heading of tone or language. A text may strike you as sad or lighthearted, formal or casual. It may make you feel nostalgic, or it may make your heart race with excitement. Somewhat more difficult, though, is isolating the elements of language that contribute to a particular tone or effect. Look for characteristic stylistic elements that create these effects. Is the diction elevated and difficult, or ordinary and simple? Are the sentences long and complex, or short and to the point? Is there dialogue? If so, how do the characters who speak this dialogue come across? Does the style stay consistent throughout the story, or does it change? What does the author leave out? Paying close attention to linguistic matters like these will take you far in your understanding of how a particular story achieves its effect.

STORIES FOR ANALYSIS

Read Charlotte Perkins Gilman's story "The Yellow Wallpaper" and Kate Chopin's "The Story of an Hour," which we have annotated below. Both stories explore issues of women's identity and freedom. The questions following the annotated story ask you to analyze how the elements of fiction work in these two stories.

CHARLOTTE PERKINS GILMAN   [1860–1935]

The Yellow Wallpaper

It is very seldom that mere ordinary people like John and myself secure ancestral halls for the summer.

A colonial mansion, a hereditary estate, I would say a haunted house and reach the height of romantic felicity—but that would be asking too much of fate!

Still I will proudly declare that there is something queer about it.

Else, why should it be let so cheaply? And why have stood so long untenanted?

John laughs at me, of course, but one expects that in marriage.

John is practical in the extreme. He has no patience with faith, an intense horror of superstition, and he scoffs openly at any talk of things not to be felt and seen and put down in figures.

John is a physician, and *perhaps*—(I would not say it to a living soul, of course, but this is dead paper and a great relief to my mind)—*perhaps* that is one reason I do not get well faster.

You see, he does not believe I am sick!

And what can one do?

If a physician of high standing, and one's own husband, assures friends and relatives that there is really nothing the matter with one but temporary nervous depression—a slight hysterical tendency—what is one to do?

My brother is also a physician, and also of high standing, and he says the same thing.

So I take phosphates or phosphites—whichever it is, and tonics, and journeys, and air, and exercise, and am absolutely forbidden to "work" until I am well again.

Personally, I disagree with their ideas.

Personally, I believe that congenial work, with excitement and change, would do me good.

But what is one to do?

I did write for a while in spite of them; but it *does* exhaust me a good deal—having to be so sly about it, or else meet with heavy opposition.

I sometimes fancy that in my condition if I had less opposition and more society and stimulus—but John says the very worst thing I can do is to think about my condition, and I confess it always makes me feel bad.

So I will let it alone and talk about the house.

The most beautiful place! It is quite alone, standing well back from the road, quite three miles from the village. It makes me think of English places that you read about, for there are hedges and walls and gates that lock, and lots of separate little houses for the gardeners and people.

There is a *delicious* garden! I never saw such a garden—large and shady, full of box-bordered paths, and lined with long grape-covered arbors with seats under them.

There were greenhouses, too, but they are all broken now.

There was some legal trouble, I believe, something about the heirs and co-heirs; anyhow, the place has been empty for years.

That spoils my ghostliness, I am afraid, but I don't care—there is something strange about the house—I can feel it.

I even said so to John one moonlight evening, but he said what I felt was a *draught*, and shut the window.

I get unreasonably angry with John sometimes. I'm sure I never used to be so sensitive. I think it is due to this nervous condition.

But John says if I feel so, I shall neglect proper self-control; so I take pains to control myself—before him, at least, and that makes me very tired.

I don't like our room a bit. I wanted one downstairs that opened on the piazza and had roses all over the window, and such pretty old-fashioned chintz hangings! but John would not hear of it.

He said there was only one window and not room for two beds, and no near room for him if he took another.

He is very careful and loving, and hardly lets me stir without special direction.

I have a schedule prescription for each hour in the day; he takes all care from me, and so I feel basely ungrateful not to value it more.

He said we came here solely on my account, that I was to have perfect rest and all the air I could get. "Your exercise depends on your strength, my dear," said he, "and your food somewhat on your appetite; but air you can absorb all the time." So we took the nursery at the top of the house.

It is a big, airy room, the whole floor nearly, with windows that look all ways, and air and sunshine galore. It was nursery first and then play-room and gymnasium, I should judge; for the windows are barred for little children, and there are rings and things in the walls.

The paint and paper look as if a boys' school had used it. It is stripped off—the paper—in great patches all around the head of my bed, about as far as I can reach, and in a great place on the other side of the room low down. I never saw a worse paper in my life.

One of those sprawling flamboyant patterns committing every artistic sin.

It is dull enough to confuse the eye in following, pronounced enough to constantly irritate and provoke study, and when you follow the lame uncertain curves for a little distance they suddenly commit suicide—plunge off at outrageous angles, destroy themselves in unheard of contradictions.

The color is repellant, almost revolting; a smouldering unclean yellow, strangely faded by the slow-turning sunlight.

It is a dull yet lurid orange in some places, a sickly sulphur tint in others.

No wonder the children hated it! I should hate it myself if I had to live in this room long.

There comes John, and I must put this away,—he hates to have me write a word.

We have been here two weeks, and I haven't felt like writing before, since that first day.

I am sitting by the window now, up in this atrocious nursery, and there is nothing to hinder my writing as much as I please, save lack of strength.

John is away all day, and even some nights when his cases are serious.

I am glad my case is not serious!

But these nervous troubles are dreadfully depressing.

John does not know how much I really suffer. He knows there is no *reason* to suffer, and that satisfies him.

Of course it is only nervousness. It does weigh on me so not to do my duty in any way!

I meant to be such a help to John, such a real rest and comfort, and here I am a comparative burden already!

Nobody would believe what an effort it is to do what little I am able,—to dress and entertain, and order things.

It is fortunate Mary is so good with the baby. Such a dear baby!

And yet I *cannot* be with him, it makes me so nervous.

I suppose John never was nervous in his life. He laughs at me so about this wallpaper!

At first he meant to repaper the room, but afterward he said that I was letting it get the better of me, and that nothing was worse for a nervous patient than to give way to such fancies.

He said that after the wallpaper was changed it would be the heavy bedstead, and then the barred windows, and then that gate at the head of the stairs, and so on.

"You know the place is doing you good," he said, "and really, dear, I don't care to renovate the house just for a three months' rental."

"Then do let us go downstairs," I said, "there are such pretty rooms there."

Then he took me in his arms and called me a blessed little goose, and said he would go down cellar, if I wished, and have it white-washed into the bargain.

But he is right enough about the beds and windows and things.

It is an airy and comfortable room as anyone need wish, and, of course, I would not be so silly as to make him uncomfortable just for a whim.

I'm really getting quite fond of the big room, all but that horrid paper.

Out of one window I can see the garden, those mysterious deep-shaded arbors, the riotous old-fashioned flowers, and bushes and gnarly trees.

Out of another I get a lovely view of the bay and a little private wharf belonging to the estate. There is a beautiful shaded lane that runs down there from the house. I always fancy I see people walking in these numerous paths and arbors, but John has cautioned me not to give way to fancy in the least. He says that with my imaginative power and habit of story-making, a nervous weakness like mine is sure to lead to all manner of excited fancies, and that I ought to use my will and good sense to check the tendency. So I try.

I think sometimes that if I were only well enough to write a little it would relieve the press of ideas and rest me.

But I find I get pretty tired when I try.

It is so discouraging not to have any advice and companionship about my work. When I get really well, John says we will ask Cousin Henry and Julia down for a long visit; but he says he would as soon put fireworks in my pillow-case as to let me have those stimulating people about now.

I wish I could get well faster.

But I must not think about that. This paper looks to me as if it *knew* what a vicious influence it had!

There is a recurrent spot where the pattern lolls like a broken neck and two bulbous eyes stare at you upside down.

I get positively angry with the impertinence of it and the everlasting-ness. Up and down and sideways they crawl, and those absurd, unblinking eyes are everywhere. There is one place where two breadths didn't match, and the eyes go all up and down the line, one a little higher than the other.

I never saw so much expression in an inanimate thing before, and we all know how much expression they have! I used to lie awake as a child and get more entertainment and terror out of blank walls and plain furniture than most children could find in a toy-store.

I remember what a kindly wink the knobs of our big, old bureau used to have, and there was one chair that always seemed like a strong friend.

I used to feel that if any of the other things looked too fierce I could always hop into that chair and be safe.

The furniture in this room is no worse than inharmonious, however, for we had to bring it all from downstairs. I suppose when this was used as a playroom they had to take the nursery things out, and no wonder! I never saw such ravages as the children have made here.

The wallpaper, as I said before, is torn off in spots, and it sticketh closer than a brother—they must have had perseverance as well as hatred.

Then the floor is scratched and gouged and splintered, the plaster itself is dug out here and there, and this great heavy bed, which is all we found in the room, looks as if it had been through the wars.

But I don't mind it a bit—only the paper.

There comes John's sister. Such a dear girl as she is, and so careful of me! I must not let her find me writing.

She is a perfect and enthusiastic housekeeper, and hopes for no better profession. I verily believe she thinks it is the writing which made me sick!

But I can write when she is out, and see her a long way off from these windows.

There is one that commands the road, a lovely shaded winding road, and one that just looks off over the country. A lovely country, too, full of great elms and velvet meadows.

This wallpaper has a kind of sub-pattern in a different shade, a particularly irritating one, for you can only see it in certain lights, and not clearly then.

But in the places where it isn't faded and where the sun is just so—I can see a strange, provoking, formless sort of figure, that seems to skulk about behind that silly and conspicuous front design.

There's sister on the stairs!

Well, the Fourth of July is over! The people are all gone and I am tired out. John thought it might do me good to see a little company, so we just had mother and Nellie and the children down for a week.

Of course I didn't do a thing. Jennie sees to everything now.

But it tired me all the same.

John says if I don't pick up faster he shall send me to Weir Mitchell° in the fall.

But I don't want to go there at all. I had a friend who was in his hands once, and she says he is just like John and my brother, only more so!

Besides, it is such an undertaking to go so far.

I don't feel as if it was worthwhile to turn my hand over for anything, and I'm getting dreadfully fretful and querulous.

I cry at nothing, and cry most of the time.

Of course I don't when John is here, or anybody else, but when I am alone.

And I am alone a good deal just now. John is kept in town very often by serious cases, and Jennie is good and lets me alone when I want her to.

So I walk a little in the garden or down that lovely lane, sit on the porch under the roses, and lie down up here a good deal.

I'm getting really fond of the room in spite of the wallpaper. Perhaps *because* of the wallpaper.

It dwells in my mind so!

I lie here on this great immovable bed—it is nailed down, I believe—and follow that pattern about by the hour. It is as good as gymnastics, I assure you. I start, we'll say, at the bottom, down in the corner over there where it has not been touched, and I determine for the thousandth time that I *will* follow that pointless pattern to some sort of a conclusion.

I know a little of the principle of design, and I know this thing was not arranged on any laws of radiation, or alternation, or repetition, or symmetry, or anything else that I ever heard of.

It is repeated, of course, by the breadths, but not otherwise.

Looked at in one way each breadth stands alone, the bloated curves and flourishes—a kind of "debased Romanesque" with *delirium tremens*—go waddling up and down in isolated columns of fatuity.

Weir Mitchell: Dr. S. Weir Mitchell (1829–1914) was an American neurologist and author who advocated "rest cures" for nervous illnesses.

But, on the other hand, they connect diagonally, and the sprawling outlines run off in great slanting waves of optic horror, like a lot of wallowing sea-weeds in full chase.

The whole thing goes horizontally, too, at least it seems so, and I exhaust myself in trying to distinguish the order of its going in that direction.

They have used a horizontal breadth for a frieze, and that adds wonderfully to the confusion.

There is one end of the room where it is almost intact, and there, when the crosslights fade and the low sun shines directly upon it, I can almost fancy radiation after all,—the interminable grotesques seem to form around a common centre and rush off in headlong plunges of equal distraction.

It makes me tired to follow it. I will take a nap I guess.

I don't know why I should write this.

I don't want to.

I don't feel able.

And I know John would think it absurd. But I *must* say what I feel and think in some way—it is such a relief!

But the effort is getting to be greater than the relief.

Half the time now I am awfully lazy, and lie down ever so much.

John says I mustn't lose my strength, and has me take cod liver oil and lots of tonics and things, to say nothing of ale and wine and rare meat.

Dear John! He loves me very dearly, and hates to have me sick. I tried to have a real earnest reasonable talk with him the other day, and tell him how I wish he would let me go and make a visit to Cousin Henry and Julia.

But he said I wasn't able to go, nor able to stand it after I got there; and I did not make out a very good case for myself, for I was crying before I had finished.

It is getting to be a great effort for me to think straight. Just this nervous weakness I suppose.

And dear John gathered me up in his arms, and just carried me upstairs and laid me on the bed, and sat by me and read to me till it tired my head.

He said I was his darling and his comfort and all he had, and that I must take care of myself for his sake, and keep well.

He says no one but myself can help me out of it, that I must use my will and self-control and not let any silly fancies run away with me.

There's one comfort, the baby is well and happy, and does not have to occupy this nursery with the horrid wallpaper.

If we had not used it, that blessed child would have! What a fortunate escape! Why, I wouldn't have a child of mine, an impressionable little thing, live in such a room for worlds.

I never thought of it before, but it is lucky that John kept me here after all, I can stand it so much easier than a baby, you see.

Of course I never mention it to them any more—I am too wise, but I keep watch of it all the same.

There are things in the wallpaper that nobody knows but me, or ever will.

Behind that outside pattern the dim shapes get clearer every day.

It is always the same shape, only very numerous.

And it is like a woman stooping down and creeping about behind that pattern. I don't like it a bit. I wonder—I begin to think—I wish John would take me away from here!

It is so hard to talk with John about my case, because he is so wise, and because he loves me so.

But I tried it last night.

It was moonlight. The moon shines in all around just as the sun does.

I hate to see it sometimes, it creeps so slowly, and always comes in by one window or another.

John was asleep and I hated to waken him, so I kept still and watched the moonlight on that undulating wallpaper till I felt creepy.

The faint figure behind seemed to shake the pattern, just as if she wanted to get out.

I got up softly and went to feel and see if the paper *did* move, and when I came back John was awake.

"What is it, little girl?" he said. "Don't go walking about like that—you'll get cold."

I thought it was a good time to talk, so I told him that I really was not gaining here, and that I wished he would take me away.

"Why, darling!" said he, "our lease will be up in three weeks, and I can't see how to leave before.

"The repairs are not done at home, and I cannot possibly leave town just now. Of course if you were in any danger, I could and would, but you really are better, dear, whether you can see it or not. I am a doctor, dear, and I know. You are gaining flesh and color, your appetite is better, I feel really much easier about you."

"I don't weigh a bit more," said I, "nor as much; and my appetite may be better in the evening when you are here but it is worse in the morning when you are away!"

"Bless her little heart!" said he with a big hug, "she shall be as sick as she pleases! But now let's improve the shining hours by going to sleep, and talk about it in the morning!"

"And you won't go away?" I asked gloomily.

"Why, how can I, dear? It is only three weeks more and then we will take a nice little trip of a few days while Jennie is getting the house ready. Really dear you are better!"

"Better in body perhaps—" I began, and stopped short, for he sat up straight and looked at me with such a stern, reproachful look that I could not say another word.

"My darling," said he, "I beg you, for my sake and for our child's sake, as well as for your own, that you will never for one instant let that idea enter your mind! There is nothing so dangerous, so fascinating, to a temperament like yours. It is a false and foolish fancy. Can you trust me as a physician when I tell you so?"

So of course I said no more on that score, and we went to sleep before long. He thought I was asleep first, but I wasn't, and lay there for hours trying to decide whether that front pattern and the back pattern really did move together or separately.

On a pattern like this, by daylight, there is a lack of sequence, a defiance of law, that is a constant irritant to a normal mind.

The color is hideous enough, and unreliable enough, and infuriating enough, but the pattern is torturing.

You think you have mastered it, but just as you get well underway in following, it turns a back-somersault and there you are. It slaps you in the face, knocks you down, and tramples upon you. It is like a bad dream.

The outside pattern is a florid arabesque, reminding one of a fungus. If you can imagine a toadstool in joints, an interminable string of toadstools, budding and sprouting in endless convolutions—why, that is something like it.

That is, sometimes!

There is one marked peculiarity about this paper, a thing nobody seems to notice but myself, and that is that it changes as the light changes.

When the sun shoots in through the east window—I always watch for that first long, straight ray—it changes so quickly that I never can quite believe it.

That is why I watch it always.

By moonlight—the moon shines in all night when there is a moon—I wouldn't know it was the same paper.

At night in any kind of light, in twilight, candlelight, lamplight, and worst of all by moonlight, it becomes bars! The outside pattern I mean, and the woman behind it is as plain as can be.

I didn't realize for a long time what the thing was that showed behind, that dim sub-pattern, but now I am quite sure it is a woman.

By daylight she is subdued, quiet. I fancy it is the pattern that keeps her so still. It is so puzzling. It keeps me quiet by the hour.

I lie down ever so much now. John says it is good for me, and to sleep all I can.

Indeed he started the habit by making me lie down for an hour after each meal.

It is a very bad habit I am convinced, for you see I don't sleep.

And that cultivates deceit, for I don't tell them I'm awake—O, no!

The fact is I am getting a little afraid of John.

He seems very queer sometimes, and even Jennie has an inexplicable look.

It strikes me occasionally, just as a scientific hypothesis,—that perhaps it is the paper!

I have watched John when he did not know I was looking, and come into the room suddenly on the most innocent excuses, and I've caught him several times *looking at the paper*! And Jennie too. I caught Jennie with her hand on it once.

She didn't know I was in the room, and when I asked her in a quiet, a very quiet voice, with the most restrained manner possible, what she was doing with the paper—she turned around as if she had been caught stealing, and looked quite angry—asked me why I should frighten her so!

Then she said that the paper stained everything it touched, that she had found yellow smooches on all my clothes and John's, and she wished we would be more careful!

Did not that sound innocent? But I know she was studying that pattern, and I am determined that nobody shall find it out but myself!

Life is very much more exciting now than it used to be. You see I have something more to expect, to look forward to, to watch. I really do eat better, and am more quiet than I was.

John is so pleased to see me improve! He laughed a little the other day, and said I seemed to be flourishing in spite of my wallpaper.

I turned it off with a laugh. I had no intention of telling him it was *because* of the wallpaper—he would make fun of me. He might even want to take me away.

I don't want to leave now until I have found it out. There is a week more, and I think that will be enough.

I'm feeling ever so much better! I don't sleep much at night, for it is so interesting to watch developments; but I sleep a good deal in the daytime.

In the daytime it is tiresome and perplexing.

There are always new shoots on the fungus, and new shades of yellow all over it. I cannot keep count of them, though I have tried conscientiously.

It is the strangest yellow, that wallpaper! It makes me think of all the yellow things I ever saw—not beautiful ones like buttercups, but old foul, bad yellow things.

But there is something else about that paper—the smell! I noticed it the moment we came into the room, but with so much air and sun it was not bad. Now we have had a week of fog and rain, and whether the windows are open or not, the smell is here.

It creeps all over the house.

I find it hovering in the dining-room, skulking in the parlor, hiding in the hall, lying in wait for me on the stairs.

It gets into my hair.

Even when I go to ride, if I turn my head suddenly and surprise it—there is that smell!

Such a peculiar odor, too! I have spent hours in trying to analyze it, to find what it smelled like.

It is not bad—at first, and very gentle, but quite the subtlest, most enduring odor I ever met.

In this damp weather it is awful, I wake up in the night and find it hanging over me.

It used to disturb me at first. I thought seriously of burning the house—to reach the smell.

But now I am used to it. The only thing I can think of that it is like is the *color* of the paper! A yellow smell.

There is a very funny mark on this wall, low down, near the mopboard. A streak that runs round the room. It goes behind every piece of furniture, except the bed, a long, straight, even *smooch*, as if it had been rubbed over and over.

I wonder how it was done and who did it, and what they did it for. Round and round and round—round and round and round—it makes me dizzy!

I really have discovered something at last.

Through watching so much at night, when it changes so, I have finally found out.

The front pattern *does* move—and no wonder! The woman behind shakes it!

Sometimes I think there are a great many women behind, and sometimes only one, and she crawls around fast, and her crawling shakes it all over.

Then in the very bright spots she keeps still, and in the very shady spots she just takes hold of the bars and shakes them hard.

And she is all the time trying to climb through. But nobody could climb through that pattern—it strangles so; I think that is why it has so many heads.

They get through, and then the pattern strangles them off and turns them upside down, and makes their eyes white!

If those heads were covered or taken off it would not be half so bad.

I think that woman gets out in the daytime!

And I'll tell you why—privately—I've seen her!

I can see her out of every one of my windows!

It is the same woman, I know, for she is always creeping, and most women do not creep by daylight.

I see her in that long shaded lane, creeping up and down. I see her in those dark grape arbors, creeping all around the garden.

I see her on that long road under the trees, creeping along, and when a carriage comes she hides under the blackberry vines.

I don't blame her a bit. It must be very humiliating to be caught creeping by daylight!

I always lock the door when I creep by daylight. I can't do it at night, for I know John would suspect something at once.

And John is so queer now, that I don't want to irritate him. I wish he would take another room! Besides, I don't want anybody to get that woman out at night but myself.

I often wonder if I could see her out of all the windows at once.

But, turn as fast as I can, I can only see out of one at one time.

And though I always see her, she *may* be able to creep faster than I can turn!

I have watched her sometimes away off in the open country, creeping as fast as a cloud shadow in a high wind.

If only that top pattern could be gotten off from the under one! I mean to try it, little by little.

I have found out another funny thing, but I shan't tell it this time! It does not do to trust people too much.

There are only two more days to get this paper off, and I believe John is beginning to notice. I don't like the look in his eyes.

And I heard him ask Jennie a lot of professional questions, about me. She had a very good report to give.

She said I slept a good deal in the daytime.

John knows I don't sleep very well at night, for all I'm so quiet!

He asked me all sorts of questions too, and pretended to be very loving and kind.

As if I couldn't see through him!

Still, I don't wonder he acts so, sleeping under this paper for three months.

It only interests me, but I feel sure John and Jennie are secretly affected by it.

Hurrah! This is the last day, but it is enough. John to stay in town over night, and won't be out until this evening.

Jennie wanted to sleep with me—the sly thing! But I told her I should undoubtedly rest better for a night all alone.

That was clever, for really I wasn't alone a bit! As soon as it was moonlight and that poor thing began to crawl and shake the pattern, I got up and ran to help her.

I pulled and she shook, I shook and she pulled, and before morning we had peeled off yards of that paper.

A strip about as high as my head and half around the room.

And then when the sun came and that awful pattern began to laugh at me, I declared I would finish it to-day!

We go away to-morrow, and they are moving all my furniture down again to leave things as they were before.

Jennie looked at the wall in amazement, but I told her merrily that I did it out of pure spite at the vicious thing.

She laughed and said she wouldn't mind doing it herself, but I must not get tired.

How she betrayed herself that time!

But I am here, and no person touches this paper but me,—not *alive*!

She tried to get me out of the room—it was too patent! But I said it was so quiet and empty and clean now that I believed I would lie down again and sleep all I could, and not to wake me even for dinner—I would call when I woke.

So now she is gone, and the servants are gone, and the things are gone, and there is nothing left but that great bedstead nailed down, with the canvas mattress we found on it.

We shall sleep downstairs to-night, and take the boat home to-morrow.

I quite enjoy the room, now it is bare again.

How those children did tear about here!

This bedstead is fairly gnawed!

But I must get to work.

I have locked the door and thrown the key down into the front path.

I don't want to go out, and I don't want to have anybody come in, till John comes.

I want to astonish him.

I've got a rope up here that even Jennie did not find. If that woman does get out, and tries to get away, I can tie her!

But I forgot I could not reach far without anything to stand on!

This bed will *not* move!

I tried to lift and push it until I was lame, and then I got so angry I bit off a little piece at one corner—but it hurt my teeth.

Then I peeled off all the paper I could reach standing on the floor. It sticks horribly and the pattern just enjoys it! All those strangled heads and bulbous eyes and waddling fungus growths just shriek with derision!

I am getting angry enough to do something desperate. To jump out of the window would be admirable exercise, but the bars are too strong even to try.

Besides I wouldn't do it. Of course not. I know well enough that a step like that is improper and might be misconstrued.

I don't like to *look* out of the windows even—there are so many of those creeping women, and they creep so fast.

I wonder if they all come out of that wallpaper as I did?

But I am securely fastened now by my well-hidden rope—you don't get *me* out in the road there!

I suppose I shall have to get back behind the pattern when it comes night, and that is hard!

It is so pleasant to be out in this great room and creep around as I please!

I don't want to go outside. I won't, even if Jennie asks me to.

For outside you have to creep on the ground, and everything is green instead of yellow.

But here I can creep smoothly on the floor, and my shoulder just fits in that long smooch around the wall, so I cannot lose my way.

Why, there's John at the door!

It is no use, young man, you can't open it!

How he does call and pound!

Now he's crying for an axe.

It would be a shame to break down that beautiful door!

"John dear!" said I in the gentlest voice, "the key is down by the front steps, under a plantain leaf!"

That silenced him for a few moments.

Then he said—very quietly indeed, "Open the door, my darling!"

"I can't," said I. "The key is down by the front door under a plantain leaf!"

And then I said it again, several times, very gently and slowly, and said it so often that he had to go and see, and he got it of course, and came in. He stopped short by the door.

"What is the matter?" he cried. "For God's sake, what are you doing!"

I kept on creeping just the same, but I looked at him over my shoulder. "I've got out at last," said I, "in spite of you and Jane. And I've pulled off most of the paper, so you can't put me back!"

Now why should that man have fainted? But he did, and right across my path by the wall, so that I had to creep over him every time!

[1892]

KATE CHOPIN   [1851–1904]

The Story of an Hour

Knowing that Mrs. Mallard was afflicted with a heart trouble, great care was taken to break to her as gently as possible the news of her husband's death.

It was her sister Josephine who told her, in broken sentences; veiled hints that revealed in half concealing. Her husband's friend Richards was there, too, near her. It was he who had been in the newspaper office when intelligence of the railroad disaster was received, with Brently Mallard's name leading the list of "killed." He had only taken the time to assure himself of its truth by a second telegram, and had hastened to forestall any less careful, less tender friend in bearing the sad message.

Her family and friends seem to think she's delicate.

She did not hear the story as many women have heard the same, with a paralyzed inability to accept its significance. She wept at once, with sudden, wild abandonment, in her sister's arms. When the storm of grief had spent itself she went away to her room alone. She would have no one follow her.

There stood, facing the open window, a comfortable, roomy armchair. Into this she sank, pressed down by a physical exhaustion that haunted her body and seemed to reach into her soul.

She could see in the open square before her house the tops of trees that were all aquiver with the new spring life. The delicious breath of rain was in the air. In the street below a peddler was crying his wares. The notes of a distant song

A beautiful day. Why does Chopin take the time to describe it in such a short story, especially one about a death?

which some one was singing reached her faintly, and countless sparrows were twittering in the eaves.

There were patches of blue sky showing here and there through the clouds that had met and piled one above the other in the west facing her window.

She sat with her head thrown back upon the cushion of the chair, quite motionless, except when a sob came up into her throat and shook her, as a child who had cried itself to sleep continues to sob in its dreams.

She was young, with a fair, calm face, whose lines bespoke repression and even a certain strength. But now there was a dull stare in her eyes, whose gaze was fixed away off yonder on one of those patches of blue sky. It was not a glance of reflection, but rather indicated a suspension of intelligent thought.

There was something coming to her and she was waiting for it, fearfully. What was it? She did not know; it was too subtle and elusive to name. But she felt it, creeping out of the sky, reaching toward her through the sounds, the scents, the color that filled the air.

Now her bosom rose and fell tumultuously. She was beginning to recognize this thing that was approaching to possess her, and she was striving to beat it back with her will—as powerless as her two white slender hands would have been.

When she abandoned herself a little whispered word escaped her slightly parted lips. She said it over and over under her breath: "free, free, free!" The vacant stare and the look of terror that had followed it went from her eyes. They stayed keen and bright. Her pulses beat fast, and the coursing blood warmed and relaxed every inch of her body.

She did not stop to ask if it were or were not a monstrous joy that held her. A clear and exalted perception enabled her to dismiss the suggestion as trivial.

She knew that she would weep again when she saw the kind, tender hands folded in death; the face that had never looked save with love upon her, fixed and gray and dead. But she saw beyond that bitter moment a long procession of years to come that would belong to her absolutely. And she opened and spread her arms out to them in welcome.

There would be no one to live for her during those coming years: she would live for herself. There would be no powerful will bending hers in that blind persistence with which men

Ominous. What could be coming? Something physical or emotional?

How could it be joy? Her emotions seem quick to change and hard to keep up with, even for her.

Was their marriage unhappy? Would her friends and family think so? Would her husband have though so?

and women believe they have a right to impose a private will upon a fellow-creature. A kind intention or a cruel intention made the act seem no less a crime as she looked upon it in that brief moment of illumination.

And yet she had loved him—sometimes. Often she had not. What did it matter! What could love, the unsolved mystery, count for in face of this possession of self-assertion which she suddenly recognized as the strongest impulse of her being!

"Free! Body and soul free!" she kept whispering.

Josephine was kneeling before the closed door with her lips to the keyhole, imploring for admission. "Louise, open the door! I beg; open the door—you will make yourself ill. What are you doing, Louise? For heaven's sake open the door."

"Go away. I am not making myself ill." No; she was drinking in a very elixir of life through that open window.

Has she become more assertive? Stronger?

Her fancy was running riot along those days ahead of her. Spring days, and summer days, and all sorts of days that would be her own. She breathed a quick prayer that life might be long. It was only yesterday she had thought with a shudder that life might be long.

She arose at length and opened the door to her sister's importunities. There was a feverish triumph in her eyes, and she carried herself unwittingly like a goddess of Victory. She clasped her sister's waist, and together they descended the stairs. Richards stood waiting for them at the bottom.

Some one was opening the front door with a latchkey. It was Brently Mallard who entered, a little travel-stained, composedly carrying his gripsack and umbrella. He had been far from the scene of accident, and did not even know there had been one. He stood amazed at Josephine's piercing cry; at Richards' quick motion to screen him from the view of his wife.

But Richards was too late.

When the doctors came they said she had died of heart disease—of joy that kills.

Surprising, ironic ending.

[1894]

QUESTIONS ON THE STORIES

☐ How would you summarize the plot of each story? What, if anything, makes it difficult to do so?

☐ Who, in your opinion, are the most sympathetic characters? Who are the most antagonistic? What kinds of information do we learn about the emotional lives of these characters?

☐ What is the point of view of each story? How would you compare the effects of these choices? What are the advantages and disadvantages of each choice?

☐ How would you describe the setting of each story? What details of setting contribute to the tone or atmosphere of the story?

☐ How would you describe the style of writing in each story? Is the prose formal? Archaic? Conversational? Melodramatic? Be as specific as possible, and note examples that bolster your claims.

☐ What kinds of symbols recur in each story? Are they fanciful? Ordinary? Conventional? Surprising? How do they move the narrative forward?

SAMPLE PAPER: AN ESSAY THAT COMPARES AND CONTRASTS

Melanie Smith was given the assignment to compare and contrast an element of her choosing in Kate Chopin's "The Story of an Hour" and Charlotte Perkins Gilman's "The Yellow Wallpaper" and to draw some conclusions about life in the nineteenth century. Rather than examining the female protagonists, Melanie chose to focus on the minor male characters in the stories. She wrote a point-by-point comparison designed to demonstrate that these men, despite the opinions of them that she heard expressed in class, were not bad people. Rather, they were led by their social training to behave in ways that were perfectly acceptable in their day, even if they now strike readers as oppressive.

Melanie Smith
Professor Hallet
English 109
18 May 2008

Good Husbands in Bad Marriages

When twenty-first-century readers first encounter literature of earlier times, it is easy for us to apply our own standards of conduct to the characters and situations. Kate Chopin's "The Story of an Hour" and Charlotte Perkins Gilman's "The Yellow Wallpaper" offer two good examples of this. Both written by American women in the last decade of the nineteenth century, the stories give us a look into the lives, and especially the marriages, of middle-class women of the time. By modern standards, the husbands of the two protagonists, particularly John in "The Yellow Wallpaper," seem almost unbearably controlling of their wives. From the vantage point of the late nineteenth century, however, their behavior looks quite different. Both men are essentially well-meaning and try to be good husbands. Their only real crime is that they adhere too closely to the conventional Victorian wisdom about women and marriage.

To begin with, both men are well respected in their communities. John in "The Yellow Wallpaper" is described as "a physician of high standing" who has "an intense horror of superstition, and he scoffs openly at any talk of things not to be felt and seen and put down in figures." These are just the qualities that we might expect to find in a respectable doctor, even today. It is less clear what Brently Mallard in "The Story of an Hour" does for a living. (In fact, Chopin's story is so short that we learn fairly little about any of the characters.) But he and his wife seem to live in a comfortable house, and they are surrounded by family and friends, suggesting a secure, well-connected lifestyle. In the nineteenth century, a man's most important job was to take care of his wife and family, and both men in these stories seem to be performing this job very well.

Melanie signals that she will focus on these two stories and makes a claim about them that she will go on to support.

Melanie's first observation about what the male characters have in common.

Smith 2

In addition to providing a comfortable life for them, it also seems that both men love their wives. When she believes her husband has died, Mrs. Mallard thinks of his "kind, tender hands folded in death; the face that had never looked save with love upon her." Her own love for him is less certain, which may be why she feels "free" when he dies, but his love for her seems genuine. The case of John in "The Yellow Wallpaper" is a bit more complicated. To a modern reader, it seems that he treats his wife more like a child than a grown woman. He puts serious restraints on her actions, and at one point he even calls her "little girl." But he also calls her "my darling" and "dear," and she does admit, "He loves me very dearly." When he has to leave her alone, he even has his sister come to look after her, which is a kind gesture, even if it seems a bit like he doesn't trust his wife. If the narrator, who is in a position to know, doesn't doubt her husband's love, what gives us the right to judge it?

A smooth transition into the next point.

To a certain extent, we must admit that both husbands do oppress their wives by being overprotective. Part of the point of both stories is to show how even acceptable, supposedly good marriages of the day could be overly confining to women. This is especially obvious when we see how much John restricts his wife — forbidding her even to visit her cousins or to write letters — and how everyone expects her to submit to his demands. Though Mrs. Mallard isn't literally confined to a house or a room the way the narrator of "The Yellow Wallpaper" is, she stays inside the house and is looking out the window longingly when she realizes she wants to be free. But it is important for a reader not to blame the husbands, because they really don't intend to be oppressive.

Melanie establishes a similarity between the husbands.

In fact, it is true that both of the wives are in somewhat frail health. Mrs. Mallard is "afflicted with a heart trouble," and the narrator of "The Yellow Wallpaper" seems to have many physical and mental problems, so it is not surprising that their husbands worry about them. It is not evil intent that leads the men to act

A point of similarity between the wives.

Smith 3

as they do; it is simply ignorance. John seems less innocent than Brently because he is so patronizing and he puts such restrictions on his wife's behavior and movement, but that kind of attitude was normal for the day, and as a doctor, John seems to be doing what he really thinks is best.

All the other characters in the stories see both men as good and loving husbands, which suggests that society would have approved of their behavior. Even the wives themselves, who are the victims of these oppressive marriages, don't blame the men at all. The narrator of "The Yellow Wallpaper" even thinks she is "ungrateful" for not appreciating John's loving care more. Once we understand this, readers should not be too quick to blame the men either. The real blame falls to the society that gave these men the idea that women are frail and need protection from the world. The men may be the immediate cause of the women's suffering, but the real cause is much deeper and has to do with cultural attitudes and how the men were brought up to protect and provide for women.

Melanie returns to her original claim.

Most people who live in a society don't see the flaws in that society's conventional ways of thinking and living. We now know that women are capable and independent and that protecting them as if they were children ultimately does more harm than good. But in the late Victorian era, such an idea would have seemed either silly or dangerously radical to most people, men and women alike. Stories like these, however, could have helped their original readers begin to think about how confining these supposedly good marriages were. Fortunately, authors such as Chopin and Gilman come along from time to time and show us the problems in our conventional thinking, so society can move forward and we can begin to see how even the most well-meaning actions should sometimes be questioned.

Melanie's conclusion argues for the idea that literature is capable of challenging the status quo.

CHAPTER 6

Writing about Poems

Poetry may be divided into several major subgenres and types. A **narrative poem**, for instance, tells a story. An **epic**, a subgenre of narrative, is a long poem that narrates heroic events. A **lyric poem** expresses the personal thoughts and feelings of a particular poet or speaker. And many other types of poems have venerable histories.

As with stories, you should be aware of certain elements as you prepare to write about poetry. Sometimes these elements are the same as for fiction. A narrative poem, for instance, will have a **plot, setting,** and **characters**, and all poems speak from a particular **point of view**. To the extent that any of the elements of fiction help you understand a poem, by all means use them in your analysis. Poetry, however, does present a special set of concerns for a reader, and elements of poetry frequently provide rich ground for analysis.

ELEMENTS OF POETRY

The Speaker

First, consider the speaker of the poem. Imagine that someone is saying the words of this poem aloud. Who is speaking, where is this **speaker**, and what is his or her state of mind? Sometimes the voice is that of the poet, but frequently a poem speaks from a different perspective, just as a short story might be from a point of view very different from the author's. It's not always apparent when this is the case, but some poets will signal who the speaker is in a title, such as "The Passionate Shepherd to His Love" and "The Love Song of J. Alfred Prufrock." Be alert to signals that will help you recognize the speaker, and remember that some poems have more than one speaker.

The Listener

Be attentive also to any other persons in the poem, particularly an implied listener. Is there a "you" to whom the poem is addressed? If the poem is being spoken aloud, who is supposed to hear it? When, early in his poem "Dover Beach," Matthew Arnold writes, "Come to the window, sweet is the night-air!" he gives us an important clue as to how to read the poem. We should imagine both the speaker and the implied listener together in a room, with a window open to the night. As we read on, we can look for further clues as to who these two people are and why they are together on this night. Many poems create a relationship between the "I" of the speaker and the "you" of the listener; however, that is not always the case. Sometimes the speaker does not address a "you" and instead provides a more philosophical meditation that isn't explicitly addressed to a listener. Consider the effect: Do they feel more abstract? More detached from the material conditions of time and place? Do they provide certainty, or resolution? The questions about the speaker and the listener are crucial to your analysis of poetry.

Imagery

Just as you should be open to the idea that there are frequently symbols in stories, you should pay special attention to the **images** in poems. Although poems are often about such grand themes as love or death, they rarely dwell long in these abstractions. Rather, the best poetry seeks to make the abstraction concrete by creating vivid images appealing directly to the senses. A well-written poem will provide the mind of an attentive reader with sights, sounds, tastes, scents, and sensations. Since poems tend to be short and densely packed with meaning, every word and image is there for a reason. Isolate these images and give some thought to what they make you think and how they make you feel. Are they typical or unexpected?

Consider these lines from John Donne's "The Good Morrow":

> My face in thine eye, thine in mine appears,
> And true plain hearts do in the faces rest;
> Where can we find two better hemispheres,
> Without sharp north, without declining west? (lines 15–18)

Here, Donne celebrates the love between the speaker and his object of desire, comparing the faces of the lovers to two "hemispheres" on globes. Elsewhere in the poem, Donne uses imagery that is borrowed from the world of navigation and mapping; here, he suggests that the lovers' faces are an improvement upon whatever instruments explorers and learned men use to understand the world. By examining the images in a poem, their placement, juxtaposition, and effect, you will have gone a long way toward understanding the poem as a whole.

Sound and Sense

Of all the genres, poetry is the one that most self-consciously highlights language, so it is necessary to pay special attention to the sounds of a poem. In fact, it is always a good idea to read a poem aloud several times, giving yourself the opportunity to experience the role that sound plays in the poem's meaning.

Rhyme

Much of the poetry written in English before the twentieth century was written in some form of **rhyme**, and contemporary poets continue to experiment with its effects. Rhymes may seem stilted or old-fashioned to our twenty-first-century ears, but keep in mind that rhymes have powerful social meanings in the cultural context in which they're written. And even today rhyme remains a viable and significant convention in popular songs, which are, after all, a form of poetry. As you read poems, ask yourself how rhymes work. Do they create **juxtapositions**? Alignments of meaning? And what is the effect of that relationship as the poem progresses?

Assonance and Consonance

While it is important to look at the end of a line to see how the poet uses sounds, it is also important to look inside the line. Poets use **assonance**, or repeated vowel sounds, to create an aural effect. Consider these opening lines from Gerard Manley Hopkins's "Pied Beauty":

> Glory be to God for dappled things —
>> For skies of couple-colour as a brinded cow;
>>> For rose-moles all in stipple upon trout that swim;
> Fresh-firecoal chestnut-falls; finches' wings;
>> Landscape plotted and pieced — fold, fallow, and plough;
>>> And all trades, their gear and tackle and trim. (lines 1–6)

Throughout these lines, Hopkins pays special attention to "uh" and "ow" sounds. Notice "couple-colour" and "cow" in line 2, "upon" and "trout" in line 3, "fallow" and "plough" in line 5. As you read through each line, ask yourself: Why does the poet align these sounds? Do these sounds speed up the tempo of the line, or slow it down? What do these sounds—and words—reveal about the poet's praise of "dappled things"?

Poets also use **consonance**, repeated consonant sounds, to create alignments and juxtapositions among consonants. Consider these first lines from Christopher Marlowe's "The Passionate Shepherd to His Love":

> Come live with me and be my love,
> And we will all the pleasures prove (lines 1-2)

In line 1, Marlowe aligns "live" with "love" to suggest that there is an equation between cohabitation and romance. In line 2, he aligns the "p" sound in "pleasures prove"; in addition, though, the **slant rhyme** of "love" and "prove" also creates meaning between the lines. What "proof" is there in love? Is love what will make the speaker feel most alive?

Meter

Poetry written in English is both **accentual** and **syllabic**. That is, poets count the number of accents as well as the number of syllables as they create each line of poetry. Patterns of syllable and accent have names like "iambic pentameter" and "dactylic tetrameter," and each meter has its own unique properties and effects. Your literature instructor may help you learn about the specifics of meter, or you can find several sites online that explain the art—called **scansion**—of determining the meter of a poem. Whether or not you have a clear understanding of the many meters of poetry in English, when you read a poem, listen to each line to find out how many accents and syllables it contains. If you can determine what that meter is, consider how the poet uses—and subverts—that formula as part of a strategy for the poem.

Form

Poets writing in English use dozens of traditional forms from a variety of traditions. Some of the most common of these forms are the **sonnet**, the **villanelle**, and the **ballad**, but there are too many to name here. As you read a poem in a traditional form, think of the form as a kind of template in which poets arrange and explore challenging emotional and intellectual material. A sonnet, for example, has a concise fourteen-line structure that allows the poet to address a religious, romantic, or philosophical argument in a very compressed space. As you read a sonnet, you might ask yourself: What does its form accomplish that is different from a looser, more extended form like a ballad? The two sample poems later in this chapter provide a good opportunity to compare a short, highly conventional form with a longer, more loosely structured one.

Note, too, that many contemporary poets write in **free verse**, which means that they don't necessarily use a strict traditional form or meter for their poems. That doesn't mean that the free verse poet is writing without rules; it just means that the poet is creating his or her own system for the unique needs of each poem.

Stanzas

A **stanza** is any grouping of lines of poetry into a unit. The term *stanza* comes from the Italian word for "room." As you read poetry, imagine each stanza as a room with its own correspondences and relationships, and consider how that stanza creates a singular effect. Sometimes a stanza can be one line long; sometimes the poet creates a block of lines with no stanza breaks. All of these choices create distinct effects for readers of poetry.

Lineation

Lineation—or how a poet uses the line breaks in the poem—is a crucial component of poetry. Sometimes poets use punctuation at the end of every line, but more often they mix end-stopped lines with enjambed lines. **Enjambment** occurs when the line is not end-stopped with a comma, dash, or period. Its meaning spills over onto the next line, creating the effect of acceleration and intensity. Poets also use **caesuras** in the middle of lines to create variety in the pattern of the line. A caesura is a deep pause created by a comma, colon, semicolon, dash, period, or white space.

Poetry written in English can have many kinds of rhyme schemes, forms, and meters. For more information, see the "Elements of Poetry" online tutorial at http://bcs.bedfordstmartins.com/virtualit/poetry/rhyme_def.html.

TWO POEMS FOR ANALYSIS

Take a few minutes to read William Shakespeare's Sonnet 116 and T. S. Eliot's "The Love Song of J. Alfred Prufrock" and consider the student annotations and the questions that follow the poems. Both of these poems are complex, though in very different ways. What elements of poetry do you notice in these poems? What insights do you have in addition to those suggested by the annotations and questions?

WILLIAM SHAKESPEARE [1564–1616]

Sonnet 116

Let me not to the marriage of true minds   *Consonance: marriage/minds.*
Admit impediments. Love is not love
Which alters when it alteration finds,   *Repetition: love/love, alters/alteration,*
Or bends with the remover to remove.   *remover/remove.*
O, no, it is an ever-fixèd mark   5
That looks on tempests and is never shaken;   *Abstract ideas become specific*
It is the star to every wandering bark,°   *images: tempests, ships.*
Whose worth's unknown, although his height be taken.°
Love's not time's fool, though rosy lips and cheeks — *Rosy lips and cheeks: clas-*
Within his bending sickle's compass come; — *sic love poem images.*   10
Love alters not with his brief hours and weeks,
But bears it out even to the edge of doom.°   *Sickle is a death image, unusual*
     If this be error and upon me proved,   *for a love poem.*
     I never writ, nor no man ever loved.   *Final rhyme is slant rhyme.*

                                                   [1609]

7. **bark:** ship
8. **taken:** is measured
12. **doom:** Judgment Day

The student who annotated noticed both structural features of the poem (such as the move from abstract to concrete language) and small-scale language features, such as consonance and repetitions of individual words. This provides a good beginning to understanding the poem; answering the questions that follow will deepen that understanding, making it easier to write a paper about the poem.

QUESTIONS ON THE POEM

☐ What images are most striking in this poem? Do they seem conventional? Surprising? Experimental? Why?

☐ A sonnet often reveals its own logic in order to argue for a point of view. What is the argument of this poem? Do you find it persuasive? If so, why? If not, why not?

☐ What is the rhyme structure of this sonnet? What words are aligned as a result of this scheme?

☐ How does Shakespeare use enjambment and caesura to manage the tempo of the poem? What effects does this create?

T. S. ELIOT   [1888–1965]

The Love Song of J. Alfred Prufrock

S'io credesse che mia risposta fosse
A persona che mai tornasse al mondo,
Questa fiamma staria senza piu scosse.
Ma percioccke giammai di questo fondo
Non torno vivo alcun, s'i'odo il vero,
Senza tema d'infamia ti rispondo.

Footnote says this is from Dante's Inferno. The speaker is in hell. Why start a "love song" with hell?

Let us go then, you and I,
When the evening is spread out against the sky
Like a patient etherised upon a table;

Who is this "you"? Where are they going?

Epigraph: "If I thought that my answer were being made to someone who would ever return to earth, this flame would remain without further movement; but since no one has ever returned alive from this depth, if what I hear is true, I answer you without fear of infamy" (Dante, *Inferno* 27.61–66). Dante encounters Guido de Montefeltro in the eighth circle of hell, where souls are trapped within flames (tongues of fire) as punishment for giving evil counsel. Guido tells Dante details about his evil life only because he assumes that Dante is on his way to an even deeper circle in hell and will never return to earth and be able to repeat what he has heard.

Let us go, through certain half-deserted streets,
The muttering retreats   5
Of restless nights in one-night cheap hotels
And sawdust restaurants with oyster-shells: *Setting grubby and seedy. Depressing.*
Streets that follow like a tedious argument
Of insidious intent
To lead you to an overwhelming question . . .   10
Oh, do not ask, "What is it?"
Let us go and make our visit.   *Who are they visiting? Why?*
    In the room the women come and go   *New setting, in a room. Visiting*
Talking of Michelangelo.   *"the women"?*

    The yellow fog that rubs its back upon the window-panes,   15
The yellow smoke that rubs its muzzle on the window-panes
Licked its tongue into the corners of the evening,   *Fog like an animal, almost*
Lingered upon the pools that stand in drains,   *a character.*
Let fall upon its back the soot that falls from chimneys,
Slipped by the terrace, made a sudden leap,   20
And seeing that it was a soft October night,
Curled once about the house, and fell asleep.   *Uses rhyme in irregular pattern.*

    And indeed there will be time
For the yellow smoke that slides along the street,
Rubbing its back upon the window-panes;   25
There will be time, there will be time   *Lots of repetition here, as*
To prepare a face to meet the faces that you meet;   *if he's fixated on these ideas*
There will be time to murder and create,   *and can't let go.*
And time for all the works and days of hands
That lift and drop a question on your plate;   30
Time for you and time for me,   *He seems obsessed with time*
And time yet for a hundred indecisions,   *and how much of it there is.*
And for a hundred visions and revisions,
Before the taking of a toast and tea.

    In the room the women come and go   *Another repetition. Same women?*   35
Talking of Michelangelo.   *Same room?*

    And indeed there will be time
To wonder, "Do I dare?" and, "Do I dare?"
Time to turn back and descend the stair,
With a bald spot in the middle of my hair—   40
(They will say: "How his hair is growing thin!")   *Physical description: aging,*
My morning coat, my collar mounting firmly to the chin,   *thin, well dressed.*
My necktie rich and modest, but asserted by a simple pin—   *Insecure.*
                                                                      Indecisive.

(They will say: "But how his arms and legs are thin!")
Do I dare   45
Disturb the universe?   *How could he "disturb the*
In a minute there is time   *universe"?*
For decisions and revisions which a minute will reverse.

  For I have known them all already, known them all: —   *He seems bored*
Have known the evenings, mornings, afternoons,   *with his life.* 50
I have measured out my life with coffee spoons;   *Maybe*
I know the voices dying with a dying fall   *depressed?*
Beneath the music from a farther room.
    So how should I presume?

  And I have known the eyes already, known them all—   55
The eyes that fix you in a formulated phrase,
And when I am formulated, sprawling on a pin,
When I am pinned and wriggling on the wall,   *Like a bug. More insecurity?*
Then how should I begin
To spit out all the butt-ends of my days and ways?   60
    And how should I presume?

  And I have known the arms already, known them all—
Arms that are braceleted and white and bare
(But in the lamplight, downed with light brown hair!)
Is it perfume from a dress   65
That makes me so digress?
Arms that lie along a table, or wrap about a shawl.
    And should I then presume?   *He asks many questions in this section. Maybe*
    And how should I begin?   *unsure of self. Women seem to make him insecure.*

                    •   •   •

Shall I say, I have gone at dusk through narrow streets   70
And watched the smoke that rises from the pipes
Of lonely men in shirt-sleeves, leaning out of windows? . . .

    I should have been a pair of ragged claws   *Earlier he was like a bug, now like a*
Scuttling across the floors of silent seas.   *crab.*

                    •   •   •

And the afternoon, the evening, sleeps so peacefully!   75
Smoothed by long fingers,
Asleep . . . tired . . . or it malingers,
Stretched on the floor, here beside you and me.
Should I, after tea and cakes and ices,

Have the strength to force the moment to its crisis?   80
But though I have wept and fasted, wept and prayed,
Though I have seen my head (grown slightly bald) brought in upon a
        platter,   *Lots of disconnected body parts:*
I am no prophet—and here's no great matter;   *eyes, arms, claws, head.*
I have seen the moment of my greatness flicker,
And I have seen the eternal Footman hold my coat, and snicker,   85
And in short, I was afraid.

                                                        Eternal Footman = Death?
    And would it have been worth it, after all,   *Again, he thinks someone is laughing*
After the cups, the marmalade, the tea,   *at him.*
Among the porcelain, among some talk of you and me,
Would it have been worth while,   90
To have bitten off the matter with a smile,
To have squeezed the universe into a ball
To roll it toward some overwhelming question,
To say: "I am Lazarus, come from the dead, —— *More about death. Who is dead*
Come back to tell you all, I shall tell you all"—   *here? Prufrock himself?*   95
If one, settling a pillow by her head,
    Should say: "That is not what I meant at all.   *Sunsets and teacups seem so*
    That is not it, at all."   *much nicer, sweeter than the grim*
                                                      cityscape earlier. Another new
    And would it have been worth it, after all,   *setting? How do they connect?*
Would it have been worth while,   100
After the sunsets and the dooryards and the sprinkled streets,
After the novels, after the teacups, after the skirts that trail along the
        floor—
And this, and so much more?—
It is impossible to say just what I mean!
But as if a magic lantern threw the nerves in patterns on a screen: 105
Would it have been worth while
If one, settling a pillow or throwing off a shawl,
And turning toward the window, should say: *Who is repeating this? "That is not*
    "That is not it at all,   *what I meant" = misunderstanding.*
    That is not what I meant, at all."   110

                    •   •   •

No! I am not Prince Hamlet, nor was meant to be;   *Why compare self to*
Am an attendant lord, one that will do   *Hamlet? He's not a prince?*
To swell a progress, start a scene or two,   *Not famous?*
Advise the prince; no doubt, an easy tool,
Deferential, glad to be of use,   115
Politic, cautious, and meticulous;

Full of high sentence, but a bit obtuse;
At times, indeed, almost ridiculous—
Almost, at times, the Fool.

Worry about aging. How old is he?

I grow old . . . I grow old . . .   120
I shall wear the bottoms of my trousers rolled.

Shall I part my hair behind? Do I dare to eat a peach?   *A peach? How is*
I shall wear white flannel trousers, and walk upon the beach.   *that daring?*
I have heard the mermaids singing, each to each.

I do not think that they will sing to me.   125

I have seen them riding seaward on the waves   *Setting changes again:*
Combing the white hair of the waves blown back   *now a beach.*
When the wind blows the water white and black.

We have lingered in the chambers of the sea   *Underwater (like the crab*
By sea-girls wreathed with seaweed red and brown   *earlier).*   130
Till human voices wake us, and we drown.   *Wake us? Is this all a dream? A
nightmare?*

[1915]

On a first reading, the student was baffled by the complexities of this
poem and felt certain that it was over her head. After annotating it on a
second read-through, however, she realized that she had gotten far more
out of it than she originally believed and that she had begun to develop
some interesting ideas about the speaker and the setting. When her class
discussed the poem, she had insightful comments to add to the discussion. The following questions build on and deepen these insights.

QUESTIONS ON THE POEM

☐ What images are most striking in this poem? What makes them striking or memorable?

☐ How do the stanza breaks work in this poem? Why do you suppose Eliot chose these particular places for breaks?

☐ The rhyme and meter of the poem are highly irregular, but it's not quite free verse. Why use rhyme and meter at all? Why not make the rhyme and meter more regular?

☐ What are the various settings of the poem? How does each contribute to your understanding of the poem?

☐ What specific words would you use to sum up the character of Prufrock?

SAMPLE PAPER: AN EXPLICATION

Patrick McCorkle, the author of the paper that follows, was given the assignment to perform a close-reading of one of the poems his class had studied. He needed first to pick a poem and then to choose specific features of its language to isolate and analyze. He chose Shakespeare's Sonnet 116 because it seemed to him to offer an interesting and balanced definition of love. After rereading the poem, he became interested in several unexpectedly negative, even unsettling images that seemed out of place in a poem about the positive emotion of love. This was a good start, and it allowed him to write a draft of the paper. When he was finished, however, the essay was a little shorter and less complex than he had hoped it would be. During a peer workshop in class, he discussed the sonnet and his draft with two classmates, and together they noticed how many positive words and images appeared in the poem as well. That was the insight Patrick needed to fill out his essay and feel satisfied with the results.

Patrick McCorkle
Professor Bobrick
English 102
10 January 2008

Shakespeare Defines Love

From the earliest written rhymes to the latest radio hit, love
is among the eternal themes for poetry. Most love poetry seems to
fall into one of two categories. Either the poet sings the praises of
the beloved and the unending joys of love in overly exaggerated
terms, or the poet laments the loss of love with such bitterness
and distress that it seems like the end of life. Anyone who has
been in love, though, can tell you that both of these views are
limited and incomplete and that real love is neither entirely joyous
nor entirely sad. In Sonnet 116, "Let me not to the marriage of
true minds," Shakespeare creates a more realistic image of love. By
balancing negative with positive images and language, this sonnet
does a far better job than thousands of songs and poems before
and since, defining love in all its complexities and contradictions.

> *Patrick identifies his topic and states his thesis.*

Like many poems, Sonnet 116 relies on a series of visual
images to paint vivid pictures for the reader, but not all of these
images are what we might expect in a poem celebrating the
pleasures of lasting love. A reader can easily picture "an ever-fixèd
mark," a "tempest," a "star," a "wandering bark" (a boat lost at
sea), "rosy lips and cheeks," and a "bending sickle." Some of
these, like stars and rosy lips, are just the sort of sunny, positive
images we typically find in love poems of the joyous variety.
Others, though, are more unexpected. Flowers and images of
springtime, for instance, are standard issue in happy love poetry,
but a sickle is associated with autumn and the death of the year,
and metaphorically with death itself in the form of the grim reaper.
Likewise, a boat tossed in a raging tempest is not exactly the
typical poetic depiction of happy love.

> *Patrick introduces the poem's contradictory imagery.*

Such pictures would hardly seem to provide an upbeat image
of what love is all about, and in fact they might be more at home

> *Patrick explains the effect of this imagery.*

in one of the sad poems about the loss of love. But these tempests and sickles are more realistic than the hearts and flowers of so many lesser love poems. In fact, they show that the poet recognizes the bad times that occur in all relationships, even those strong enough to inspire love sonnets. And the negative images are tempered because of the contexts in which they occur. The "wandering bark," for instance, might represent trouble and loss, but love itself is seen as the star that will lead the boat safely back to calm waters. Meanwhile, the beloved's "rosy lips and cheeks" may fade, but real love outlives even the stroke of death's sickle, lasting "to the edge of doom."

Just as positive and negative images are juxtaposed, so are positive and negative language. The first four lines of Sonnet 116 are made up of two sentences, both negatives, beginning with the words "Let me not" and "Love is not." The negatives of the first few lines continue in phrases like "Whose worth's unknown" and "Love's not time's fool." From here, the poem goes on to dwell in abstract ideas such as "alteration," "impediments," and "error." None of this is what readers of love poems have been led to expect in their previous reading, and we might even wonder if the poet finds this love thing worth the trouble. This strange and unexpected language continues on through the last line of the poem, which contains no fewer than three negative words: "never," "nor," and "no."

Patrick integrates direct quotations from the poem into his close-reading.

Where, a reader might ask, are the expected positive descriptions of love? Where are the summer skies, the smiles and laughter? Clearly, Shakespeare doesn't mean to sweep his readers up in rosy images of a lover's bliss. Ultimately, though, even with the preponderance of negative images and words, the poem strikes a hopeful tone. The hedging about what love isn't and what it can't do are balanced with positive words and phrases, saying clearly what love is: "it is an ever-fixèd mark" and "it is the star." Love, it would seem, does not make our lives perfect, but it gives us the strength, stability, and direction to survive the bad times.

Though more than four hundred years have passed since

McCorkle 3

Shakespeare wrote his sonnets, some things never change, and among these is the nature of complex human emotions. In a mere fourteen lines, Shakespeare succeeds where many others have failed through the years, providing a much more satisfying definition of love than one normally sees in one-dimensional, strictly happy or sad poetry. The love he describes is the sort that not everyone is lucky enough to find — a "marriage of true minds" — complicated, unsettling, and very real.

In his conclusion, Patrick suggests that the poem is successful because of the juxtapositions he has discussed.

CHAPTER 7

Writing about Plays

Perhaps the earliest literary critic in the Western tradition was Aristotle, who, in the fifth century B.C.E., set about explaining the power of the genre of **tragedy** by identifying the six **elements of drama** and analyzing the contribution each of these elements makes to the functioning of a play as a whole. The elements Aristotle identified as common to all dramas were plot, characterization, theme, diction, melody, and spectacle. Some of these are the same as or very similar to the basic components of prose fiction and poetry, but others are either unique to drama or expressed differently in dramatic texts.

ELEMENTS OF DRAMA

Plot, Character, and Theme

The words *plot*, *character*, and *theme* mean basically the same thing in drama as they do in fiction, though there is a difference in how they are presented. A story *tells* you about a series of events, whereas a play *shows* you these events happening in real time. The information that might be conveyed in descriptive passages in prose fiction must be conveyed in a play through **dialogue** (and to a lesser extent through **stage directions** and the **set** and character descriptions that sometimes occur at the start of a play). The "How to Read a Play" section later in this chapter gives suggestions and advice for understanding these special features of drama.

Diction

When Aristotle speaks of **diction**, he means the specific words that a playwright chooses to put into the mouth of a character. In a well-written play, different characters will have different ways of speaking, and these will tell us a good deal about their character and personality. Does one character sound very formal and well educated? Does another speak in slang or dialect? Does someone hesitate or speak in fits and starts, perhaps indicating distraction or nervousness? Practice paying attention to these nuances. And keep in mind that just because a character says something, that doesn't make it true. As in real life, some characters might be mistaken in what they say, or they may be hiding the truth or even telling outright lies.

Melody and Spectacle

When Aristotle writes of **melody**, he is referring to the fact that Greek drama was written in verse and was chanted or sung onstage. The role of melody varies substantially with the work created in different cultures and time periods. In the English Renaissance, Shakespeare and his contemporaries used iambic pentameter and occasional end-rhymes to create dramas in verse, and staged productions have often used some kind of music, whether it be instrumental, vocal, or a mix of both. Melody is much less significant in drama today, though some plays do contain songs, of course. In musical theater, and even more in opera, songs carry much of the meaning of the play. Even in a play with no overt musical component, though, the rhythm of spoken words is important, just as it is in a poem. Even an actor's tone of voice can be considered a part of melody in the Aristotelian sense.

Spectacle refers to what we actually see onstage when we go to a play—the costumes, the actors' movements, the sets, the lights, and so forth. All of these details make a difference in how we understand and interpret a play's message. Hamlet's famous "To be or not to be" soliloquy will resonate differently with an audience if the actor playing Hamlet is wearing ripped jeans and a T-shirt, or a modern military uniform, rather than the conventional Renaissance doublet and hose. In reading a play, it is important to remember that it was not written to be read only, but rather so that it would be seen onstage in the communal setting of a theater. Reading with this in mind and trying to imagine the spectacle of a real production will increase your enjoyment of plays immensely. Specific suggestions for this sort of reading can be found in the "How to Read a Play" section of this chapter.

Setting

Setting, which Aristotle ignores completely, is just as important in drama as it is in fiction. But again, in drama it must be either displayed onstage or alluded to through the characters' words rather than being described as it might be in a story or a poem. The texts of modern plays often (though not always) begin with elaborate descriptions of the stage, furniture, major props, and so forth, which can be very useful in helping you picture a production. These tend to be absent in older plays, so in some cases you will have to use your imagination to fill in these gaps. In Act 4 of *Hamlet*, the characters are in a castle one moment and on a windswept plain the next. The only way a reader can be aware of this shift, though, is by paying close attention to the words and actions that characters use to signal a change of locale.

HOW TO READ A PLAY

Very few of us read plays for pleasure in the same way that we might take a novel with us to the beach. This isn't surprising: most playwrights, in fact, never intend for their plays to be read in this way. Drama is a living art, and if you read the play text on the page, you are getting only one part of what has made drama so important to all cultures across many time periods. Plays are written for the stage and are meant to be experienced primarily in live performance. This means that as a reader you must be especially attentive to nuances of language in a play, which often means imagining what might be happening onstage during a particular passage of speech. Using your imagination in this way—in effect, staging the play in your mind—will help you with some of the difficulties inherent in reading plays.

If you have access to film versions of the play that you are examining, be sure to watch them. Do bear in mind, though, that play scripts usually undergo substantial rewriting to adapt them for film, so you will still need to read the play in its original form, perhaps making comparisons between the stage and film versions. If you are reading a Shakespeare play, you can usually choose from several film versions, many of which might be in your library's collection. Live drama, of course, is different from film. Check the listings of local theaters to see what they are staging; you might find that a theater company is performing the play that you have to read for your class.

Some of the most skilled readers of plays are theater directors. These professionals have developed the ability to read a play and instantly see and hear in their minds the many possibilities for how the play might look and sound onstage. Directors understand that a play script is just one piece of a large, collaborative process involving playwright, director, designers, actors, backstage crew, and audience. Every new production of a play is different—sometimes vastly different—from the productions that have gone before, and every play script yields nearly endless possibilities for creative staging. By altering the look and feel of a play, a director puts his or her individual stamp on it, connecting with the audience in a unique way and helping that audience understand the playwright's and the director's messages. The questions that follow are the sort that a director would consider when reading a play. As you read plays for your literature class, these questions can help you formulate a consistent and strong interpretation.

DIRECTOR'S QUESTIONS FOR PLAY ANALYSIS

☐ What is the main message or theme of the play? What thoughts and/or feelings could be stirred up in an audience during a performance?

☐ In what kind of theater would you like to stage this play? A large, high-tech space with room to accommodate a huge audience? Or something more intimate?

☐ What sort of audience would you hope to attract to a production of this play? Older people? Young adults? Kids? Urban or rural? A mix? Who would get the most from the play's messages and themes?

☐ What sort of actors would you cast in the lead roles? Think about the sort of people you want for the various roles in terms of age, physical description, and so on. What should their voices sound like? Loud and commanding? Soft and timid?

☐ What kind of physical movement, blocking, or choreography would you want to see onstage? What are the most dramatic moments in the script? The most quiet or subtle?

☐ What would the set design look like? Would it change between acts and scenes or remain the same for the duration of the play?

☐ How would the characters be costumed? Period clothes? Modern dress? Something totally different? How could costuming contribute to character development?

☐ How much spectacle do you want? Would there be vivid sound and lighting effects? Or are you looking for a more naturalistic feel? How would this help portray the play's message?

SUSAN GLASPELL   [1882–1948]

Trifles

Characters
GEORGE HENDERSON, *county attorney*
HENRY PETERS, *sheriff*
LEWIS HALE, *a neighboring farmer*
MRS. PETERS
MRS. HALE

Scene: *The kitchen in the now abandoned farmhouse of John Wright, a gloomy kitchen, and left without having been put in order—the walls covered with a faded wall paper. Down right is a door leading to the parlor. On the right wall above this door is a built-in kitchen cupboard with shelves in the upper portion and drawers below. In the rear wall at right, up two steps is a door opening onto stairs leading to the second floor. In the rear wall at left is a door to the shed and from there to the outside. Between these two doors is an old-fashioned black iron stove. Running along the left wall from the shed door is an old iron sink and sink shelf, in which is set a hand pump. Downstage of the sink is an uncurtained window. Near the window is an old wooden rocker. Center stage is an unpainted wooden kitchen table with straight chairs on either side. There is a small chair down right. Unwashed pans under the sink, a loaf of bread outside the breadbox, a dish towel on the table—other signs of incompleted work. At the rear the shed door opens and the Sheriff comes in followed by the County Attorney and Hale. The Sheriff and Hale are men in middle life, the County Attorney is a young man; all are much bundled up and go at once to the stove. They are followed by the two women—the Sheriff's wife, Mrs. Peters, first: she is a slight wiry woman, a thin nervous face. Mrs. Hale is larger and would ordinarily be called more comfortable looking, but she is disturbed now and looks fearfully about as she enters. The women have come in slowly, and stand close together near the door.*

COUNTY ATTORNEY (*at stove rubbing his hands*): This feels good. Come up to the fire, ladies.

MRS. PETERS (*after taking a step forward*): I'm not—cold.

SHERIFF (*unbuttoning his overcoat and stepping away from the stove to right of table as if to mark the beginning of official business*): Now, Mr. Hale, before we move things about, you explain to Mr. Henderson just what you saw when you came here yesterday morning.

COUNTY ATTORNEY (*crossing down to left of the table*): By the way, has anything been moved? Are things just as you left them yesterday?

SHERIFF (*looking about*): It's just about the same. When it dropped below zero last night I thought I'd better send Frank out this morning to make a fire for us—(*sits right of center table*) no use getting pneumonia with a big case on, but I told him not to touch anything except the stove—and you know Frank.

COUNTY ATTORNEY: Somebody should have been left here yesterday.

SHERIFF: Oh—yesterday. When I had to send Frank to Morris Center for that man who went crazy—I want you to know I had my hands full yesterday. I knew you could get back from Omaha by today and as long as I went over everything here myself———

COUNTY ATTORNEY: Well, Mr. Hale, tell just what happened when you came here yesterday morning.

HALE (*crossing down to above table*): Harry and I had started to town with a load of potatoes. We came along the road from my place and as I got here I said, "I'm going to see if I can't get John Wright to go in with me on a party telephone." I spoke to Wright about it once before and he put me off, saying folks talked too much anyway, and all he asked was peace and quiet—I guess you know about how much he talked himself; but I thought maybe if I went to the house and talked about it before his wife, though I said to Harry that I didn't know as what his wife wanted made much difference to John———

COUNTY ATTORNEY: Let's talk about that later, Mr. Hale. I do want to talk about that, but tell now just what happened when you got to the house.

HALE: I didn't hear or see anything; I knocked at the door, and still it was all quiet inside. I knew they must be up, it was past eight o'clock. So I knocked again, and I thought I heard someone say, "Come in." I wasn't sure, I'm not sure yet, but I opened the door—this door (*indicating the door by which the two women are still standing*) and there in that rocker—(*pointing to it*) sat Mrs. Wright. (*They all look at the rocker down left.*)

COUNTY ATTORNEY: What—was she doing?

HALE: She was rockin' back and forth. She had her apron in her hand and was kind of—pleating it.

COUNTY ATTORNEY: And how did she—look?

HALE: Well, she looked queer.

COUNTY ATTORNEY: How do you mean—queer?

HALE: Well, as if she didn't know what she was going to do next. And kind of done up.

COUNTY ATTORNEY (*takes out notebook and pencil and sits left of center table*): How did she seem to feel about your coming?

HALE: Why, I don't think she minded—one way or other. She didn't pay much attention. I said, "How do, Mrs. Wright, it's cold, ain't it?" And she said, "Is it?"—and went on kind of pleating at her apron. Well, I was surprised: she didn't ask me to come up to the stove, or to set down, but just sat there, not even looking at me, so I said, "I want to see John." And then she—laughed. I guess you would call it a laugh. I thought of Harry and the team outside, so I said a little sharp: "Can't I see John?" "No," she says, kind o' dull like. "Ain't he home?" says I. "Yes," says she, "he's home." "Then why can't I see him?" I asked her, out of patience. "'Cause he's dead," says she. "*Dead?*" says I. She just nodded her head, not getting a bit excited, but rockin' back and forth. "Why—where is he?" says I, not knowing what to say. She just pointed upstairs—like that. (*Himself pointing to the room above.*) I started for the stairs, with the idea of going up there. I walked from there to here—then I says, "Why, what did he die of?" "He died of a rope round his neck," says she, and just went on pleatin' at her apron. Well, I went out and called Harry. I thought I might—need help. We went upstairs and there he was lyin'———

County Attorney: I think I'd rather have you go into that upstairs, where you can point it all out. Just go on now with the rest of the story.

Hale: Well, my first thought was to get that rope off. It looked . . . (*stops: his face twitches*) . . . but Harry, he went up to him, and he said, "No, he's dead all right, and we'd better not touch anything." So we went right back downstairs. She was still sitting that same way. "Has anybody been notified?" I asked. "No," says she, unconcerned. "Who did this, Mrs. Wright?" said Harry. He said it businesslike—and she stopped pleatin' of her apron. "I don't know," she says. "You don't *know*?" says Harry. "No," says she. "Weren't you sleepin' in the bed with him?" says Harry. "Yes," says she, "but I was on the inside." "Somebody slipped a rope round his head and strangled him and you didn't wake up?" says Harry. "I didn't wake up," she said after him. We must 'a' looked as if we didn't see how that could be, for after a minute she said, "I sleep sound." Harry was going to ask her more questions but I said maybe we ought to let her tell her story first to the coroner, or the sheriff, so Harry went fast as he could to Rivers' place, where there's a telephone.

County Attorney: And what did Mrs. Wright do when she knew that you had gone for the coroner?

Hale: She moved from the rocker to that chair over there (*pointing to a small chair in the down right corner*) and just sat there with her hands held together and looking down. I got a feeling that I ought to make some conversation, so I said I had come in to see if John wanted to put in a telephone, and at that she started to laugh, and then she stopped and looked at me—scared. (*The County Attorney, who has had his notebook out, makes a note.*) I dunno, maybe it wasn't scared. I wouldn't like to say it was. Soon Harry got back, and then Dr. Lloyd came and you, Mr. Peters, and so I guess that's all I know that you don't.

County Attorney (*rising and looking around*): I guess we'll go upstairs first—and then out to the barn and around there. (*To the Sheriff.*) You're convinced that there was nothing important here—nothing that would point to any motive?

SHERIFF: Nothing here but kitchen things. (*The County Attorney, after again looking around the kitchen, opens the door of a cupboard closet in right wall. He brings a small chair from right—gets on it and looks on a shelf. Pulls his hand away, sticky.*)

COUNTY ATTORNEY: Here's a nice mess. (*The women draw nearer up to center.*)

MRS. PETERS (*to the other woman*): Oh, her fruit; it did freeze. (*To the Lawyer.*) She worried about that when it turned so cold. She said the fire'd go out and her jars would break.

SHERIFF (*rises*): Well, can you beat the woman! Held for murder and worryin' about her preserves.

COUNTY ATTORNEY (*getting down from chair*): I guess before we're through she may have something more serious than preserves to worry about. (*Crosses down right center.*)

HALE: Well, women are used to worrying over trifles. (*The two women move a little closer together.*)

COUNTY ATTORNEY (*with the gallantry of a young politician*): And yet, for all their worries, what would we do without the ladies? (*The women do not unbend. He goes below the center table to the sink, takes a dipperful of water from the pail, and pouring it into a basin, washes his hands. While he is doing this the Sheriff and Hale cross to cupboard, which they inspect. The County Attorney starts to wipe his hands on the roller towel, turns it for a cleaner place.*) Dirty towels! (*Kicks his foot against the pans under the sink.*) Not much of a housekeeper, would you say, ladies?

MRS. HALE (*stiffly*): There's a great deal of work to be done on a farm.

COUNTY ATTORNEY: To be sure. And yet (*with a little bow to her*) I know there are some Dickson County farmhouses which do not have such roller towels. (*He gives it a pull to expose its full-length again.*)

MRS. HALE: Those towels get dirty awful quick. Men's hands aren't always clean as they might be.

COUNTY ATTORNEY: Ah, loyal to your sex, I see. But you and Mrs. Wright were neighbors. I suppose you were friends, too.

MRS. HALE (*shaking her head*): I've not seen much of her of late years. I've not been in this house—it's more than a year.

COUNTY ATTORNEY (*crossing to women up center*): And why was that? You didn't like her?

MRS. HALE: I liked her all well enough. Farmer's wives have their hands full, Mr. Henderson. And then——

COUNTY ATTORNEY: Yes——?

MRS. HALE (*looking about*): It never seemed a very cheerful place.

COUNTY ATTORNEY: No—it's not cheerful. I shouldn't say she had the homemaking instinct.

MRS. HALE: Well, I don't know as Wright had, either.

COUNTY ATTORNEY: You mean that they didn't get on very well?

MRS. HALE: No, I don't mean anything. But I don't think a place'd be any cheerfuller for John Wright's being in it.

COUNTY ATTORNEY: I'd like to talk more of that a little later. I want to get the lay of things upstairs now. (*He goes past the women to up right where the steps lead to a stair door.*)

SHERIFF: I suppose anything Mrs. Peters does'll be all right. She was to take in some clothes for her, you know, and a few little things. We left in such a hurry yesterday.

COUNTY ATTORNEY: Yes, but I would like to see what you take, Mrs. Peters, and keep an eye out for anything that might be of use to us.

MRS. PETERS: Yes, Mr. Henderson. (*The men leave by up right door to stairs. The women listen to the men's steps on the stairs, then look about the kitchen.*)

MRS. HALE (*crossing left to sink*): I'd hate to have men coming into my kitchen, snooping around and criticizing. (*She arranges the pans under sink which the lawyer had shoved out of place.*)

MRS. PETERS: Of course it's no more than their duty. (*Crosses to cupboard up right.*)

MRS. HALE: Duty's all right, but I guess that deputy sheriff that came out to make the fire might have got a little of this on. (*Gives the roller towel a pull.*) Wish I'd thought of that sooner. Seems mean to talk about her for not having things slicked up when she had to come away in such a hurry. (*Crosses right to Mrs. Peters at cupboard.*)

MRS. PETERS (*who has been looking through cupboard, lifts one end of towel that covers a pan*): She had bread set. (*Stands still.*)

MRS. HALE (*eyes fixed on a loaf of bread beside the breadbox, which is on a low shelf of the cupboard*): She was going to put this in there. (*Picks up loaf, abruptly drops it. In a manner of returning to familiar things.*) It's a shame about her fruit. I wonder if it's all gone. (*Gets up on chair and looks.*) I think there's some here that's all right, Mrs. Peters. Yes—here; (*holding it toward the window*) this is cherries, too. (*Looking again.*) I declare I believe that's the only one. (*Gets down, jar in hand. Goes to the sink and wipes it off on the outside.*) She'll feel awful bad after all her hard work in the hot weather. I remember the afternoon I put up my cherries last summer. (*She puts the jar on the big kitchen table, center of the room. With a sigh, is about to sit down in the rocking chair. Before she is seated realizes what chair it is; with a slow look at it, steps back. The chair which she has touched rocks back and forth. Mrs. Peters moves to center table and they both watch the chair rock for a moment or two.*)

MRS. PETERS (*shaking off the mood which the empty rocking chair has evoked. Now in a businesslike manner she speaks*): Well I must get those things from the front room closet. (*She goes to the door at the right but, after looking into the other room, steps back.*) You coming with me, Mrs. Hale? You could help me carry them. (*They go in the other room; reappear, Mrs. Peters carrying a dress, petticoat, and skirt, Mrs. Hale following with a pair of shoes.*) My, it's cold in there. (*She puts the clothes on the big table and hurries to the stove.*)

MRS. HALE (*right of center table examining the skirt*): Wright was close. I think maybe that's why she kept so much to herself. She didn't even belong to the Ladies' Aid. I suppose she felt she couldn't do her part, and then you don't enjoy things when you feel shabby. I heard she used to wear pretty clothes and be lively, when she was Minnie Foster, one of the town girls singing in the choir. But that—oh, that was thirty years ago. This all you want to take in?

MRS. PETERS: She said she wanted an apron. Funny thing to want, for there isn't much to get you dirty in jail, goodness knows. But I suppose just to make her feel more natural. (*Crosses to cupboard.*) She said they was in the top drawer in this cupboard. Yes, here. And then her little shawl that always hung behind the door. (*Opens stair door and looks.*) Yes, here it is. (*Quickly shuts door leading upstairs.*)

MRS. HALE (*abruptly moving toward her*): Mrs. Peters?

MRS. PETERS: Yes, Mrs. Hale? (*At up right door.*)

MRS. HALE: Do you think she did it?

MRS. PETERS (*in a frightened voice*): Oh, I don't know.

MRS. HALE: Well, I don't think she did. Asking for an apron and her little shawl. Worrying about her fruit.

MRS. PETERS (*starts to speak, glances up, where footsteps are heard in the room above. In a low voice*): Mr. Peters says it looks bad for her. Mr. Henderson is awful sarcastic in a speech and he'll make fun of her sayin' she didn't wake up.

MRS. HALE: Well, I guess John Wright didn't wake when they was slipping that rope under his neck.

MRS. PETERS (*crossing slowly to table and placing shawl and apron on table with other clothing*): No, it's strange. It must have been done awful crafty and still. They say it was such a—funny way to kill a man, rigging it all up like that.

MRS. HALE (*crossing to left of Mrs. Peters at table*): That's just what Mr. Hale said. There was a gun in the house. He says that's what he can't understand.

MRS. PETERS: Mr. Henderson said coming out that what was needed for the case was a motive: something to show anger, or—sudden feeling.

MRS. HALE (*who is standing by the table*): Well, I don't see any signs of anger around here. (*She puts her hand on the dish towel, which lies on the table, stands looking down at table, one-half of which is clean, the other half messy.*) It's wiped to here. (*Makes a move as if to finish work, then turns and looks at loaf of bread outside the breadbox. Drops towel. In that voice of coming back to familiar things.*) Wonder how they are finding things up-stairs. (*Crossing below table to down right.*) I hope she had it a little more red-up up there. You know, it seems kind of *sneaking*. Locking her up in town and then coming out here and trying to get her own house to turn against her!

MRS. PETERS: But, Mrs. Hale, the law is the law.

MRS. HALE: I s'pose 'tis. (*Unbuttoning her coat.*) Better loosen up your things, Mrs. Peters. You won't feel them when you go out. (*Mrs. Peters takes off her fur tippet, goes to hang it on chair back left of table, stands look-ing at the work basket on floor near down left window.*)

MRS. PETERS: She was piecing a quilt. (*She brings the large sewing basket to the center table and they look at the bright pieces, Mrs. Hale above the table and Mrs. Peters left of it.*)

MRS. HALE: It's a log cabin pattern. Pretty, isn't it? I wonder if she was goin' to quilt it or just knot it? (*Footsteps have been heard coming down the stairs. The Sheriff enters followed by Hale and the County Attorney.*)

SHERIFF: They wonder if she was going to quilt it or just knot it! (*The men laugh, the women look abashed.*)

COUNTY ATTORNEY (*rubbing his hands over the stove*): Frank's fire didn't do much up there, did it? Well, let's go out to the barn and get that cleared up. (*The men go outside by up left door.*)

MRS. HALE (*resentfully*): I don't know as there's anything so strange, our takin' up our time with little things while we're waiting for them to get the evidence. (*She sits in chair right of table smoothing out a block with decision.*) I don't see as it's anything to laugh about.

MRS. PETERS (*apologetically*): Of course they've got awful important things on their minds. (*Pulls up a chair and joins Mrs. Hale at the left of the table.*)

MRS. HALE (*examining another block*): Mrs. Peters, look at this one. Here, this is the one she was working on, and look at the sewing! All the rest of it has been so nice and even. And look at this! It's all over the place! Why, it looks as if she didn't know what she was about! (*After she has said this they look at each other, then start to glance back at the door. After an instant Mrs. Hale has pulled at a knot and ripped the sewing.*)

MRS. PETERS: Oh, what are you doing, Mrs. Hale?

MRS. HALE (*mildly*): Just pulling out a stitch or two that's not sewed very good. (*Threading a needle.*) Bad sewing always made me fidgety.

MRS. PETERS (*with a glance at the door, nervously*): I don't think we ought to touch things.

MRS. HALE: I'll just finish up this end. (*Suddenly stopping and leaning for-ward.*) Mrs. Peters?

MRS. PETERS: Yes, Mrs. Hale?

MRS. HALE: What do you suppose she was so nervous about?

MRS. PETERS: Oh—I don't know. I don't know as she was nervous. I sometimes sew awful queer when I'm just tired. (*Mrs. Hale starts to say something, looks at Mrs. Peters, then goes on sewing.*) Well, I must get these things wrapped up. They may be through sooner than we think. (*Putting apron and other things together.*) I wonder where I can find a piece of paper, and string. (*Rises.*)

MRS. HALE: In that cupboard, maybe.

MRS. PETERS (*crosses right looking in cupboard*): Why, here's a bird-cage. (*Holds it up.*) Did she have a bird, Mrs. Hale?

MRS. HALE: Why, I don't know whether she did or not—I've not been here for so long. There was a man around last year selling canaries cheap, but I don't know as she took one; maybe she did. She used to sing real pretty herself.

MRS. PETERS (*glancing around*): Seems funny to think of a bird here. But she must have had one, or why would she have a cage? I wonder what happened to it?

MRS. HALE: I s'pose maybe the cat got it.

MRS. PETERS: No, she didn't have a cat. She's got that feeling some people have about cats—being afraid of them. My cat got in her room and she was real upset and asked me to take it out.

MRS. HALE: My sister Bessie was like that. Queer, ain't it?

MRS. PETERS (*examining the cage*): Why, look at this door. It's broke. One hinge is pulled apart. (*Takes a step down to Mrs. Hale's right.*)

MRS. HALE (*looking too*): Looks as if someone must have been rough with it.

MRS. PETERS: Why, yes. (*She brings the cage forward and puts it on the table.*)

MRS. HALE (*glancing toward up left door*): I wish if they're going to find any evidence they'd be about it. I don't like this place.

MRS. PETERS: But I'm awful glad you came with me, Mrs. Hale. It would be lonesome for me sitting here alone.

MRS. HALE: It would, wouldn't it? (*Dropping her sewing.*) But I tell you what I do wish, Mrs. Peters. I wish I had come over sometimes when she was here. I—(*looking around the room*)—wish I had.

MRS. PETERS: But of course you were awful busy, Mrs. Hale—your house and your children.

MRS. HALE (*rises and crosses left*): I could've come. I stayed away because it weren't cheerful—and that's why I ought to have come. I—(*looking out left window*)—I've never liked this place. Maybe it's because it's down in a hollow and you don't see the road. I dunno what it is, but it's a lonesome place and always was. I wish I had come over to see Minnie Foster sometimes. I can see now—(*Shakes her head.*)

MRS. PETERS (*left of table and above it*): Well, you mustn't reproach yourself, Mrs. Hale. Somehow we just don't see how it is with other folks until—something turns up.

MRS. HALE: Not having children makes less work—but it makes a quiet house, and Wright out to work all day, and no company when he did come in. (*Turning from window.*) Did you know John Wright, Mrs. Peters?

MRS. PETERS: Not to know him; I've seen him in town. They say he was a good man.

MRS. HALE: Yes—good; he didn't drink, and kept his word as well as most, I guess, and paid his debts. But he was a hard man, Mrs. Peters. Just to pass the time of day with him—(*Shivers.*) Like a raw wind that gets to the bone. (*Pauses, her eye falling on the cage.*) I should think she would 'a' wanted a bird. But what do you suppose went with it?

MRS. PETERS: I don't know, unless it got sick and died. (*She reaches over and swings the broken door, swings it again, both women watch it.*)

MRS. HALE: You weren't raised round here, were you? (*Mrs. Peters shakes her head.*) You didn't know—her?

MRS. PETERS: Not till they brought her yesterday.

MRS. HALE: She—come to think of it, she was kind of like a bird her-self—real sweet and pretty, but kind of timid and—fluttery. How—she—did—change. (*Silence: then as if struck by a happy thought and relieved to get back to everyday things. Crosses right above Mrs. Peters to cupboard, replaces small chair used to stand on to its original place down right.*) Tell you what, Mrs. Peters, why don't you take the quilt in with you? It might take up her mind.

MRS. PETERS: Why, I think that's a real nice idea, Mrs. Hale. There couldn't possibly be any objection to it could there? Now, just what would I take? I wonder if her patches are in here—and her things. (*They look in the sewing basket.*)

MRS. HALE (*crosses to right of table*): Here's some red. I expect this has got sewing things in it. (*Brings out a fancy box.*) What a pretty box. Looks like something somebody would give you. Maybe her scissors are in here. (*Opens box. Suddenly puts her hand to her nose.*) Why———(*Mrs. Peters bends nearer, then turns her face away.*) There's something wrapped up in this piece of silk.

MRS. PETERS: Why, this isn't her scissors.

MRS. HALE (*lifting the silk*): Oh, Mrs. Peters—it's———(*Mrs. Peters bends closer.*)

MRS. PETERS: It's the bird.

MRS. HALE: But, Mrs. Peters—look at it! Its neck! Look at its neck! It's all—other side *to*.

MRS. PETERS: Somebody—wrung—its—neck. (*Their eyes meet. A look of growing comprehension, of horror. Steps are heard outside. Mrs. Hale slips box under quilt pieces, and sinks into her chair. Enter Sheriff and County Attorney. Mrs. Peters steps down left and stands looking out of window.*)

COUNTY ATTORNEY (*as one turning from serious things to little pleasant-ries*): Well, ladies, have you decided whether she was going to quilt it or knot it? (*Crosses to center above table.*)

MRS. PETERS: We think she was going to—knot it. (*Sheriff crosses to right of stove, lifts stove lid, and glances at fire, then stands warming hands at stove.*)

COUNTY ATTORNEY: Well, that's interesting, I'm sure. (*Seeing the bird-cage.*) Has the bird flown?

MRS. HALE (*putting more quilt pieces over the box*): We think the—cat got it.

COUNTY ATTORNEY (*preoccupied*): Is there a cat? (*Mrs. Hale glances in a quick covert way at Mrs. Peters.*)

MRS. PETERS (*turning from window takes a step in*): Well, not *now*. They're superstitious, you know. They leave.

COUNTY ATTORNEY (*to Sheriff Peters, continuing an interrupted conversation*): No sign at all of anyone having come from the outside. Their own rope. Now let's go up again and go over it piece by piece. (*They start upstairs.*) It would have to have been someone who knew just the———(*Mrs. Peters sits down left of table. The two women sit there not looking at one another, but as if peering into something and at the same time holding back. When they talk now it is in the manner of feeling their way over strange ground, as if afraid of what they are saying, but as if they cannot help saying it.*)

MRS. HALE (*hesitatively and in hushed voice*): She liked the bird. She was going to bury it in that pretty box.

MRS. PETERS (*in a whisper*): When I was a girl—my kitten—there was a boy took a hatchet, and before my eyes—and before I could get there———(*Covers her face an instant.*) If they hadn't held me back I would have—(*catches herself, looks upstairs where steps are heard, falters weakly*)—hurt him.

MRS. HALE (*with a slow look around her*): I wonder how it would seem never to have had any children around. (*Pause.*) No, Wright wouldn't like the bird—a thing that sang. She used to sing. He killed that, too.

MRS. PETERS (*moving uneasily*): We don't know who killed the bird.

MRS. HALE: I knew John Wright.

MRS. PETERS: It was an awful thing was done in this house that night, Mrs. Hale. Killing a man while he slept, slipping a rope around his neck that choked the life out of him.

MRS. HALE: His neck. Choked the life out of him. (*Her hand goes out and rests on the bird-cage.*)

MRS. PETERS (*with rising voice*): We don't know who killed him. We don't know.

MRS. HALE (*her own feelings not interrupted*): If there'd been years and years of nothing, then a bird to sing to you, it would be awful—still, after the bird was still.

MRS. PETERS (*something within her speaking*): I know what stillness is.

When we homesteaded in Dakota, and my first baby died—after he was two years old, and me with no other then——

MRS. HALE (*moving*): How soon do you suppose they'll be through look-ing for the evidence?

MRS. PETERS: I know what stillness is. (*Pulling herself back.*) The law has got to punish crimes, Mrs. Hale.

MRS. HALE (*not as if answering that*): I wish you'd seen Minnie Foster when she wore a white dress with blue ribbons and stood up there in the choir and sang. (*A look around the room.*) Oh, I *wish* I'd come over here once in a while! That was a crime! That was a crime! Who's going to punish that?

MRS. PETERS (*looking upstairs*): We mustn't—take on.

MRS. HALE: I might have known she needed help! I know how things can be—for women. I tell you, it's queer, Mrs. Peters. We live close to-gether and we live far apart. We all go through the same things—it's all just a different kind of the same thing. (*Brushes her eyes, noticing the jar of fruit, reaches out for it.*) If I was you I wouldn't tell her her fruit was gone. Tell her it ain't. Tell her it's all right. Take this in to prove it to her. She—she may never know whether it was broke or not.

MRS. PETERS (*takes the jar, looks about for something to wrap it in; takes pet-ticoat from the clothes brought from the other room, very nervously begins winding this around the jar. In a false voice*): My, it's a good thing the men couldn't hear us. Wouldn't they just laugh! Getting all stirred up over a little thing like a—dead canary. As if that could have anything to do with—with—wouldn't they *laugh*! (*The men are heard coming down-stairs.*)

MRS. HALE (*under her breath*): Maybe they would—maybe they wouldn't.

COUNTY ATTORNEY: No, Peters, it's all perfectly clear except a reason for doing it. But you know juries when it comes to women. If there was some definite thing. (*Crosses slowly to above table. Sheriff crosses down right. Mrs. Hale and Mrs. Peters remain seated at either side of table.*) Some-thing to show—something to make a story about—a thing that would connect up with this strange way of doing it——(*The women's eyes meet for an instant. Enter Hale from outer door.*)

HALE (*remaining by door*): Well, I've got the team around. Pretty cold out there.

COUNTY ATTORNEY: I'm going to stay awhile by myself. (*To the Sheriff.*) You can send Frank out for me, can't you? I want to go over everything. I'm not satisfied that we can't do better.

SHERIFF: Do you want to see what Mrs. Peters is going to take in? (*The Lawyer picks up the apron, laughs.*)

COUNTY ATTORNEY: Oh, I guess they're not very dangerous things the la-dies have picked out. (*Moves a few things about, disturbing the quilt pieces which cover the box. Steps back.*) No, Mrs. Peters doesn't need supervising. For that matter a sheriff's wife is married to the law. Ever think of it that way, Mrs. Peters?

MRS. PETERS: Not—just that way.

SHERIFF (*chuckling*): Married to the law. (*Moves to down right door to the other room.*) I just want you to come in here a minute, George. We ought to take a look at these windows.

COUNTY ATTORNEY (*scoffingly*): Oh, windows!

SHERIFF: We'll be right out, Mr. Hale. (*Hale goes outside. The Sheriff follows the County Attorney into the room. Then Mrs. Hale rises, hands tight together, looking intensely at Mrs. Peters, whose eyes make a slow turn, finally meeting Mrs. Hale's. A moment Mrs. Hale holds her, then her own eyes point the way to where the box is concealed. Suddenly Mrs. Peters throws back quilt pieces and tries to put the box in the bag she is carrying. It is too big. She opens box, starts to take bird out, cannot touch it, goes to pieces, stands there helpless. Sound of a knob turning in the other room. Mrs. Hale snatches the box and puts it in the pocket of her big coat. Enter County Attorney and Sheriff, who remains down right.*)

COUNTY ATTORNEY (*crosses to up left door facetiously*): Well, Henry, at least we found out that she was not going to quilt it. She was going to—what is it you call it, ladies?

MRS. HALE (*standing center below table facing front, her hand against her pocket*): We call it—knot it, Mr. Henderson.

[1916]

SAMPLE PAPER: AN ANALYSIS

Sarah Johnson was free to choose the topic and focus of her paper. In the same semester as her literature class, she was enrolled in a philosophy course on ethics where she was introduced to the idea of situational ethics, the notion that exterior pressures often cause people to act in ways they might normally deem unethical, often to prevent or allay a worse evil. This philosophical concept was on Sarah's mind when she read Susan Glaspell's play *Trifles*. She noticed that the character of Mrs. Peters does indeed end up behaving in a way she would probably never have imagined for herself. This seemed an interesting concept to pursue, so Sarah decided to trace the development of Mrs. Peters' journey away from her original moral certainty.

Sarah Johnson

Professor Riley

English 253

24 October 2007

Moral Ambiguity and Character Development
in *Trifles*

What is the relationship between legality and morality? Susan Glaspell's short play *Trifles* asks us to ponder this question, but it provides no clear answers. Part murder mystery, part battle of the sexes, the play makes its readers confront and question many issues about laws, morals, and human relationships. In the person of Mrs. Peters, a sheriff's wife, the play chronicles one woman's moral journey from a certain, unambiguous belief in the law to a more situational view of ethics. Before it is over, this once legally minded woman is even willing to cover up the truth and let someone get away with murder.

At the beginning of the play, Mrs. Peters believes that law, truth, and morality are one and the same. Though never unkind about the accused, Mrs. Wright, Mrs. Peters is at first firm in her belief that the men will find the truth and that the crime will be punished as it should be. Mrs. Hale feels the men are "kind of *sneaking*" as they look about Mrs. Wright's abandoned house for evidence against her, but Mrs. Peters assures her that "the law is the law." It is not that Mrs. Peters is less sympathetic toward women than her companion, but she is even more sympathetic toward the lawmen, because her version of morality is so absolute. When the men deride the women's interest in so-called trifles, like sewing and housework, Mrs. Hale takes offense. But Mrs. Peters, convinced that the law must prevail, defends them, saying, "It's no more than their duty," and later, "They've got awful important things on their minds."

As she attempts to comply with the requirements of the law, Mrs. Peters is described in a stage direction as "businesslike," and she tries to maintain a skeptical attitude as she waits for the truth

Sarah focuses on Mrs. Peters right away.

Sarah uses direct quotations from the play text as backup for her claims.

to emerge. Asked if she thinks Mrs. Wright killed her husband, she says, "Oh, I don't know." She seems to be trying to convince herself that the accused is innocent until proven guilty, though she admits that her husband thinks it "looks bad for her." She seems to have absorbed her husband's attitudes and values and to be keeping a sort of legalistic distance from her feelings about the case.

Mrs. Hale is less convinced of the rightness of the men or the law. Even before the two women discover a possible motive for the murder, Mrs. Hale is already tampering with evidence, tearing out the erratic sewing stitches that suggest Mrs. Wright was agitated. Mrs. Peters says, "I don't think we ought to touch things," but she doesn't make any stronger move to stop Mrs. Hale, who continues to fix the sewing. At this point, we see her first beginning to waver from her previously firm stance on right and wrong.

It is not that Mrs. Peters is unsympathetic to the hard life that Mrs. Wright has led. She worries with Mrs. Hale about the accused woman's frozen jars of preserves, her half-done bread, and her unfinished quilt. But she tries to think, like the men, that these things are "trifles" and that what matters is the legal truth. But when she sees a bird with a wrung neck, things begin to change in a major way. She remembers the boy who killed her kitten when she was a child, and the sympathy she has felt for Mrs. Wright begins to turn to empathy. The empathy is enough to prompt her first lie to the men. When the county attorney spies the empty birdcage, she corroborates Mrs. Hale's story about a cat getting the bird, even though she knows there was no cat in the house.

In this paragraph, Sarah analyzes a turning point in the play text: a moment in which Mrs. Peters experiences a transformation.

Even after she has reached that point of empathy, Mrs. Peters tries hard to maintain her old way of thinking and being. Alone again with Mrs. Hale, she says firmly, "We don't know who killed the bird," even though convincing evidence points to John Wright. More important, she says of Wright himself, "We don't know who killed him. We don't *know*." But her repetition and her "rising

Johnson 3

voice," described in a stage direction, show how agitated she has
become. As a believer in the law, she should feel certain that everyone is innocent until proven guilty, but she thinks she knows the
truth, and, perhaps for the first time in her life, legal truth does not
square with moral truth. Her empathy deepens further still when
she thinks about the stillness of the house in which Mrs. Wright
was forced to live after the death of her beloved pet, which brought
song to an otherwise grim life. She knows Mrs. Wright is childless,
and she now remembers not just the death of her childhood kitten
but also the terrible quiet in her own house after her first child
died. She reaches a moment of crisis between her two ways of thinking when she says, "I know what stillness is. (*Pulling herself back.*)
The law has got to punish crimes, Mrs. Hale." This is perhaps the
most important line in the chronicle of her growth as a character.
First she expresses her newfound empathy with the woman she
believes to be a murderer; then, as the stage directions say, she
tries to pull herself back and return to the comfortable moral certainty that she felt just a short time before. It is too late for that,
though.

*Here and else-
where, Sarah
relies on stage
directions as
evidence for her
claims about
Mrs. Peters.*

In the end, Mrs. Peters gives in to what she believes to be
emotionally right rather than what is legally permissible. She collaborates with Mrs. Hale to cover up evidence of the motive and hide
the dead canary. Though very little time has gone by, she has undergone a major transformation. She may be, as the county attorney
says, "married to the law," but she is also divorced from her old
ideals. When she tries to cover up the evidence, a stage direction
says she "goes to pieces," and Mrs. Hale has to help her. By the
time she pulls herself together, the new woman she is will be a very
different person from the old one. She, along with the reader, is
now in a world where the relationship between legality and morality is far more complex than she had ever suspected.

*Sarah isolates
this passage to
emphasize the
complexity of
Mrs. Peters.*

CHAPTER 8

Writing a Literary Research Paper

Writing a literary research paper draws on the same set of skills as writing any other paper—choosing a topic, developing a thesis, gathering and organizing support, and so on. The main difference between research writing and other sorts of writing lies in the number and types of sources from which one's support comes. All writing about literature begins with a **primary source**—the poem, story, or play on which the writing is based. Research papers also incorporate **secondary sources**, such as biographical, historical, and critical essays.

As you begin the process of research writing, the most important thing to remember is that you are writing a critical argument. Your paper should not end up reading like a book report or a catalog of what others have said about the literature. Rather, it should begin and end by making an original point based on your own ideas, and like any other paper, it needs a clear, sharply focused thesis. The sources, both primary and secondary, are there to support your thesis, not to take over the paper.

The method laid out below seems very linear and straightforward: find and evaluate sources for your paper, read them and take notes, and then write a paper integrating material from these sources. In reality, the process is rarely, if ever, this neat. As you read and write, you will discover gaps in your knowledge, or you will ask yourself new questions that will demand more research. Be flexible. Keep in mind that the process of research is recursive, requiring a writer to move back and forth between various stages. Naturally, this means that for research writing, even more than for other kinds of writing, you should start early and give yourself plenty of time to complete the project.

FINDING SOURCES

For many students, research is more or less synonymous with the Internet. It may be easy to think that all the information anybody could ever want is available online, readily and easily accessible to the public. But when it comes to literary research, this is not the case at all. True, there are plenty of Web sites and newsgroups devoted to literary figures, but the type of information available on these sites tends to be limited to a narrow range—basic biographies of authors, plot summaries, and so forth—and the quality of information is highly variable. Though serious literary scholarship does exist on the Web, proprietary online databases (available through a library portal) and print books and journals are still the better sources for you in most cases.

Online Indexes

You can begin to locate sources for your research paper by using the online indexes and databases available through your college or university library. These services sort and index journal and magazine articles to help researchers find what they are looking for. Although using these indexes is somewhat similar to using an Internet search engine, the two should not be confused. The Internet links to an array of documents— some of very high quality, some worse than useless—that are available for free to the public. By contrast, college, university, and many public libraries pay a fee to allow their users access to the more specialized and highly vetted sources found in various indexes and databases. When you use these services, you are assured that any articles you locate have been published by reliable, respected sources.

Your library probably subscribes to dozens of databases covering many fields of knowledge. These are some of the most useful ones for literary research:

- *Academic OneFile* and *Expanded Academic ASAP* (both from InfoTrac) index a combination of scholarly journals and popular magazines and provide a good starting point for articles of general interest.

- *Literary Reference Center* (EBSCO) provides full-text articles from specialized encyclopedias and reference works, including author biographies, synopses of major literary works, and articles on literary history and criticism.

- *MLA International Bibliography* (EBSCO) indexes scholarly books and articles on modern languages, literature, folklore, and linguistics; many have full-text links.

- *Humanities Index* (H. W. Wilson) indexes periodicals in the humanities, including scholarly journals and lesser-known specialized magazines; many have full-text links.

- *JSTOR* provides searchable, full-text articles digitized from more than a thousand academic journals, some dating back to the nineteenth century.

The indexes listed on page 131 are just a sampling of those most generally applicable to literary research. Depending on your particular topic or interests, you may find yourself drawn to one of the many more specialized indexes, such as *GenderWatch* (for topics related to feminism and other gender issues), *GreenFile* (for environmental topics), and *Hispanic American Periodicals Index*, to name just a few.

If you do not know how to access or use these sources, ask the reference librarian on duty at your college library. Helping students find what they need is this person's principal job, and you will likely learn a lot from him or her. Both your librarian and your instructor can also suggest additional indexes to point you toward good secondary sources. One of the great advantages of databases and indexes is that results can be filtered and sorted according to a wide array of criteria. You can find articles written in a particular year or in a particular language; you can choose to look only at articles that have been peer-reviewed (the process that assures scholarly legitimacy); or you can select any of a number of other filters to help you find exactly what you need.

When you begin searching, use fairly specific search terms to help the database focus on what you really need and to filter out irrelevant material. Let's say you are researching the nature of love in Shakespeare's sonnets. If you perform a search on the keyword or topic *Shakespeare*, you will get many thousands of hits, many of them about topics unrelated to yours. Searching on both *Shakespeare* and *sonnet*, however, will get you closer to what you want, while searching on *Shakespeare*, *sonnet*, and *love* will yield far fewer and far better, more targeted results. If your search nets you fewer results than you expected, try again with different terms (substitute *romance* for *love*, for example). Be patient, and don't be afraid to ask your instructor or librarian for help if you are experiencing difficulty.

Once you have a screen full of results, you will be able to access a **text**, an abstract, or a citation. Some results will give you a link to the complete text of an article; just click on the link, and you can read the article on-screen, print it out, or e-mail it to yourself. Frequently, a link is provided to an abstract, a brief summary (generally just a few sentences) of the content of the full article. Reading an abstract is a good way of finding out whether it is worth tracking down the whole article for your paper. A citation gives only the most basic information about an article—its title, its author, the date of publication, and its page numbers—and it is up to you to then find and read the whole article.

It may be tempting to settle on only those articles available immediately in full-text versions. Don't fall into this trap. Even in this electronic age, scholars and specialists still write books, as well as articles for academic journals that are not always available in electronic versions. Many of the best sources of literary research are available only in print, and the only way to obtain these is to follow the citation's lead and locate the book or journal in the library stacks. If a title or an abstract looks promising, go and retrieve the article. If you think getting up and tracking down a journal is frustrating or time-consuming, imagine how frustrating and time-consuming it will be to attempt to write a research paper without great sources.

Periodicals

At this point, you should be aware of the distinction between two types of periodicals that your search may lead to: magazines, which are directed at a general readership, and scholarly journals, which are written by and for specialists in various academic fields. *Scientific American*, for instance, is a well-respected magazine available on newsstands, whereas *The Journal of Physical Chemistry* is a scholarly journal, generally available only by subscription and read mainly by chemists and chemistry students. In the field of literary studies, there are hundreds of journals, ranging from publications covering a general period or topic (*American Literary Realism, Modern Drama*) to those devoted to specific authors (*Walt Whitman Review, Melville Society Extracts*).

While magazines like *Time* and *Newsweek* are sometimes appropriate research sources, and you certainly should not rule them out, the highest-quality and most sophisticated literary criticism tends to appear in journals. If you are uncertain whether you are looking at a scholarly journal, look for the following typical characteristics:

- Scholarly journal articles tend to be *longer* than magazine articles, ranging anywhere from five to more than fifty pages.
- Journal articles are *written by specialists* for researchers, professors, and college students. The author's professional credentials and institutional affiliation are often listed.
- Journal articles tend to be written in a given profession's *special language* and can be difficult for nonspecialists to understand. Articles in literary journals use the specialized language of literary theory and criticism.
- Journal articles are usually *peer-reviewed* or refereed, meaning that other specialists have read them and determined that they make a significant contribution to the field. Peer referees are often listed as an editorial board on the journal's masthead page.
- Journal articles usually include *footnotes or endnotes* and an often substantial references, *bibliography*, or works cited section.

Books

As mentioned earlier, many scholars still publish their most important work in print books, and the place to look for these is in your college or university library's catalog. (Public libraries, no matter how well run, seldom carry the sorts of specialized sources needed for college-level research.) Start by looking for one or two good books on your topic. Books tend to be more general in their scope than journal articles, and they can be useful at the early stages of your research to help you focus and refine your thinking. If you have given yourself sufficient time for the process, take a book or two home and skim them to determine which parts would be most useful for you. When you return to the library to perform more research, you will have a clearer sense of what you are looking for and therefore will be more efficient at completing the rest of your search.

Interlibrary Loan

If you find a promising lead but discover that your library doesn't have a particular book or has no subscription to the needed periodical, you still may be in luck. Nearly all libraries offer interlibrary loan services, which can track down books and articles from a large network of other libraries and send them to your home institution, generally free of charge. Of course, this process takes time—usually, a couple of days to a couple of weeks—and this is yet another reason to get started as early as possible on your research.

The Internet

Lastly, if your quest for books and periodicals has not yielded all the results you want, search the World Wide Web. As with a search of a specialized index, you will do better and filter out a lot of low-quality sources if you come up with some well-focused search terms in advance. Be sure to ask your instructor or reference librarian about authoritative Web sites. Your librarian may have already created a special page on the library's Web site that provides links to the best Web sites for students of English. If you use the Web for your research, look especially for scholarly sites, written by professors or researchers and maintained by colleges and universities. For example, if you want to research the poetry and artwork of William Blake, you might check The Blake Archive, an online project sponsored by the Library of Congress and the University of North Carolina, Chapel Hill: http://www.blakearchive.org/blake/. If you are interested in learning more about Walt Whitman's life and work, check The Walt Whitman Archive, a project developed and edited by Ed Folsom and Kenneth M. Price, both of whom are eminent Whitman scholars: http://www.whitmanarchive.org/. If you want to read the 1603 printing of *Hamlet*, check the British Library's Web site: http://www.bl.uk/treasures/ shakespeare/homepage.html. Also potentially useful are the online equivalents of scholarly journals, as well as discussion groups or newsgroups dedicated to particular authors, literary schools, or periods.

How do you know when you have enough sources? Many instructors specify a minimum number of sources for research papers, and many students find exactly that number of sources and then look no further. Your best bet is to stop looking for sources when you think you have enough material to write a top-quality paper. Indeed, it is far better to gather up too many sources and end up not using them all than to get too few and find yourself wanting more information as you write. And remember that any "extra" research beyond what you actually cite in your paper isn't really wasted effort—every piece of information you read contributes to your background knowledge and overall understanding of your topic, making your final paper sound smarter and better informed.

EVALUATING SOURCES

As you locate research sources, you should engage in a continual process of evaluation to determine both the reliability of the potential source and its appropriateness to your particular topic and needs. Keep the following questions in mind to help you evaluate both print and electronic sources:

- **Who is the author, and what are his or her credentials?** If this information is not readily available, you might ask yourself why not. Is the author or publisher trying to hide something?
- **What is the medium of publication?** Books, journals, magazines, newspapers, and electronic publications all have something to offer a researcher, but they do not all offer the same thing. A good researcher will usually seek out a variety of sources.
- **How respectable is the publisher?** Not all publishers are created equal, and some have a much better reputation than others for reliability. Just because something is published, that doesn't make it accurate—think of all those supermarket tabloids publishing articles about alien autopsies. In general, your best sources are books from university presses and major, well-established publishers; scholarly journal articles; and articles from well-regarded magazines and newspapers such as the *Atlantic Monthly* or the *New York Times*.

- If you are not sure how respectable or reliable a particular publisher or source might be, ask your instructor or librarian.

- **If it's an online publication, who is hosting the site?** Though commercial sites (whose Web addresses end in *.com*) should not be ruled out, keep in mind that these sites are often driven by profit as much as a desire to educate the public. Sites hosted by educational institutions, nonprofit organizations, or the government (*.edu*, *.org*, and *.gov*, respectively) tend to be more purely educational, though they likely won't be free of an agenda either.

- **How recent is the publication?** While older publications can often be appropriate—you may be doing historical research, or you may want to refer to a classic in a certain field—newer ones are preferable, all other things being equal. Newer publications take advantage of more recent ideas and theories, and they often summarize or incorporate older sources.

- **How appropriate is the source to your specific project?** Even the highest-quality scholarly journal or a book by the top expert in a given field will be appropriate for only a very limited number of research projects. Let your topic, your tentative thesis, and your common sense be your guides.

WORKING WITH SOURCES

You now have a stack of articles and printouts of electronic sources, and perhaps a book or two as well. How do you work through these to get the support you need for your paper?

- *First*, sort the various sources by expected relevance, with those you think will be most informative and useful to you on the top of the list.

- *Next*, skim or read through everything quickly, highlighting or making note of the parts that seem most directly applicable to your paper. (Obviously, you should not mark up or otherwise deface library materials—take notes on a separate piece of paper.)

- *Then*, slow down and reread the important passages again, this time taking careful notes.

- *When taking notes*, keep yourself scrupulously well organized, making sure that you always know which of your notes refers to which source.

If you are taking notes by hand, it's a good idea to start a separate page for each source. If you are using a computer to take notes, start a separate file or section for each new source you read.

Notes will generally fall into one of four categories: quotations, paraphrases, summaries, and commentaries.

Quotations

While quotations are useful, and you will almost certainly incorporate several into your paper, resist the urge to transcribe large portions of text from your sources. Papers that rely too heavily on quotations can be unpleasant reading, with a cluttered or choppy style that results from moving back and forth between your prose and that of the various authors you quote. Reserve direct quoting for those passages that are especially relevant and that you simply can't imagine phrasing as clearly or elegantly yourself. When you do make note of a quotation, be sure also to note the pages on which it appears in the source material so that later you will be able to cite it accurately.

Paraphrases and Summaries

Most often, you should take notes in the form of **paraphrase** or summary. To paraphrase, simply put an idea or opinion drawn from a source into your own words. Generally, a paraphrase will be about equal in length to the passage being paraphrased, while a summary will be much shorter, capturing the overall point of a passage while leaving out supporting details. Here is a brief passage from *Britannica Online*'s biography of Emily Dickinson, followed by a paraphrase and a summary:

> She began writing in the 1850s; by 1860 she was boldly experimenting with language and prosody, striving for vivid, exact words and epigrammatic concision while adhering to the basic quatrains and metres of the Protestant hymn. The subjects of her deceptively simple lyrics, whose depth and intensity contrast with the apparent quiet of her life, include love, death, and nature. Her numerous letters are sometimes equal in artistry to her poems.

Paraphrase

> Dickinson began writing poetry in the 1850s, and within ten years she had begun experimenting with poetic styles and forms. She used meters that were familiar to her from church hymns, but her words were chosen to be especially concise and vivid. She wrote about love, death, and nature in ways that seem simple but contain a great deal of emotional depth and intensity. She was also an avid letter-writer, and her letters show the same care and artistry as her poems.

Summary

In both her poems and her many letters, Dickinson used formal experimentation and precision to get to the heart of the themes of love, death, and nature.

Paraphrasing and summarizing are usually superior to quoting for two reasons. First, if you can summarize or paraphrase with confidence, then you know you have really understood what you have read. Second, a summary or paraphrase will be more easily transferred from your notes to your paper and will fit in well with your individual prose style. (For more on the use of summary, see pages 51–52.) Just as with quotations, make a note of the page numbers in the source material from which your summaries and paraphrases are drawn.

Commentaries

Finally, some of your notes can be written as commentaries. When something you read strikes you as interesting, you can record your reaction to it. Do you agree or disagree strongly? Why? What exactly is the connection between the source material and your topic or tentative thesis? Making copious commentaries will help you keep your own ideas in the forefront and will keep your paper from devolving into a shopping list of other writers' priorities. Be sure to note carefully when you are commenting rather than summarizing or paraphrasing. When you are drafting your paper, you will want to distinguish carefully between which ideas are your own and which are borrowed from others.

Keeping Track of Your Sources

As you take notes on the substance of your reading, it is also essential that you record the source's author, title, and publication information for later use in compiling your works cited list, or bibliography. Nothing is more frustrating than having to retrace your research steps on a computer, or even to return to the library, just to get a page reference or the full title of a source. Most accomplished researchers actually put together their works cited list as they go along rather than waiting until the essay is drafted. Such a strategy will ensure that you have all the information you need, and it will save you from the painstaking (and potentially tedious) task of having to create the list all at once at the end of your process.

WRITING THE PAPER

After what may seem like a long time spent gathering and working with your sources, you are now ready to begin the actual writing of your paper.

Refine Your Thesis

Start by looking again at your tentative thesis. Now that you have read a lot and know much more about your topic, does your proposed thesis still seem compelling and appropriate? Is it a little too obvious, something that other writers have already said or have taken for granted? Do you perhaps need to refine or modify it in order to take into account the information you have learned and opinions you have encountered? If necessary—and it usually is—refine or revise your tentative thesis so that it can help you stay focused as you write. (For advice on what makes a good thesis, see pages 23–26.)

Organize Your Evidence

Just as with any other essay, you will need to organize the evidence in support of your thesis. Follow whatever process for organization you have used successfully in writing other papers, while bearing in mind that this time you will probably have more, and more complex, evidence to deal with. You will likely need an outline—formal or informal—to help you put your materials in a coherent and sensible order. But, once again, flexibility is the key here. If, as you begin to work your way through the outline, some different organizational strategy begins to make sense to you, revise your outline rather than forcing your ideas into a preconceived format.

Start Your Draft

The actual drafting of the research paper is probably the part you will find most similar to writing other papers. Try to write fairly quickly and fluently, knowing you can and will add examples, fill in explanations, eliminate redundancies, and work on style during the revision phase. As with your other papers, you may want to write straight through from beginning to end, or you may want to save difficult passages like the introduction for last. Interestingly, many writers find that the process of drafting a research paper actually goes a bit more quickly than does drafting other papers, largely because their considerable research work has left them so well versed in the topic that they have a wealth of ideas for writing.

What might slow you down as you draft your research papers are the citations, which you provide so that a reader knows which ideas are your own and which come from outside sources. Before you begin drafting, familiarize yourself with the conventions for MLA in-text citations (see pages 146–149). Each time you incorporate a quotation, paraphrase, or summary into your essay, you will need to cite the author's name and the relevant page numbers (if available) from the source material. Do not, however, get hung up at this stage trying to remember how to format and punctuate citations. There will be time to hammer out these details later, and it is important as you write to keep your focus on the big picture.

Revise

As you go through the revision process, you should do so with an eye toward full integration of your source material. Are all connections between quotations, paraphrases, or summaries and your thesis clear? Do you include sufficient commentary explaining the inclusion of all source material? Is it absolutely clear which ideas come from which research source? Most important, is the paper still a well-focused argument, meant to convince an audience of the validity of your original thesis? Bearing these questions in mind, you will be ready to make the same sorts of global revision decisions that you would for any other paper— what to add, what to cut, how to reorganize, and so forth. (See pages 32–35 for a reminder of what to look for.)

Edit and Proofread

During the final editing and proofreading stage, include one editorial pass just for checking quotations and documentation format. Make sure each quotation is accurate and exact. Ensure that each reference to a source has an appropriate in-text citation and that your list of works cited (bibliography) is complete and correct. Double-check manuscript format and punctuation issues with the guidelines included in this book or with another appropriate resource. After putting so much time and effort into researching and writing your paper, it would be a shame to have its effectiveness diminished by small inaccuracies or errors.

UNDERSTANDING AND AVOIDING PLAGIARISM

Everyone knows that **plagiarism** is wrong. Buying or borrowing someone else's work, downloading all or part of a paper from the Web, and similar practices are beyond reprehensible. Most colleges and universities

have codes of academic honesty forbidding such practices and imposing severe penalties—including expulsion from the institution in some
cases—on students who are caught breaking them. Many educators feel
these penalties are, if anything, not severe enough. Instructors tend to be
not only angered but also baffled by students who plagiarize. In addition
to the obvious wrongs of cheating and lying (nobody likes being lied to),
students who plagiarize are losing out on a learning opportunity, a waste
of the student's time as well as the instructor's.

Not everyone, though, is altogether clear on what plagiarism entails,
and a good deal of plagiarism can actually be unintentional on the part
of the student. A working definition of plagiarism will help to clarify
what plagiarism is:

- presenting someone else's ideas as your own
- using information from any print or electronic source without fully
  citing the source
- buying or "borrowing" a paper from any source
- submitting work that someone else has written, in whole or in part
- having your work edited to the point that it is no longer your work
- submitting the same paper for more than one class without the express permission of the instructors involved

Some of this is obvious. You know it is cheating to have a friend do
your homework or to download a paper from the Web and submit it as
your own. But the first and last items on the list are not as clear-cut or
self-explanatory. What exactly does it mean to present someone else's
ideas as your own? Many students believe that as long as they rephrase
an idea into their own words, they have done their part to avoid plagiarism; however, they are mistaken. Readers assume, and reasonably so,
that everything in your paper is a product of your own thinking, not just
your own phrasing, unless you share credit with another by documenting your source. No matter how it is phrased, an original idea belongs to
the person who first thought of it and wrote it down; in fact, the notion
of possession in this context is so strong that the term applied to such
ownership is *intellectual property*.

As an analogy, imagine you invented a revolutionary product, patented
it, and put it up for sale. The next week, you find that your neighbor has
produced the same product, painted it a different color, changed the
name, and is doing a booming business selling the product. Is your
neighbor any less guilty of stealing your idea just because he or she is
using a new name and color for the product? Of course not. Your intellectual property, the idea behind the product, has been stolen. And you
are no less guilty of plagiarism if you glean a piece of information, an

opinion, or even an abstract concept from another person, put it into your own words, and "sell" it in your paper without giving proper credit.

Let us say, for example, that you find this passage about William Butler Yeats:

> Religious by temperament but unable to accept orthodox Christianity, Yeats throughout his life explored esoteric philosophies in search of a tradition that would substitute for a lost religion. He became a member of the Theosophical Society and the Order of the Golden Dawn, two groups interested in Eastern occultism, and later developed a private system of symbols and mystical ideas.

Drawing from this passage, you write:

> Yeats rejected the Christianity of his native Ireland, but he became interested in occultism and Eastern philosophy. From these sources, he developed his own system of mystical symbols that he used in his poetry.

Clearly the words of this new passage are your own, and some elements of the original have been streamlined while other information has been added. However, the essential line of reasoning and the central point of both passages are largely the same. If this second passage appears in your paper without an acknowledgment of the original source, *this is plagiarism.*

Finally, let's look at the last item on the list: submitting the same paper for more than one class without the express permission of the instructors involved. Sometimes, you will find substantial overlap in the subject matter of two or more of your classes. A literature class, for instance, has elements of history, psychology, sociology, and other disciplines, and once in a while you might find yourself working on writing projects in courses that share common features. You might be tempted to let your research and writing in such a case do double duty, and there is not necessarily anything wrong with that. However, if you wish to write a paper on a single topic for more than one class, clear these plans with both instructors first. And, of course, even if you use the same research sources for both assignments, you will almost certainly need to write two separate essays, tailoring each to meet the specifications of individual classes and disciplines.

WHAT TO DOCUMENT AND WHAT *NOT* TO DOCUMENT

Everything borrowed from another source needs to be documented. Obviously, you should document every direct quotation of any length from primary or secondary sources. Equally important is the documentation of all your paraphrases and summaries of ideas, information, and opinions, citing authors and page numbers. The rule of thumb is that if you didn't make it up yourself, you should probably document it.

The word *probably* in the previous sentence suggests that there are exceptions, and indeed there are. You do not need to document proverbial sayings ("Live and let live") or very familiar quotations ("I have a dream"), though in the case of the latter you may want to allude to the speaker in your text. You also do not need to document any information that can be considered **common knowledge**. Common knowledge here refers not only to information that you would expect nearly every adult to know immediately (that Shakespeare wrote *Hamlet*, for instance, or that George Washington was the first president of the United States). Common knowledge also encompasses undisputed information that you could look up in a general or specialized reference work. The average person on the street probably couldn't tell you that T. S. Eliot was born in 1888, but you don't need to say where that piece of information comes from, as it is widely available to anyone who wishes to find it.

Use both your common sense and your sense of fairness to make any necessary decisions about whether or not to document something. When in doubt, ask your instructor, and remember, it's better to document something unnecessarily than to be guilty of plagiarism.

DOCUMENTING SOURCES: MLA FORMAT

This section includes information on how to document the following:

In-Text Citations, p. 146
   Citing Author and Page Number in Parentheses, p. 146
   Citing the Author in Body Text and Only the Page Number in Parentheses, p. 147
   Citing Multiple Pages in a Source, p. 147
   Citing a Source without Page Numbers, p. 148
   Citing Multiple Sources at Once, p. 148
   Citing Two or More Sources by the Same Author, p. 148
   Citing a Quotation or Source within a Source, p. 149

Preparing Your Works Cited List, p. 149
  General Guidelines, p. 150
  Citing Books, p. 151
    A Book by a Single Author, p. 152
    A Book by Two or Three Authors, p. 152
    A Book by Four or More Authors, p. 152
    A Book by an Unknown or Anonymous Author, p. 153
    A Book by a Corporate Author, p. 153
    Two or More Books by the Same Author, p. 153
    A Work in an Anthology or Compilation, p. 153
    Two or More Works in a Single Anthology or Compilation, p. 153
    An Article in a Reference Work, p. 154
    An Introduction, Preface, Foreword, or Afterword, p. 154
  Citing Periodicals, p. 154
    An Article in a Scholarly Journal, p. 154
    An Article in a Magazine, p. 154
    An Article in a Newspaper, p. 154
    A Review, p. 154
  Citing Electronic Sources, p. 156
    An Article from an Online Subscription Database or Index, p. 156
    A CD-ROM, p. 156
    An Online Scholarly Project or Database, p. 156
    An Online Journal or Magazine, p. 156
    A Professional or Personal Web Page, p. 157
    A Page on a Web Site, p. 157
    A Blog, p. 157
    A Wiki, p. 157
    An E-book, p. 158
    A Posting to a Discussion List or Newsgroup, p. 158
  Citing Other Miscellaneous Sources, p. 158
    A Television or Radio Program, p. 158
    A Film, Video, or DVD, p. 158
    An Interview, p. 158
    A Lecture or Speech, p. 159
    A Letter or E-mail, p. 159
    A Work of Visual Art, p. 160

Some students seem to believe that English teachers find footnotes and bibliographies and textual citations fun and interesting. In truth, few people know better than those who have to teach it how tedious format and documentation can be for a writer. Chances are your instructor will insist that you document your sources. There are at least three reasons for requiring documentation. First, a sense of fair play demands that we give proper credit to those whose ideas benefit us. Second, by documenting your sources, you make it possible for your readers to find the sources themselves and follow up if they become interested in something in your paper. Third, documenting your sources, and doing it accurately, enhances your credibility as a writer by highlighting your professionalism and thoroughness.

As you read the following pages, and as you work on documenting sources in your own papers, don't say that you don't understand it or that you can't learn this. If you learned the difficult and abstract skills of reading and writing, you can certainly learn something as concrete as documentation. Actually, documentation is the easy part of research writing, since there is only one right way to do it. The hard part is the creative work of discovering and presenting your original ideas and integrating them fluently with the work of others. And, of course, you don't need to actually memorize the specifics of format. Nobody does. When you need to know how to cite an anonymous newspaper article or what to include in a bibliographic entry for a radio broadcast, for instance, you can look it up. That's what professional writers do all the time.

There are many different forms and formulas for documenting sources—the APA (American Psychological Association) format commonly used in the social sciences, the CBE (Council of Biology Editors) format used in the life sciences, the *Chicago* (*Chicago Manual of Style*) format used in history, and so on. Each system highlights the type of information most relevant to experts in a particular field. If you have received contradictory instructions about documentation format for research projects in the past—include dates in your in-text references or don't; use footnotes or use endnotes—chances are you were working in different documentation systems. The format most often used in the humanities is MLA, the system developed by the Modern Language Association.

MLA format breaks down into two main elements: in-text citations and a works cited list (bibliography). In-text citations are parenthetical references that follow each quotation, paraphrase, or summary and give the briefest possible information about the source, usually the author's last name and a page number. The works cited list, which comes at the end of the paper, gives more detailed information about all sources used. The idea is that a reader coming across a parenthetical reference in your text can easily turn to the works cited list and get full details about the type of publication from which the material comes, the date of publication, and so on. (Some writers use a third element of MLA style, content endnotes, which come between the end of the paper and the works cited list and contain extra information not readily integrated into the paper. Although you may use endnotes if you wish, they are not necessary.)

The following pages describe the major types of sources you are likely to encounter and how to reference those sources both in the text of your research paper and in your works cited list. The information here, however, is not exhaustive. If you want to cite a source not covered here, or if you would like more information about MLA style and citation format, turn to:

MLA Handbook for Writers of Research Papers. 7th ed. New York: MLA, 2009. Print.

In-Text Citations

The purpose of an in-text citation is to give a very brief acknowledgment of a source within the body of your essay. In MLA format, in-text citations take the form of brief parenthetical interruptions directly following each quotation, paraphrase, or summary. Some students find these interruptions a bit distracting at first, but you will quickly find that you grow accustomed to them and that soon they will not slow your reading or comprehension. The following explanations and examples of in-text citations should cover most instances you will encounter.

Citing Author and Page Number in Parentheses

Typically, a citation will contain the last name of the author being cited and a page number. The first example here shows a direct quotation, the second a paraphrase.

> One reviewer referred to *Top Girls* as, "among other things, a critique of bourgeois feminism" (Munk 33).

> When English wool was in demand, the fens were rich, but for many years now they have been among the poorest regions in England (Chamberlain 13).

Coming across these references in your text, your readers will know that they can turn to your works cited list and find out the full names of Munk and Chamberlain; the titles of what they have written; and where, when, and in what medium the works were published.

Please note:

- **In-text references contain no extraneous words or punctuation.** There is no comma between the name and the page number. Neither the word *page* nor the abbreviation *p.* precede the number. There are no extra spaces, just the name and the number.
- **Quotation marks close *before* the citation.** The in-text citation is not part of a direct quotation, so it does not belong inside the quotation marks.
- **The period that ends the sentence is placed *after* the citation.** Probably the most common error students make in MLA in-text citation is to put the period (or other closing punctuation mark) at the end of the quotation or paraphrase and then give the reference in parentheses. Doing so, however, makes the citation the beginning of the next sentence rather than the end of the one being cited.

Citing the Author in Body Text and Only the Page Number in Parentheses

If you have already named the author in your own text, for instance in a lead-in phrase, you do not need to repeat the name in parentheses, as your reader will already know which author to look for in your works cited. In this case, the parenthetical reference need only contain the page number. The two examples already given could be rewritten as follows:

> Reviewer Erika Munk referred to *Top Girls* as, "among other things, a critique of bourgeois feminism" (33).

> Martha Chamberlain writes that when English wool was in demand, the fens were rich, but for many years now they have been among the poorest regions in England (13).

Citing Multiple Pages in a Source

You may find yourself wanting to make a brief summary of an extended passage, in which case you might need to cite the inclusive pages of the summarized material.

> John McGrath's Scottish theater company was destroyed by the end of government subsidies, as Elizabeth MacLennan chronicles in *The Moon Belongs to Everyone* (137-99).

Citing a Source without Page Numbers

Many electronic publications do not have page numbers. If you are citing one of these sources, simply give the author's last name either in parentheses or in a signal phrase before the quotation or summary.

> Critics have noted that "Dickinson declined to make the public confession of faith that would admit her to the church" (Yezzi).

or

> David Yezzi writes that "Dickinson declined to make the public confession of faith that would admit her to the church."

Citing Multiple Sources at Once

Sometimes several different sources say roughly the same thing, or at least there is substantial overlap in the parts you want to cite. Following are two ways of handling this situation; use whichever one best suits your needs.

> This particular passage in the play has been the source of much critical speculation, especially by Freudian critics (Anders 19; Olsen 116; Smith 83-84; Watson 412).

> A number of Freudian critics have commented on this passage, including Anders (19), Olsen (116), Smith (83-84), and Watson (412).

Citing Two or More Sources by the Same Author

It is common for one author to write multiple books or articles on the same general topic, and you might want to use more than one of them in your paper. In this case, a shortened version of the title must appear in the parenthetical reference, to show which work by the author is being quoted or cited. In citations for an article and a book about playwright Caryl Churchill, both by the author Geraldine Cousin, one would give the first word of the work's title (other than *the* or *a*, etc.). As seen here, *Common* and *Churchill* are the first words in the title of the article and the book, respectively.

> Churchill claims that this sentiment was expressed to her by one of the gangmasters she encountered in the fens (Cousin, "Common" 6).

Churchill's notebooks from her visit to the fens record her seeing baby prams parked around the fields in which the women worked (Cousin, *Churchill* 47).

Note the comma between the author's name and the title. Note that these shortened titles are formatted (with italics or quotation marks) just as they would be in the works cited list or elsewhere in your writing, in quotation marks for an article and in italics (or underscored) for a book.

If the author is named in a signal phrase, only the shortened title and page number are needed in the parenthetical reference.

"Violence," says Ruby Cohn, "is the only recourse in these brutalized lives on the Fen" (*Retreats* 139).

Citing a Quotation or Source within a Source

On page 58 of his book about Margaret Thatcher, Charles Moser writes:

In a speech to Parliament in June of 1983, Thatcher said, "A return to Victorian values will encourage personal responsibility, personal initiative, self-respect, and respect for others and their property."

Let us say you do not have the text of Thatcher's original speech and that Moser doesn't make reference to a primary source that you can track down. But Moser is a reliable author, so you believe the Thatcher quotation is accurate and want to use a portion of it in your paper. This is done by giving the original speaker's name (in this case Margaret Thatcher) in your text and using the abbreviation *qtd. in* and the author from whom you got the quote (in this case Charles Moser) in the parenthetical citation.

These "Victorian values," Thatcher claimed, would "encourage personal responsibility, personal initiative, self-respect, and respect for others" (qtd. in Moser 58).

Preparing Your Works Cited List

It is a good idea to begin preparing your list of works cited during the research process, adding new entries each time you find a source that might be useful to you. That way, when the time comes to finalize your paper, you can just edit the list you already have, making sure it contains all the necessary entries and no extraneous ones, and checking each for accuracy and format. If you wait until the end to create your works cited list, you will have to compile the whole list from scratch at a time when you are most tired and therefore least able to focus your attention on this necessary, detailed work.

A number of online resources exist to help you compose and format your works cited. Two of the best respected are *easybib.com* and *citationmachine.net*. These sites allow you to select the type of source from a menu and then enter information about author names, titles, and so on in a form. Once all the information is entered, the software formats and punctuates it appropriately, and you can then save it to your document. You can choose from MLA, APA, or other popular formats. Most instructors do not mind you using these services (ask if you are unsure how your instructor feels about this), but a word of caution is needed. These services can format and punctuate, but they cannot proofread. They will use the information exactly as you enter it, so you must double-check for accuracy before submitting the information for formatting. Many word processing programs also have bibliography generators, but these are usually not adequate for specialized, scholarly sources and are therefore not recommended.

General Guidelines

- **Begin your list of works cited on a new page.** Continue paginating as you have throughout the paper, with your last name and the page number appearing in the upper right corner.
- **Center the heading Works Cited at the top of the page** in capital and lowercase letters; do not use italics, boldface print, or quotation marks.
- **Arrange the sources alphabetically, by the last name of the source's author** (or by title, in the case of anonymous works), regardless of the order in which the sources are cited in your paper.
- **Begin each entry flush with the left margin.** When an entry takes up more than one line, all lines after the first are indented one-half inch. (For an example, see the works cited list in the research paper by Jarrad Nunes, on page 161.) This is called a hanging indent, and all major word processing programs can be set to format your entries this way.
- **Double-space the entire list.**
- **Do not put extra line spaces between entries.**
- **As always, carefully follow any additional or contrary instructions provided by your instructor.**

Citing Books

To list books in your works cited, include as much of the following information as is available and appropriate, in the following order and format. Each bulleted element here should be separated by a period. If no other formatting (quotation marks, italics, etc.) is specified, then none should be added.

- **The name of the author or editor**, last name first for the first author or editor listed. Names of additional authors or others listed, anywhere in the entry, should appear in the regular order (first name first). (Multiple authors or editors should be listed in the order in which they appear on the book's title page. Use initials or middle names, just as they appear. You need not include titles, affiliations, and any academic degrees that precede or follow names.)
- **Title of a part of the book**, in quotation marks. Needed only if you cite a chapter, an introduction, or other part of a book written by someone other than the principal author or editor listed on the title page. See "A work in an anthology or compilation," "An article in a reference work," or "An introduction, preface, foreword, or afterword" on the following pages.
- **The title of the book**, italicized. If there is a subtitle, put a colon after the main title, and follow this with the full subtitle. This is the standard format for a works cited entry, even if no colon appears on the book's title page. (If the main title ends in a question mark, an exclamation point, or a dash, however, do not add a colon between the main title and the subtitle.)
- **Name of the editor** (for books with both an author and an editor), **translator**, or **compiler**, if different from the primary author(s), with the abbreviation *Ed.*, *Trans.*, or *Comp.*, as appropriate.
- **Edition used**, if other than the first.
- **Volume used**, if a multivolume work.
- **City or place of publication**, followed by a colon (if more than one city is listed on the title page, use only the first one); **name of the publisher**, followed by a comma; **year of publication** (if multiple copyright dates are listed, use the most recent one).
- **Page numbers.** Needed only if you cite a chapter, an introduction, or other part of a book written by someone other than the principal author or editor listed on the title page. See "A work in an anthology or compilation," "An article in a reference work," or "An introduction, preface, foreword, or afterword" on the following pages.

- **Medium of publication**, such as Print, Web, CD, DVD, Film, Lecture, Performance, Radio, Television, or E-mail.
- **Series name**, if the book is part of a series.

Copy your entries directly from the book's title page, which provides more complete and accurate information than does a cover or another bibliography. The following examples cover most of the sorts of books you are likely to encounter.

A book by a single author. The simplest entry is a single-volume book by a single author, not part of a series, and without additional editors, translators, or compilers.

> Alexie, Sherman. *The Absolutely True Diary of a Part-Time Indian*. New York: Little, 2007. Print.

If a book has an editor, a translator, or a compiler in addition to an author, identify this person by role and by name, between the book's title and the place of publication.

> Sebald, W. G. *The Rings of Saturn*. Trans. Michael Hulse. New York: New Directions, 1998. Print.

The following example cites a third-edition book by a single author.

> Richter, David H. *The Critical Tradition: Classic Texts and Contemporary Trends*. 3rd ed. Boston: Bedford, 2007. Print.

A book by two or three authors. Note that in the following example only the first author's name appears in reverse order. UP (with no periods) is the abbreviation for University Press. Note also the series title, Oxford Shakespeare Topics, is included when citing a book in a series.

> Gurr, Andrew, and Mariko Ichikawa. *Staging in Shakespeare's Theaters*. Oxford: Oxford UP, 2000. Print. Oxford Shakespeare Topics.

A book by four or more authors. If four or more authors or editors are listed on a book's title page, you can list all names or give only the name of the first, followed by *et al.* (Latin for "and others").

> Gardner, Janet E., et al., eds. *Literature: A Portable Anthology*. 3rd ed. Boston: Bedford, 2013. Print.

A book by an unknown or anonymous author. Simply include all the other information, beginning with the title.

> *Gilgamesh: A New English Version*. Trans. Stephen Mitchell. New York: Free,
>   2006. Print.

A book by a corporate author. Corporate authorship refers to a book that lists an organization rather than an individual as its author. This is especially common with publications from government and nonprofit organizations. GPO stands for the Government Printing Office, which publishes most U.S. federal documents.

> Bureau of the Census. *Historical Statistics of the United States, 1789-1945: A
>   Supplement to the Statistical Abstract of the United States*. Washington:
>   GPO, 1945. Print.

Two or more books by the same author. If you cite more than one work by a single author, alphabetize the entries by title. For the second and all subsequent entries by the same author, replace the author's name with three hyphens.

> Bloom, Harold. *Hamlet: Poem Unlimited*. New York: Riverhead-Penguin, 2003.
>   Print.
>
> ---. *Shakespeare's Poems and Sonnets*. Broomall: Chelsea, 1999. Print.
>   Bloom's Major Poets.

A work in an anthology or compilation. The first example that follows is a citation from a literature anthology; the second is from a scholarly work in which each chapter is written by a different author. The title of the work or chapter being cited is usually enclosed in quotation marks. However, if the piece is a play or novel, you should italicize its title instead.

> Baldwin, James. "Sonny's Blues." *Literature: A Portable Anthology*. Ed. Janet
>   E. Gardner et al. 3rd ed. Boston: Bedford, 2013. 250-76. Print.
>
> Keyishian, Harry. "Shakespeare and the Movie Genre: The Case of *Hamlet*."
>   *The Cambridge Companion to Shakespeare on Film*. Ed. Russell Jackson.
>   Cambridge: Cambridge UP, 2000. 72-81. Print.

Two or more works in a single anthology or compilation. If you cite two or more works from a single anthology or collection, you can create a cross-reference, citing the full publication information for the collection as a whole and cross-referencing the individual pieces using only the name of the editor and page numbers of the particular work within the anthology or compilation.

Chopin, Kate. "The Story of an Hour." Gardner et al. 59-61.

Gardner, Janet E., et al., eds. *Literature: A Portable Anthology*. 2nd ed. Boston: Bedford, 2009. Print.

Gilman, Charlotte Perkins. "The Yellow Wallpaper." Gardner et al. 76-89.

An article in a reference work. The format for citing material from dictionaries, encyclopedias, or other specialized reference works is similar to that for a work in an anthology, but the name of the reference work's editor is omitted. Often, such reference articles are anonymous anyway. The first example is for a signed article in a print book, the second for an anonymous entry in an electronic encyclopedia.

Brown, Andrew. "Sophocles." *The Cambridge Guide to Theatre*. Cambridge: Cambridge UP, 1988. 899-900. Print.

"Browning, Elizabeth Barrett." *Encyclopaedia Britannica Online*. Encyclopaedia Britannica, 2008. Web. 4 Feb. 2008.

An introduction, preface, foreword, or afterword. After the author's name, give the name of the part of the book being cited, capitalized but neither italicized nor in quotation marks, followed by the title of the book and all relevant publication information.

Bode, Carl. Introduction. *The Portable Thoreau*. By Henry David Thoreau. Ed. Bode. Revised ed. Harmondsworth, Eng.: Penguin, 1977. 1-27. Print. Viking Portable Library.

Citing Periodicals

An article in a scholarly journal. Most scholarly journals publish several issues in each annual volume and paginate continuously throughout the entire volume. (In other words, if one issue ends on page 230, the next will begin with page 231.) Your works cited entry should list the author, article title, journal title, volume number (in arabic numerals, even if it appears in roman numeral form on the journal cover), issue number, year (in parentheses), page numbers, and medium. Follow the punctuation shown here exactly.

> Miller, Greg. "The Bottom of Desire in Suzan-Lori Parks's Venus." *Modern Drama* 45.1 (2002): 125-37. Print.

An article in a magazine. For an article in a magazine, omit the volume and issue numbers (if given) and include the date of publication. The first example here shows the format for a monthly, bimonthly, or quarterly magazine; the second, which includes the date as well as the month, is appropriate for weekly and biweekly magazines.

> McChesney, Robert W., and John Nichols. "Holding the Line at the FCC." *Progressive* Apr. 2003: 26-29. Print.

> Welch, Jilly. "Campaign Spells Out Concern for Literacy." *People Management* 18 Apr. 1996: 6-7. Print.

An article in a newspaper. When a newspaper is separated into sections, note the letter or number designating the section as a part of the page reference. Newspapers and some magazines frequently place articles on nonconsecutive pages. When this happens, give the number of the first page only, followed by the plus sign (+). For locally published newspapers, state the city of the publication if not included in the paper's name. Do this by adding the city in square brackets after the newspaper's name: *Argus Leader* [Sioux Falls]. If the masthead notes a specific edition, add a comma after the date and list the edition (for example, *natl. ed., late ed.*). Different editions of the same issue of a newspaper contain different material, so it's important to note which edition you are using.

> Mahren, Elizabeth. "University's 'Leap of Faith' Becomes Lesson in Community." *Los Angeles Times* 16 Mar. 2003: A1+. Print.

A review. To cite a review, you must include the title and author of the work being reviewed between the review title and the periodical title. The first entry that follows is for a book review in a magazine. The second is an untitled review in a scholarly journal that includes the name of an adaptor as well as the place and date of the play's production.

> Ilan Stavans. "Familia Faces." Rev. of *Caramelo*, by Sandra Cisneros. *Nation* 10 Feb. 2003: 30-34. Print.

> Sofer, Andrew. Rev. of *Lysistrata*, by Aristophanes. Adapt. Robert Brustein. Amer. Repertory Theatre, Cambridge, 28 May 2002. *Theater Journal* 55.1 (2003): 137-38. Print.

Citing Electronic Sources

Sometimes online sources do not list all the information required for a complete citation. They are, for instance, frequently anonymous, and they do not always record the dates when they were written or updated. Give as much of the information as you can find, using the formats that follow. Note that entries for online sources generally contain two dates. The first is the date when the document was posted or updated; the second is the date the researcher accessed the document.

An article from an online subscription database or index. When you access an article through an online index or database (*MLA International Bibliography*, *JSTOR*, etc.), treat it as you would a print source, with the addition of the title of the database (italicized), the medium of publication, and the date you accessed the material.

> Farland, Maria Magdalena. "'That Tritest/Brightest Truth': Emily Dickinson's Anti-Sentimentality." *Nineteenth-Century Literature* 53.3 (1998): 364-89. *JSTOR*. Web. 21 Mar. 2010.

> Shaw, Mary Neff. "Dickinson's 'Because I could not stop for Death.'" *Explicator* 50.1 (1991): 20-21. *MLA International Bibliography*. Web. 20 Mar. 2010.

A CD-ROM. An entry for a CD-ROM resembles a book entry, with the addition of the acronym *CD-ROM* inserted at the end as the medium of publication.

> *Shakespeare: His Life, Times, Works, and Sources.* Princeton: Films for the Humanities and Sciences, 1995. CD-ROM.

An online scholarly project or database. A full entry for an online scholarly project or database includes the editor's name; the title of the project, italicized; the name of the sponsoring organization or institution; the date of the project's most recent update; the medium; and the date that you accessed the project.

> Folsom, Ed, and Kenneth M. Price, eds. *The Walt Whitman Archive.* Walt Whitman Archive, 2009. Web. 1 Apr. 2009.

An online journal or magazine. The first entry that follows is from an online scholarly journal that does not have issue numbers or page numbers; the second is from the online version of a popular magazine.

Fukuda, Tatsuaki. "Faulknerian Topography." *The Faulkner Journal of Japan* 4 (2002): n. pag. Web. 20 Mar. 2003.

Keegan, Rebecca Winters. "Redeeming Roman Polanski." *Time.* Time Inc., 24 Jan. 2008. Web. 4 Feb. 2008.

A professional or personal Web page. Include as much of the following information as appropriate and available: the author of the document or site; the document title, in quotation marks (if the site is divided into separate documents); the name of the site, italicized; the sponsoring organization or institution; the date of creation or most recent update; the medium; and your date of access. If the site has no official title, provide a brief identifying phrase, neither italicized nor in quotation marks, as in the second example below.

Werner, Liz. "A Brief History of the Dickinson Homestead." *The Dickinson Homestead: Home of Emily Dickinson.* Amherst Coll., 2001. Web. 12 June 2003.

Korista, Kirk. Home page. Western Michigan U, 3 June 2008. Web. 20 Oct. 2008.

A page on a Web site. For an individual page on a Web site, list the author (if given), followed by the rest of the information for the entire Web site, as above.

Arthur, Luke. "Financial Advice for Young Adults." *eHow.com.* eHow, 31 May 2011. Web. 10 Aug. 2011.

A blog. An entry for a blog citation includes the blogger's name (or online handle), the title of the posting, blog title, date of posting, medium, and date of access.

Curran, Kevin. "The Newspaper and the Culture of Print in the Early American Republic." *Textual Studies, 1500-1800,* Blogger, 7 Jan. 2008. Web. 14 Jan. 2008.

A wiki. An entry for a wiki citation begins with the title of the wiki page, followed by the wiki title (italicized), sponsor or publisher, date of posting, medium, and date of access.

"Cornelius Eady." *Wikipedia.* Wikimedia Foundation, 7 Apr. 2009. Web. 20 Apr. 2009.

An e-book. Treat e-books as you would print books, changing only the medium.

> Enterline, Lynn. *The Rhetoric of the Body from Ovid to Shakespeare*. Cambridge: Cambridge UP, 2000. *Northwestern University Ebrary*. Web. 30 Nov. 2007.

A posting to a discussion list or newsgroup. Give the author's name, the title of the posting (in quotation marks) taken from the subject line, the title of the site on which the forum is found (italicized), the sponsor of the site, the date of posting, the medium, and your date of access. If the posting has no title, use the identifying phrase *Online posting*.

> Arnove, Anthony. "Query Regarding Arthur Miller." *Campaign against Sanctions on Iraq*. Iraq Analysis Group, 28 Jan. 2000. Web. 20 Apr. 2003.

Citing Other Miscellaneous Sources

A television or radio program. Begin with the name of the author or another individual (director, narrator, etc.), only if you refer primarily to the work of a particular individual. Otherwise, begin with the title of a segment or episode (if appropriate), in quotation marks; the title of the program, italicized; the title of the series (if applicable), italicized; the name of the network; the call letters and city of the local station (if applicable); the date of broadcast; and the medium. The first entry that follows is a citation of a segment of a radio broadcast. The second is a citation of an episode of a television program.

> Alison, Jay. "For Sale." *This American Life*. Public Radio Intl. WCAI, Woods Hole, MA, 11 Oct. 2002. Radio.

> "The Undertaking." *Frontline*. PBS. WGBH, Boston, 30 Oct. 2007. Television.

A film, video, or DVD. Film citations begin with the film title (italicized), followed by *Dir.* and the director's name, the year the film was originally released, the distributor, the year of release, and the medium (Videocassette, DVD, etc.).

> *Hamlet*. Dir. Laurence Olivier. 1948. Home Vision Entertainment, 2000. DVD.

An interview. Begin with the name of the person interviewed. For a published interview, give the title, if any, in quotation marks (if there is no title, simply use the designation *Interview*, neither in quotation marks nor italicized), followed by the name of the interviewer, publication information, and medium. The first example that follows is for an interview published in a magazine. The second example is for an interview conducted personally by the author of the research paper and gives the name of the person interviewed.

> Shields, David. "The Only Way Out Is Deeper In." Interview by Andrew C.
> Gottlieb. *Poets & Writers* July/Aug. 2002: 27-31. Print.

> Smith, Stephen. Personal interview. 20 Mar. 2002.

A lecture or speech. To cite a speech or lecture that you've attended, use the following format, listing the speaker's name; the title of the presentation, in quotation marks (if announced or published); the sponsoring organization; the location; the date; and a descriptive label such as *Address* or *Lecture*. The first example given here is for a speech with an announced title. The second is for an untitled address.

> Cohen, Amy R. "Sharing the Orchestra: How Modern Productions Reveal
> Ancient Conventions." Sixth Natl. Symposium on Theater in Academe.
> Washington and Lee U, Lexington, VA. 15 Mar. 2003. Speech.

> Nader, Ralph. U of Massachusetts Dartmouth, North Dartmouth. 24 Mar.
> 2003. Address.

To cite a lecture, speech, or address you've seen in a film or TV broadcast or heard on the radio, use the appropriate format for the medium of transmission. Generally speaking, you do not need to cite a class lecture; to quote or otherwise refer to something an instructor says in class, you may do so simply by crediting the instructor in the text of your essay.

A letter or e-mail. There are three kinds of letters: published, unpublished (in archives), and personal. A published letter includes the writer's name, the recipient's name (in quotation marks), the date of the letter, the number of the letter (if assigned by the editor), and publication information for the book or periodical in which it appears.

> Thomas, Dylan. "To Donald Taylor." 28 Oct. 1944. *Dylan Thomas: The Col-
> lected Letters*. Ed. Paul Ferris. New York: Macmillan, 1985. 529-30. Print.

In citing an unpublished letter, give the writer's name, the title or a description of the material (for example, *Letter to Havelock Ellis*), the date, the medium (*MS* for a handwritten letter, *TS* for a letter composed on a machine), and any identifying number assigned to it. Include the name and location of the library or institution housing the material.

> Sanger, Margaret. Letter to Havelock Ellis. 14 July 1924. MS. Margaret Sanger
> Papers. Sophia Smith Collection, Smith Coll., Northampton, MA.

To cite a letter you received personally, include the author, the designation *Letter to the author*, the date posted, and the medium (*MS* for a handwritten letter, *TS* for a letter composed on a machine). To cite an e-mail you received personally, include the author, the designation *Message to the author*, the date of the message, and the designation *E-mail*.

> Green, Barclay. Letter to the author. 1 Sept. 2008. TS.

> Kapadia, Parmita. Message to the author. 12 Mar. 2010. E-mail.

A work of visual art. Give the artist's name, the title of the artwork (in italics), the date of composition, the medium of composition, and, if you saw the original artwork in person, the name and location of the institution that houses the artwork. If you used a reproduction of the artwork in a print or electronic source, provide appropriate bibliographic information for that source.

> Goya, Francisco. *The Family of Charles IV.* 1800. Oil on canvas. Museo del
> Prado, Madrid.

> Evans, Walker. *Bud Fields and His Family.* Photograph. 1935. "A Photo Essay
> on the Great Depression." *Modern American Poetry.* U of Illinois, 2011.
> Web. 5 Aug. 2011.

SAMPLE RESEARCH PAPER

When choosing a research paper topic, Jarrad Nunes recalled how interesting he had found Emily Dickinson's poem "Because I could not stop for Death" (page 10), which seemed to defy his expectations of literature about death and dying. Jarrad decided to see what professional literary critics had to say on the subject and how closely their ideas matched his own. His paper, which follows, is a type of **reader-response criticism**, because it attends to reader expectations and how Dickinson manipulates these, and it combines a close-reading of the primary literary text with research from a variety of secondary sources.

Jarrad S. Nunes
Professor Gardner
English 204
2 April 2010

Emily Dickinson's "Because I could not stop for Death": Challenging Readers' Expectations

With a keen eye for detail and a well-known conciseness and compression, Emily Dickinson's poetry records the abstractions of human life so matter-of-factly that her readers often take her technical skill for granted. Take, for example, the six-stanza poem "Because I could not stop for Death" — a detached, but never completely dispassionate, recollection of a human's journey to its final conclusion. The verse is crafted so succinctly and with such precision that its complex and vivid images are made even more extraordinary and meaningful. At least one critic has pointed out how Dickinson employs "rhetorical strategies that resist and contest dominant cultural conceptions of death and immortality" (Farland 370). We might expect literature on the theme of death to invoke religious imagery, stillness, and a sense of dread or foreboding, but none of this is the case. Instead, the poem challenges the preconceptions Dickinson's contemporaries had about death, and in doing so it makes us challenge ours as well.

Jarrad focuses in on one Dickinson poem.

From the start, Dickinson infuses this often-grim topic with a palpable humanity, beginning with her personification of death as the courteous, careful carriage driver bearing the speaker's body to rest. Literary critic Harold Bloom asserts, "The image here of a woman and her escort, Death, meditating on the prospect of eternity, is neither one of despair nor loss nor outrage, but of resignation" (37). This "resignation," though, does not come across as the predictable acceptance of God's will. In fact, any mention of God or the soul is remarkably absent from this poem about death and eternity. This suggests the uneasy relationship Dickinson had with the strict religious beliefs of her society and

Because he mentions Bloom at the beginning of the sentence, Jarrad does not have to include Bloom's name in the in-text citation.

her family. "Raised during the period of New England Revivalism," writes David Yezzi, "Dickinson declined to make the public confession of faith that would admit her to the church (her father made his twice) and by the age of thirty she left off attending services altogether." Clearly at odds with familial and social expectations, Dickinson nonetheless fearlessly expresses her religious "doubt, which her poems later absorbed as ambiguity and contradiction" (Yezzi).

Jarrad integrates Yezzi's quotation with his own writing in order to provide some cultural context.

Dickinson's narrator does not fear death, perhaps because death is associated here not so much with endings or divine judgment but instead with a very human journey. The driver seems affable, "kindly stopp[ing]" and driving slowly. In stanza 2, the narrator puts her work away to observe the driver calmly. It may seem unlikely that she would be trusting of so ominous a character, but as critic Betsy Erikkila explains it, "Death himself comes courting as an aristocratic gentleman with horses and a carriage" (9). David Baker carries this one step further, noting "[h]ow homely and comfortable is this ride" and comparing it to "a mild 19th-century date." Indeed, the fact that the carriage driver has stopped for the narrator on a day when she was too busy to do the same emphasizes his courtesy and thoughtfulness as a character. This is an original and deeply humanistic perception of death, in which the personified entity is neither a black-cloaked grim reaper nor a stern servant of God.

Along with its deep humanity, Dickinson's image of Death has a fluidity and graceful movement that is, at first, juxtaposed against our more frightening preconceptions of the idea. This tangible sense of motion is perhaps best illustrated in the poem's perfectly constructed third stanza. Here, a series of images metaphorically re-creates a natural progression — childish play gives way to growing grain and, eventually, to the setting of the sun (lines 9-12). One critic has demonstrated how these three images might represent childhood, maturity, and old age (Shaw 20). The very fact that the narrator views these scenes from a

Jarrad paraphrases Shaw's point in his own words and then provides an appropriate in-text citation.

slowly rolling carriage lends the passage a clear sense of movement and an unexpected vitality. The absurdity of this meandering vessel passing "the Setting Sun" perhaps suggests a sense of quickening as death draws near, or it may even signal the dissolution of temporal reality altogether. Regardless, the steady progression of this section is undeniable.

The strong sense of motion is continued in the fourth stanza, though with some differences. Here, the movement is less concrete, as the narrator herself moves from a life marked by careful self-control into a position in which she all but succumbs to outside forces. As "[t]he Dews drew quivering and chill" (14), the narrator has lost the ability to keep herself warm. Her earthly garments do not provide adequate protection. From her philosophical viewpoint, however, these difficulties, like death itself, are to be calmly accepted rather than feared. Indeed, before this point, there is not a single truly fearful image in this remarkable poem about death, and even here any sense of foreboding is muted.

Jarrad's smooth transition provides a link between his analyses of two stanzas.

As the poem moves into its fifth stanza, the momentum is halted temporarily, and a more traditional death image is finally introduced with the lines "We paused before a House that seemed / A Swelling of the Ground" (17-18). At this point, the character of Death seems to bid his passenger a rather unceremonial good-bye at the foot of her earthen grave. As the resting place is described, he retreats, returning to the world of the living to repeat his duty with another passenger. While the sparse but vivid description of the grave should invoke a paralyzing loneliness, Dickinson again thwarts our expectations, tempering the reader's fear by having her narrator merely pause at the sight, as if staying for a short while at a hotel or a friend's house. Once again, a usual symbol of finality is given a transitive purpose.

Jarrad consistently chooses important quotations from the poem as evidence for his claims.

The final stanza brings the narrator to a new place, Eternity. However, as one critic explains it, "Eternity, for Dickinson, is not a place at which one arrives. It is rather a journey-towards, a continual evolving" (Baker). Once again Dickinson has thwarted readers' expectations. While this should certainly be the logical end of her journey, Dickinson's exquisite use of language suggests that the entire account may simply be a daydream — a mental dress rehearsal for the real death to come. Consider this account of the poem's final stanza:

> All of this poetically elapsed time "Feels shorter than the Day," the day of death brought to an end by the setting sun of the third stanza. . . . "Surmised," carefully placed near the conclusion, is all the warranty one needs for reading this journey as one that has taken place entirely in her mind . . . the poem returns to the very day, even the same instant, when it started. (Anderson 245)

Jarrad indents this long quotation to set it apart from his own prose.

Thus even the most basic facts about death — its finality and permanence — are brought into question.

Finally, "Because I could not stop for Death" indicates both Dickinson's precise and vivid style and her unwillingness to settle for the ordinary interpretation. Death no longer conforms to the readers' preconceptions, as religion, stillness, and finality give way to humanist philosophy, motion, and continuity. The poet observes, experiences, and recounts her perceptions in metaphor. She opens up many questions about the nature of death, yet she provides no easy answers to her readers. Instead, we are provided with an account of death that weaves in and out of time, finally looping back on its own structure to provide a stunningly dramatic conclusion. In six short stanzas, Dickinson cleverly exposes what she saw as fundamental flaws in the traditional conception of death, burial, and the eternal afterlife, and in doing so, she opens up new pathways of thought for us all.

In his conclusion, Jarrad reinforces his claim: that the poem challenges nineteenth-century notions of death.

Works Cited

Anderson, Charles R. *Emily Dickinson's Poetry: Stairway of Surprise.*   *A print book.*
    New York: Holt, 1960. Print.

Baker, David. "Elegy and Eros." *Virginia Quarterly Review* 81.2
    (2005): 207-20. *MLA International Bibliography.* Web. 20 Mar.
    2010.

Bloom, Harold. *Emily Dickinson.* New York: Chelsea, 1999. Print.   *Book in a series.*
    Bloom's Major Poets.

Dickinson, Emily. "Because I could not stop for Death." *Literature:*   *A poem reprinted*
    A Portable Anthology. Ed. Janet E. Gardner et al. 3rd ed.   *in an anthology.*
    Boston: Bedford, 2013. 523-24. Print.

Erikkila, Betsy. "Emily Dickinson and Class." *American Literary*   *Articles accessed*
    History 4.1 (1992): 1-27. *JSTOR.* Web. 21 Mar. 2010.   *through online*
    database service.

Farland, Maria Magdalena. "'That Tritest/Brightest Truth': Emily
    Dickinson's Anti-Sentimentality." *Nineteenth-Century Literature*
    53.3 (1998): 364-89. *JSTOR.* Web. 21 Mar. 2010.

Shaw, Mary Neff. "Dickinson's 'Because I could not stop for Death.'"
    Explicator 50.1 (1991): 20-21. *MLA International Bibliography.*
    Web. 20 Mar. 2010.

Yezzi, David. "Straying Close to Home." *Commonweal.* Commonweal   *An online ver-*
    Foundation, 9 Oct. 1998. Web. 20 May 2009.   *sion of a maga-*
    zine article.

CHAPTER 9

Literary Criticism and Literary Theory

Anytime you sit down to write about literature, or even to discuss a story, play, or poem with classmates, you are acting as a literary critic. The word *criticism* is often interpreted as negative and faultfinding. But literary criticism is a discipline and includes everything from a glowing review to a scathing attack to a thoughtful and balanced interpretation. Criticism can be broken down into two broad categories: evaluative and interpretive. Evaluative criticism seeks to determine how accomplished a work is and what place it should hold in the evolving story of literary history. Book reviews are the most common form of evaluative criticism. Interpretive criticism comprises all writing that seeks to explain, analyze, clarify, or question the meaning and significance of literature. Although you may engage in a certain amount of evaluative criticism in your literature class, and while your attitude about the value of literature will likely be apparent in your writing, the criticism you write for class will consist largely of interpretation.

All literary critics, including you, begin with some form of literary theory. Just as you may not have thought of yourself as a literary critic, you probably haven't thought of yourself as using literary theory. But you are doing so every time you write about literature, and it is a good idea to become familiar with some of the most prevalent types of theory. This familiarity will help you understand why so many respected literary critics seem to disagree with one another and why they write such different analyses of the same work of literature. It may also help to explain why you might disagree with your classmates, or even your instructor, in your interpretation of a particular story, poem, or play. Perhaps you are simply starting from a different theoretical base. You will be able to explain your thinking more eloquently if you understand that base.

Literary theory has the reputation of being incredibly dense and difficult. Indeed, the theories—sometimes called *schools* of criticism—discussed in the following pages are all complex, but here they are presented in their most basic, stripped-down forms. As such, these explanations are necessarily incomplete and selective. You should not feel you need to master the complexities of literary theory right now. You need only be aware of the existence of these various schools and watch for them as you read and write. Doing so will give you a better sense of what you're reading and hearing about the literature you explore, and it will make your writing more informed and articulate. There are many other schools and subschools in addition to those described here, but these are the most significant—the ones you are most likely to encounter as you continue to explore literature.

Focusing on Jamaica Kincaid's "Girl" (page 53) and T. S. Eliot's "The Love Song of J. Alfred Prufrock" (page 102), the last paragraph of each entry offers a few directions one might take in a critical reading, with the specific critical theory applied to the analysis. While these notes are by no means exhaustive, they might help spark ideas for a paper, or at least grant greater insight into the literature and theory discussed.

FORMALISM AND NEW CRITICISM

For a large part of the twentieth century, literary criticism was dominated by various types of theory that can broadly be defined as **formalism** and **New Criticism**. (New Criticism is no longer new, having begun to fall out of prominence in the 1970s, but its name lives on.) Formalist critics focus their attention on the formal elements of a literary text—things like **structure, tone, characters, setting, symbols,** and linguistic features. Explication and close-reading (explained on page 56) are techniques of formalist criticism. While poetry, which is quite self-consciously formal in its structure, lends itself most obviously to formalist types of criticism, prose fiction and drama are also frequently viewed through this lens.

Perhaps the most distinguishing feature of formalism and New Criticism is that they focus on the text itself and not on extratextual factors. Formalist critics are interested in how parts of a text relate to one another and to the whole, and they seek to create meaning by unfolding and examining these relationships. Excluded from consideration are questions about the author, the reader, history or culture, and the relationship of the literary text to other texts or artwork. Chances are you have written some formalist criticism yourself, either in high school or in college. If you have ever written a paper on **symbolism,** character development, or the relationship between sound patterns and sense in a poem, you have been a formalist critic.

A formalist critic of Jamaica Kincaid's story "Girl" might choose to focus on how the language used by the speaker of this monologue illuminates her character, while a formalist critic of T. S. Eliot's "The Love

Song of J. Alfred Prufrock" might focus on Eliot's irregular use of rhyme and meter in the poem.

FEMINIST AND GENDER CRITICISM

Have you ever had a classroom discussion of a piece of literature in which the focus was on the roles of women in the literature or the culture, or on the relationships between men and women? If so, you have engaged in **feminist criticism**. Some version of feminist criticism has been around for as long as readers have been interested in gender roles, but the school rose to prominence in the 1970s at the same time the modern feminist movement was gaining steam. Most feminist criticism from this time was clearly tied to raising consciousness about the patriarchy in which many women felt trapped. Some feminist critics sought to reveal how literary texts demonstrated the repression and powerlessness of women in different periods and cultures. Others had a nearly opposite agenda, showing how female literary characters could overcome the sexist power structures that surround them and exercise power in their worlds. Still others looked to literary history and sought to rediscover and promote writing by women whose works had been far less likely than men's to be regarded as "great" literature.

Before long, however, some critics began to point out that women were not alone in feeling social pressure to conform to gender roles. Over the years, men have usually been expected to be good providers, to be strong (both physically and emotionally), and to keep their problems and feelings more or less to themselves. Though the expectations are different, men are socialized no less than women to think and behave in certain ways, and these social expectations are also displayed in works of literature. Feminist criticism has expanded in recent years to become **gender criticism**. Any literary criticism that highlights gender roles or relationships between the sexes can be a type of gender criticism, whether or not it is driven by an overt feminist agenda.

The story "Girl" would be an obvious choice for a feminist critic, since it focuses on how a young girl is socialized into the domestic roles expected of women in her society. A gender critic might also be interested in "Prufrock" and in the ways that the poem's aging speaker feels his masculinity called into question.

QUEER THEORY

Queer theory is one of the more recent and more challenging critical schools to emerge out of critical interest in gender. It came into prominence in the 1990s, when some gay and lesbian literary critics perceived a need for a critical school that reflected their own particular circumstances and viewpoints. Some queer theorists insist that sexuality—or even the binary male/female division of gender itself—is culturally constructed rather than determined by physical characteristics present at birth. Many of these critics and theorists seek to destabilize the cultural norm that suggests that certain sexual preferences, marriage and family customs, and so forth are "normal" or "natural" while others are "deviant."

Queer theorists, like all literary critics, differ substantially in their focus. Some are interested in studying literary texts written by authors known or suspected to be gays, lesbians, bisexual, or transgender, particularly if these authors have been devalued in the past because of their sexual identity. Other queer theorists are interested in portrayals of gay or lesbian characters in literature by either gay or straight authors. Still others seek a "queer subtext" in canonical works of literature that have long been considered hetero-normative. (Included in this latter category are the many critics who have asked whether Shakespeare's Hamlet had something more than a traditional heterosexual friendship with his close confidante Horatio.)

At first glance, Jamaica Kincaid's "Girl" might not look like a promising candidate for examination by queer theory. But a queer theorist might, in fact, be interested in how the very possibility of homosexuality is erased by the narrator, the way the young girl is assumed to have an interest in "wharf-rat boys" and a need to know "how to love a man," though she never expresses these heterosexual urges.

MARXIST CRITICISM

Just as feminist criticism and queer theory came into their own because of the political agenda of certain critics, so too did **Marxist criticism**, which originally sought to use literature and criticism to forward a socialist political program. Early Marxist critics began with Karl Marx's (1818–1883) insistence that human interactions are economically driven and that the basic model of human progress is based on a struggle for power between different social classes. For Marxist critics, then, literature was just another battleground, another venue for the ongoing quest for individual material gain. Literary characters could be divided into powerful oppressors and their powerless victims, and literary plots and themes could be examined to uncover the economic forces that drove them. According to this model, the very acts of writing and reading literature can be characterized as production and consumption, and some Marxist critics have studied the external forces that drive education, publication, and literary tastes.

The sort of Marxist criticism that ignores all forces but socioeconomic ones is sometimes referred to as *vulgar* Marxism because, in its single-mindedness, it ignores certain complexities of individual thought and action. Its sole purpose is to expose the inequalities that underlie all societies and to thus raise the consciousness of readers and move society closer to a socialist state. Such Marxist criticism tends to be full of the language of Marxist political analysis—references to *class struggle*, to the economic *base* and *superstructure*, to the *means of production*, to worker *alienation* and *reification* (the process whereby oppressed workers lose their sense of individual humanity), and so forth.

But just as feminist criticism soon opened up into the broader and more complex school of gender criticism, so too did most Marxist criticism break free of a single-minded political agenda. You no longer have to be a committed Marxist to engage in Marxist criticism; all you need to do is acknowledge that socioeconomic forces do, in fact, affect people's lives. If you notice inequalities in power between characters in a work of literature, if you question how the class or educational background of an author affects his or her work, or if you believe that a certain type of literature—a Shakespearean sonnet, say, or a pulp western novel— appeals more to readers of a particular social background, then you are, at least in part, engaging in Marxist criticism.

Social class roles, one of the primary interests of Marxist critics, are visible in the apparently modest circumstances of the characters in "Girl" (where class and gender have a clear overlap) as well as in the more bourgeois world of porcelain teacups and perfumed dresses on display in "Prufrock."

CULTURAL STUDIES

Cultural studies is the general name given to a wide variety of critical practices, some of which might seem on the surface to have little in common with one another. Perhaps the best way to understand cultural studies is to begin with the notion that certain texts are privileged in our society while others are dismissed or derided. Privileged texts are the so-called great works of literature commonly found in anthologies and on course syllabi. Indeed, when we hear the word *literature*, these are probably the works we imagine. All other writing—from pulp romance novels to the slogans on bumper stickers—belongs to a second category of texts, those generally overlooked by traditional literary critics.

One major trend in cultural studies is the attempt to broaden the **canon**—those texts read and taught again and again and held up as examples of the finest expressions of the human experience. Critics have pointed out that canonical authors—Shakespeare, Milton, Keats, Steinbeck—tend (with obvious exceptions) to be from a fairly narrow segment of society: they are usually middle to upper-middle class, well educated, heterosexual white males. Some cultural critics, therefore, have sought out and celebrated the writing of historically disadvantaged groups such as African Americans or gay and lesbian authors. Other proponents of cultural studies turn their attention to the works of various social "outsiders," like prisoners, schoolchildren, or mental patients. This attempt at broadening the canon is designed to provide students and scholars alike with a more inclusive definition of what art and literature are all about.

Cultural critics seek to blur or erase the line separating "high" art from "low" art in the minds of the literary establishment. Some cultural critics believe that all texts are to some extent artistic expressions of a culture and that any text can therefore give us vital insights into the human experience. Rather than traditional literary objects, then, a cultural critic might choose to study such things as movies and television shows, advertisements, religious tracts, graffiti, and comic books. These texts—and virtually any other visual or verbal works you can imagine—are submitted to the same rigorous scrutiny as a sonnet or a classic novel. Some cultural critics suggest that English departments should become departments of cultural studies, in which a course on hip-hop culture would be valued as much as a course on Victorian poetry.

The poems of T. S. Eliot, including "The Love Song of J. Alfred Prufrock," occupy an important place in the early-twentieth-century literary canon. A cultural critic might seek to explain how and why Eliot came to be so firmly associated with high culture.

POSTCOLONIAL CRITICISM

One very active branch of cultural studies is **postcolonial criticism**, which focuses on writing from former British (and other, mostly European) colonies around the world. Postcolonial criticism is most strongly associated with the Indian subcontinent (India, Pakistan, and Bangladesh), large portions of Africa and the Middle East, parts of Asia (such as Singapore and Vietnam), the Caribbean, and Latin America. In such places, indigenous authors often possess attitudes, tastes, and literary traditions very different from those of their former colonial masters. Postcolonial criticism seeks to discover these attitudes and tastes, to recover literary history that was ignored or suppressed during the colonial period, and to celebrate indigenous cultures of storytelling, drama, and poetry. At the same time, it attempts to understand how occupation by a more powerful colonizing nation disrupted and changed the course of history in a particular place.

In a colonial setting, members of the ruling group tend to see as natural and ordinary attitudes that might be better understood as racist, classist, and/or religiously intolerant, such as assuming that indigenous traditions are "superstitious" or "primitive" compared to the more "civilized" culture of the imperialists. Postcolonial theorists demand that indigenous attitudes and customs be treated with full respect and understanding. Postcolonial literary theory is situated within a larger move to comprehend the effect of colonial culture on history, art, architecture, politics, law, philosophy, sociology, sex and race relations, and daily life.

A postcolonial critic reading "Girl" would likely focus his or her attention on the details of language and culture—*benna* music, for instance, or the belief that blackbirds might really be spirits—that locate the story in a particular postcolonial Caribbean setting.

HISTORICAL CRITICISM AND NEW HISTORICISM

If you have ever written a research paper that involved some background reading about the life and times of an author, you have already engaged in a form of **historical criticism**. Literary scholars have long read history books and various sorts of historical documents—from newspaper articles to personal letters—to gain insights into the composition and significance of a given work. The explanatory footnotes that often appear in literary reprints and anthologies are one obvious manifestation of this type of sleuthing. Indeed, some works of literature would be virtually inexplicable if we did not understand something of the times in which they were written and first read. If you did not know that Walt Whitman's "When Lilacs Last in the Dooryard Bloom'd" was an elegy written upon the assassination of Abraham Lincoln, it would be difficult to make any sense at all of the poem, since neither the president's name nor the cause of his death actually appear in the poem.

Likewise, historians have long turned to literary works and the visual arts in order to gain insights into the periods they study. While archives and contemporary documents can teach us a lot about the broad sweep of history—wars, leaders, the controversies of the day—it is often difficult to see from these documents what life was like for ordinary people, whose interior lives were not often documented. We may be able to learn from parish burial records, for example, how common childhood mortality was at a particular time in English history, but only when we read Ben Jonson's poem "On My First Son" (page 15) do we begin to understand how this mortality may have affected the parents who lost their children. Likewise, the few pages of James Joyce's story "Araby" may tell us more about how adolescent boys lived and thought in early-twentieth-century Dublin than would several volumes of social history.

One school of historical criticism, known as **New Historicism**, takes account of both what history has to teach us about literature *and* what literature has to teach us about history. (New Historicism has been around since the 1960s, and as with New Criticism, the name of the school is no longer as accurate as it once was.) New Historicists are sometimes said to read literary and nonliterary texts *in parallel*, attempting to see how each illuminates the other. Typically, New Historicists examine many different types of documents—government records, periodicals, private diaries, bills of sale—in order to re-create, as much as possible, the rich cultural context that surrounded both an author and that author's original audience. In doing so, they seek to give modern audiences a reading experience as rich and informed as the original readers of a literary work.

A historical critic of "Prufrock" might be able to untangle the meaning of certain lines or images that have little meaning for contemporary readers. These would include, for instance, what Prufrock means when he describes his "necktie rich and modest, but asserted by a simple pin" (line 43) or says, "I shall wear the bottoms of my trousers rolled" (121).

PSYCHOLOGICAL THEORIES

Early in the twenty-first century, it is easy to underestimate the enormous influence that the theories of the psychoanalyst Sigmund Freud (1856–1939) have had on our understanding of human behavior and motivation. For many modern readers, Freud seems to have little to say; his work is too focused on sex and too thoroughly bound by the norms of the bourgeois Viennese society in which he lived. But if you have ever wondered what the buried significance of a dream was or whether someone had a subconscious motivation for an action, you have been affected by Freudian thinking. Freud popularized the notions that the mind can be divided into conscious and unconscious components and that we are often motivated most strongly by the unconscious. He taught us to think in terms of overt and covert desires (often referred to in Freudian language as *manifest* and *latent*) as the basis of human actions.

Like many intellectual movements of the twentieth century, psychology, and specifically Freudian psychology, has had a major influence on literary criticism. The most typical **psychological literary criticism** examines the internal mental states, the desires, and the motivations of literary characters. (In fact, Freud himself used Shakespeare's Hamlet as an example of a man whose life was ruled by what the psychoanalyst called an Oedipal complex—man's unhealthy, but not uncommon, interest in his mother's sexuality.) Another subject of psychological criticism can be the author. A critic may examine the possible unconscious urges that drove an author to write a particular story or poem. Finally, a critic might examine the psychology of readers, trying to determine what draws us to or repels us from certain literary themes or forms. If any of these aspects of literature have ever interested you, you have engaged in psychological literary criticism.

Psychological critics often interpret literature as a psychologist might interpret a dream or a wish. Special attention is often paid to symbols as the manifest representation of a deeper, less obvious meaning. Attention is also focused on the unstated motives and unconscious states of mind of characters, authors, or readers. Freud is not the only psychological theorist whose ideas are frequently used in literary analysis. Other important figures include Carl Jung (1875–1961), who gave us the notion of the collective unconscious and the influence of **archetypes** on our thinking, and Jacques Lacan (1901–1981), who had a special interest in the unconscious and the nature of language. However, you don't need to be well versed in the intricacies of psychoanalytic theory in order to be interested in the inner workings of the human mind or the ways in which they manifest themselves in literature.

The narrator of "Prufrock" is an excellent candidate for psychological study, displaying many signs of social anxiety, depression, and other recognizable psychological conditions. Or a Jungian critic of this poem might focus on archetypal symbols such as the animalistic fog early in the poem or the mermaids that appear near the end.

READER-RESPONSE THEORIES

You no doubt have heard the old question: If a tree falls in the forest and nobody hears it, did the tree make a sound? Let us rephrase that question: If a book sits on a shelf and nobody reads it, is it still a book? If you use **reader-response criticism**, your answer to that question will be a resounding *no*. Of course, the book exists as a physical object, a sheaf of paper bound in a cover and printed with symbols. But, say reader-response critics, as a work of art or a conduit for meaning, no text exists without a reader.

A text, according to the various theories of reader-response criticism, is not a container filled with meaning by its author but rather an interaction between an author and a reader, and it can never be complete unless readers bring to it their own unique insights. These insights come from a number of sources, including the reader's life experience, as well as his or her beliefs, values, state of mind at the time of the reading, and, of course, previous reading experience. Reading is not a passive attempt to understand what lies within a text but an act of creation, no less so than the writing itself. Reader-response critics try to understand the process by which we make meaning out of words on a page. If you have ever wondered why a classmate or friend saw something entirely different than you did in a story or poem, then you have been a reader-response critic.

Two key terms associated with reader-response criticism are *gaps* and *process*. Gaps are those things that a text doesn't tell us, that we need to fill in and work out for ourselves. Let us say, for instance, that you read a story told from the perspective of a child, but the author never explicitly mentions the child's age. How, then, do you imagine the narrator as you read? You pay attention to his or her actions and thoughts, and you compare this to your experience of real children you have known and others whose stories you have read. In doing so, you fill in a *gap* in the text and help solidify the text's meaning. Imagine, though, that as the story continues, new clues emerge and you need to adjust your assumptions about the child's age. This highlights the idea that reading is a *process*, that the meaning of the text is not fixed and complete but rather evolving as the text unfolds in the time it takes to read.

Some reader-response critics focus on the ways that meanings of a text change over time. To illustrate this idea, let us look at a specific example. Contemporary readers of Kate Chopin's short novel *The Awakening*, first published in 1899, tend to find the book's treatment of the heroine's sexuality subtle or even invisible. Such readers are often shocked or amused to learn that the book was widely condemned at the time of its publication as tasteless and overly explicit. Expectations and tastes change over time and place, and we can tell a lot about a society by examining how it responds to works of art. Reader-response critics, therefore, sometimes ask us to look at our own reactions to literature and to ask how, if at all, they match up with those of earlier readers. When we look at reactions to *The Awakening* at the end of the nineteenth century and then at the beginning of the twenty-first, we learn not only about Chopin's culture but also about our own.

The response paper written by Tom Lyons (pages 55–56) shows how a student with no formal background in literary theory might still approach "Girl" in a way that gives credence to the core reader-response tenet that readers bring their own meanings to literary texts.

STRUCTURALISM

Structuralism, as the name implies, is concerned with the structures that help us understand and interpret literary texts. This may sound like a return to formalism, which, as we saw earlier, examines the formal and linguistic elements of a text. But the elements scrutinized by structuralist critics are of a different order entirely—namely, the structures that order our thinking rather than the interior architecture of poems, stories, and plays. Structuralist criticism actually derives from the work of anthropologists, linguists, and philosophers of the mid-twentieth century who sought to understand how humans think and communicate. The basic insight at the heart of the movement is the realization that we understand nothing in isolation but rather that every piece of our knowledge is part of a network of associations. Take, for instance, the question "Is Jim a good father?" In order to form a simple yes or no answer to this question, we must consider, among other things, the spectrum of "good" and "bad," the expectations our culture holds for fathers, and all we know of Jim's relationship with his children.

For a structuralist literary critic, questions about literature are answered with the same sort of attention to context. Two different types of context are especially salient—the cultural and the literary. Cultural context refers to an understanding of all aspects of an author's (and a reader's) culture, such as the organizing structures of history, politics, religion, education, work, and family. Literary context refers to all related texts, literary and nonliterary, that affect our ability to interpret a text. What had the author read that might have affected the creation of the text? What have we read that might affect our interpretation? What are the norms of the textual genre, and how does this piece of literature conform to or break from those norms?

According to structuralist critics, then, we can understand a text only by placing it within the broader contexts of culture (that of both the reader and the author) and other texts (literary and nonliterary). To fully understand one of Shakespeare's love sonnets to the mysterious "dark lady," for example, we would need to understand the conventions of romantic love, the conceptions of dark versus fair women in culturally accepted standards of beauty, and the acceptable interactions between men and women in Shakespeare's England. We would also need to relate the sonnet to the history of love poems generally, to the development of the sonnet form specifically, and to the other works in Shakespeare's cycle of 154 sonnets.

A structuralist reading of "Prufrock," then, would be likely to consider, among other things, the types of poetry that were in vogue in 1915, when the poem was first published, as well as the specific poems and poets that Eliot, who wrote literary criticism as well as poetry, most admired.

POSTSTRUCTURALISM AND DECONSTRUCTION

Poststructuralism, it will come as no surprise, begins with the insights of structuralism but carries them one step further. If, as the structuralists insist, we can understand things only in terms of other things, then perhaps there is no center point of understanding but only an endlessly interconnected web of ideas leading to other ideas leading to still other ideas. This is the starting point of poststructuralist criticism, which posits that no text has a fixed or real meaning because no meaning exists outside of the network of other meanings to which it is connected. Meaning, then, including literary meaning, is forever shifting and altering as our understanding of the world changes. The best-known version of poststructuralism is **deconstruction**, a school of philosophy and literary criticism that first gained prominence in France and that seeks to overturn the very basis of Western philosophy by undermining the notion that reality has any stable existence.

At its worst, of course, this school of thought leads to the most slippery sort of relativism. What does it matter what I think of this poem or this play? I think what I want; you think what you want. Perhaps next week I will think something different. Who cares? Every interpretation is of equal value, and none has any real value at all. At its best, though, poststructuralist criticism can lead toward truly valuable insights into literature. It reminds us that meaning within a text is contingent on all sorts of exterior understandings; it allows for several interpretations, even contradictory interpretations, to exist simultaneously; and, by insisting that no text and no meaning are absolute, it allows for a playful approach to even the most "serious" of literary objects. Indeed, one of the recurrent themes of deconstructionist criticism is the French term *jouissance*, often translated as *bliss*, which refers to a free-spirited, almost sexual enjoyment of literary language.

Having thus briefly described deconstruction, we would do well to dispel a common misconception about the word. In recent years, many people, both within and outside of academia, have begun to use *deconstruct* as a synonym for *analyze*. You might hear, for instance, "We completely deconstructed that poem in class—I understand it much better now," or "The defense attorney deconstructed the prosecutor's argument." In both these cases, what the speaker likely means has little if anything to do with the literary critical practice of deconstruction. When we take apart a text or an argument and closely examine the parts, we are engaging not in deconstruction but in analysis.

A deconstructionist reading of "Girl" might call into question the very basis for our belief in gender divisions, class structure, or the need for the socialization of young people by their elders.

These are only some of the many varieties of literary theory and criticism. In addition, you might encounter eco-criticism, which focuses on the environment and human beings' relationship with the rest of nature; religious (for example, Christian, Muslim, or Buddhist) criticism; comparative literature, which compares related works from different languages and/or cultures; various schools of critical inquiry based on race and ethnicity; and many, many more. There are even literary critics who perform textual analysis using sophisticated computer programs.

By now you may be wondering what sort of literary critic you are. You may feel that you have been a formalist one day and a psychological critic the next. This is not surprising, and it should cause you no worry, as virtually none of these schools are mutually exclusive. Indeed, most professional critics mix and match the various schools in whatever way best suits their immediate needs. The close-reading techniques of the New Critics, for instance, are frequently adopted by those who would fervently reject the New Critical stance that social and political context be excluded from consideration. If you wished to write about the social decline of Mme. Loisel in Guy de Maupassant's story "The Necklace," you might well find yourself in the position of a Marxist–feminist–New Historicist critic. That's fine. Writing with the knowledge that you are drawing from Marxism, feminism, and New Historicism, you will almost certainly write a better-organized, better-informed, and more thorough paper than you would have had you begun with no conscious basis in literary theory.

Take a look at the annotations and notes you have made on literary works, the notes you have taken in class, and any exams or papers you have written. Are there particular themes and issues to which you keep returning, particular genres or literary features that continue to attract or interest you? If so, you may have the beginning of an answer to the question: *What sort of literary critic am I?*

Glossary of Critical and Literary Terms

This glossary provides definitions for important literary terms used in this book. Words and phrases highlighted in **boldface** in individual entries are defined elsewhere in the glossary.

Abstract language Any language that employs intangible, nonspecific concepts. *Love, truth,* and *beauty* are abstractions. Abstract language is the opposite of **concrete language**. Both types have different effects and are important features of an author's style.

Absurd, theater of the Theatrical style prominent in the mid-twentieth century that seeks to dramatize the absurdity of modern life. **Conventions** of the style include disjointed or elliptical plot lines, disaffected characters, non-**naturalistic** dialogue, and, often, **black comedy**. Proponents include Eugene Ionesco and Samuel Beckett.

Accent The stress, or greater emphasis, given to some syllables of words relative to that received by adjacent syllables.

Accentual meter A metrical system in which the number of accented, or stressed, syllables per line is regular—all lines have the same number, or the corresponding lines of different stanzas have the same number—while the number of unstressed syllables in lines varies randomly. Accentual meter consisting of two accented syllables in each half line linked by a system of alliteration was the hallmark of Old English poetry (up to the eleventh century),

and some modern poets, such as W. H. Auden, have sought to revive it. Gerard Manley Hopkins developed a unique variety of accentual verse he called *sprung rhythm.*

Accentual-syllabic verse Verse whose meter takes into account both the number of syllables per line and the pattern of accented and unaccented syllables. The great majority of metrical poems in English are accentual-syllabic. Cf. **quantitative verse.**

Act One of the principal divisions of a full-length play. Plays of the Renaissance are commonly divided into five acts. Although four acts enjoyed a brief period of popularity in the nineteenth century, two or three acts are more typical of modern and contemporary dramas.

Agon The central conflict in a play. In Greek drama, the agon is a formal structural component, often a debate between two characters or parts of the **chorus.**

Alexandrine A poetic line with six iambic feet (iambic hexameter).

Allegory (1) An extended **metaphor** in which characters, events, objects, settings, and actions stand not only for themselves but also for abstract concepts, such as death or knowledge. Allegorical plays, often religious, were popular in medieval times; a famous example is *Everyman*. (2) A form or manner, usually narrative, in which objects, persons, and actions make coherent sense on a literal level but also are equated in a sustained and obvious way with (usually) abstract meanings that lie outside the story. A classic example in prose is John Bunyan's *The Pilgrim's Progress*; in narrative poetry, Edmund Spenser's *The Faerie Queene*.

Alliteration The repetition of identical consonant sounds in the stressed syllables of words relatively near to each other (in the same line or adjacent lines, usually). Alliteration is most common at the beginnings of words ("as the *g*rass was *g*reen") but can involve consonants within words ("*g*reen and care*f*ree, *f*amous among the barns"). Alliteration applies to sounds, not spelling: "And honoured among *f*oxes and *ph*easants" is an example. (The examples are from Dylan Thomas's "Fern Hill.") Cf. **consonance**.

Allusion A figure of speech that echoes or makes brief reference to a literary or artistic work or a historical figure, event, or object, as, for example, the references to Lazarus and Hamlet in "The Love Song of J. Alfred Prufrock" (p. 102). It is usually a way of placing one's poem within or alongside a context that is evoked in a very economical fashion. See also **intertextuality**.

Alternative theater Any theater— most often political or experimental— that sets itself up in opposition to the **conventions** of the mainstream theater of its time.

Ambiguity In expository prose, an undesirable doubtfulness or uncertainty of meaning or intention resulting from imprecision in the use of one's words or the construction of one's sentences. In poetry, the desirable condition of admitting more than one possible meaning resulting from the capacity of language to function on levels other than the literal. Related terms sometimes employed are *ambivalence* and *polysemy*.

Anagnorisis A significant recognition or discovery by a character, usually the **protagonist**, that moves the **plot** forward by changing the circumstances of a play.

Anapest A metrical **foot** consisting of three syllables, with two unaccented syllables followed by an accented one (˘˘ˊ). In *anapestic meter*, anapests are the predominant foot in a line or poem. The following line from William Cowper's "The Poplar Field" is in anapestic meter: "Ănd thĕ whĭs | pĕrĭng soúnd | ŏf thĕ cóol | cŏlŏnnáde."

Anaphora Repetition of the same word or words at the beginning of two or more lines, clauses, or sentences. Walt Whitman employs anaphora extensively in "Song of Myself."

Antagonist The character (or, less often, the force) that opposes the **protagonist**.

Anticlimax In drama, a disappointingly trivial occurrence where a **climax** would usually happen. An anticlimax can achieve comic effect or disrupt audience expectations of dramatic structure. In poetry, an anticlimax is an arrangement of details such that one of lesser importance follows one or ones of greater importance, where something of greater significance is expected. A well-known example is "Not louder shrieks to pitying heaven are cast, / When husbands die, or when lapdogs breathe their last" (Alexander Pope, *The Rape of the Lock*).

Antihero, antiheroine A character playing a hero's part but lacking the grandeur typically associated with a **hero**. Such a character may be comic or may exist to force the audience to reconsider its notions of heroism.

Antistrophe The second part of a choral **ode** in Greek drama. The antistrophe was traditionally sung as the **chorus** moved from **stage left** to **stage right**.

Antithesis A figure of speech in which contrasting words, sentences, or ideas are expressed in balanced, parallel grammatical structures; "She had some horses she loved. / She had some horses she hated," from Joy Harjo's poem "She Had Some Horses," illustrates antithesis.

Apostrophe A figure of speech in which an absent person, an abstract quality, or a nonhuman entity is addressed as though present. It is a particular type of personification. See, for example, Ben Jonson's "On My First Son" (p. 15).

Approximate rhyme See **slant rhyme**.

Archetype An image, symbol, character type, or plot line that occurs frequently enough in literature, religion, myths, folktales, and fairy tales to be recognizable as an element of universal experience and that evokes a deep emotional response. In "Spring and Fall," Gerard Manley Hopkins develops the archetypes in his title, those of spring (archetype for birth and youth) and fall (archetype for old age and the approach of death).

Aside A brief bit of dialogue spoken by a character to the audience or to him- or herself and assumed to be unheard by other characters onstage.

Assonance The repetition of identical or similar vowel sounds in words relatively near to one another (usually within a line or in adjacent lines) whose consonant sounds differ. It can be initial ("*a*pple . . . *a*nd h*a*ppy *a*s") or, more commonly, internal ("gr*ee*n and car*e*fr*ee*," "T*i*me held m*e* gr*ee*n and d*y*ing"). (Examples taken from Dylan Thomas's "Fern Hill.")

Aubade A dawn song, ordinarily expressing two lovers' regret that day has come and they must separate.

Ballad A poem that tells a story and was meant to be recited or sung; originally, a folk art transmitted orally, from person to person and from generation to generation. Many of the popular ballads were not written down and published until the eighteenth century, though their origins may have been centuries earlier.

Ballad stanza A quatrain in iambic meter rhyming *abcb* with (usually) four feet in the first and third lines, three in the second and fourth. See, for example, Robert Burns's "A Red, Red Rose."

Black comedy A type of comedy in which the traditional material of tragedy (that is, suffering, or even death) is staged to provoke laughter.

Blank verse Lines of unrhymed **iambic pentameter**. Blank verse is the most widely used verse form of poetry in English because it is closest to the natural rhythms of English speech. Shakespeare's plays, as well as Milton's *Paradise Lost* and *Paradise Regained*, and countless other long poems were composed in blank verse because it is well suited to narrative, dialogue, and reflection.

Blocking The process of determining the stage positions, movement, and groupings of actors. Blocking generally is proposed in rehearsal by the director and may be negotiated and reworked by the actors themselves.

Brainstorming An information-gathering process in which a group or an individual writes down any and all ideas that come to mind regarding the topic of a given paper or project. The list is later fine-tuned during the organizing stage of the project.

Cacophony A harsh or unpleasant combination of sounds, as in Alexander Pope's poem "An Essay on Criticism": "But when loud surges lash the sounding shore, / The hoarse, rough verse should like the torrent roar." Cf. **euphony**.

Caesura A pause or break within a line of verse, usually signaled by a mark of punctuation.

Canon The group of literary works that form the backbone of a cultural tradition.

Carpe diem A Latin phrase from an ode by Horace meaning "seize the day." It became the label for a theme common in literature, especially in sixteenth- and seventeenth-century English love poetry, that life is short and fleeting and that therefore one must make the most of present pleasures.

Catastrophe The final movement of a **tragedy**, which brings about the fall or death of the **protagonist**. In plays other than classical tragedy, a **denouement** takes the place of a catastrophe.

Catharsis A purging of the emotions of pity and fear. Aristotle argued in *Poetics* that catharsis is the natural, and beneficial, outcome of viewing a **tragedy**.

Characters,   characterization Broadly speaking, characters are usually the people of a work of literature—although characters may be animals or some other beings. In fiction, characterization means the development of a character or characters throughout a story. Characterization includes the narrator's description of what characters look like and what they think, say, and do (these are sometimes very dissimilar). Their own actions and views of themselves, and other characters' views of and behavior toward them, are also means of characterization. Characters may be minor, like Goody Cloyse, or major, like Goodman Brown, both of Hawthorne's story "Young Goodman Brown." Depending on the depth of characterization, a character may be simple or complex, flat or round. Character is one of the six **elements of drama** identified by Aristotle, and characterization is the process by which writers and actors make a character distinct and believable to an audience.

Chaucerian stanza A seven-line iambic stanza rhyming *ababbcc*, sometimes having an **alexandrine** (hexameter) closing line. See, for example, Sir Thomas Wyatt's poem "They flee from me."

Chorus In classical Greek theater, a group of actors who perform in the **orchestra** and whose functions might include providing **exposition**, confronting or questioning the **protagonist**, and commenting on the action of the play. Much of the **spectacle** of Greek drama lay in the chorus's singing and dancing. In theater of other times and places, particularly that of the Renaissance, the functions of the Greek chorus are sometimes given to a single character identified as "Chorus."

Climax In drama, the turning point at which a play switches from **rising action** to **falling action**. In fiction, the moment of greatest intensity and conflict in the action of a story. In Nathaniel Hawthorne's "Young Goodman Brown," events reach their climax when Brown and his wife stand together in the forest, at the point of conversion.

Closed form Any structural pattern or repetition of meter, rhyme, or stanza. Cf. **open form**.

Closet drama A play intended to be read rather than performed.

Comedy Originally, any play that ended with the characters in a better condition than when the play began, though the term is now used more frequently to describe a play intended to be funny. Traditional comedy is generally distinguished by low or ordinary characters (as opposed to the great men and women of tragedy), a

humble style, a series of events or role reversals that create chaos and upheaval, and a conclusion or **denouement** that marks a return to normalcy and often a reintegration into society (such as with a wedding or other formal celebration).

Comic relief A funny scene or character appearing in an otherwise serious play, intended to provide the audience with a momentary break from the heavier themes of tragedy.

Commedia dell'arte Semi-improvised comedy relying heavily on **stock characters** and **stage business**, performed originally by traveling Italian players in the sixteenth and seventeenth centuries.

Complication One of the traditional elements of **plot**. Complication occurs when someone or something opposes the **protagonist**.

Compression The dropping of a syllable to make a line fit the meter, sometimes marked with an apostrophe (e.g., William Shakespeare, Sonnet 73, line 13: "This thou perceiv'st"). Another common device is elision, the dropping of a vowel at the beginning or end of a word (e.g., in lines 7 and 28 of John Donne's "A Valediction: Forbidding Mourning": "'Twere profanation of our joys" and "To move, but doth, if th' other do").

Conceit A figure of speech that establishes a striking or far-fetched analogy between seemingly very dissimilar things, either the exaggerated, unrealistic comparisons found in love poems (such as in Shakespeare's Sonnet 18) or the complex analogies of metaphysical wit (as in John Donne's "A Valediction: Forbidding Mourning").

Concrete language Any specific, physical language that appeals to one or more of the senses—sight, hearing, taste, smell, or touch. *Stones, chairs,* and *hands* are concrete words. Concrete language is the opposite of **abstract language.** Both types are important features of an author's style.

Concrete poem A poem shaped in the form of the object the poem describes or discusses. See, for example, George Herbert's "Easter-wings."

Confessional poetry Poetry about personal, private issues in which a poet usually speaks directly, without the use of a **persona.** See, for example, Robert Lowell's "Skunk Hour" and Sylvia Plath's "Daddy."

Confidant A character, major or minor, to whom another character confides secrets so that the audience can "overhear" the transaction and be apprised of unseen events.

Conflict Antagonism between characters, ideas, or lines of action; between a character and the outside world; or between different aspects of a character's nature. Conflict is essential in a traditional plot, as in the conflict between Montresor and Fortunato in Edgar Allan Poe's story "The Cask of Amontillado." Shakespeare's play Hamlet is in conflict both with his stepfather Claudius for killing his father and with himself as he tries to decide a course of action.

Connotation The range of emotional implications and associations a word may carry outside of its dictionary definitions. Cf. **denotation.**

Consonance The repetition of consonant sounds in words whose vowels are different. In perfect consonance, all consonants are the same—*live, love; chitter, chatter; reader, rider;* words in which all consonants following the main vowels are identical also are considered consonant—*dive, love; swatter, chitter; sound, bond; gate, mat; set, pit.*

Convention An unstated rule, code, practice, or characteristic established by usage. In drama, tacit acceptance of theatrical conventions prevents the audience from being distracted by unrealistic features that are necessarily part of any theater experience. Greek audiences, for instance, accepted the convention of the **chorus,** while today's audiences readily accept the convention of the **fourth wall** in realistic drama and of songs in musical comedy.

Couplet Two consecutive lines of poetry with the same **end-rhyme. English** (Shakespearean) **sonnets** end with a couplet; for an entire poem in tetrameter couplets, see Andrew Marvell's "To His Coy Mistress." See also **heroic couplets.**

Cruelty, theater of Term coined by Antonin Artaud in the early twentieth century to describe a type of theater using light, sound, **spectacle,** and other primarily nonverbal forms of communication to create images of cruelty and destruction intended to shock audiences out of complacency.

Cultural context The milieu that gives rise to a work of literature.

Cultural studies A general name given to a wide variety of critical practices that examine and challenge why certain texts are privileged in our society while others are dismissed or derided. Rather than focusing on traditional literary objects, cultural studies critics might choose to study movies, television shows, advertisements, graffiti, or comic books, often in conjunction with **canonical** works of literature.

Dactyl A metrical **foot** consisting of three syllables, an accented one followed by two unaccented ones (–᷉᷉). In "dactylic meter," dactyls are the predominant foot of a line or poem. The following lines from Thomas Hardy's "The Voice" are in dactylic meter: "Wómăn mŭch | miśsed, hŏw yŏu | cáll tŏ mĕ, | cáll tŏ mĕ, / Sáyĭng thăt | nów yŏu aŕe | nót ăs yŏu | wére."

Deconstruction A variety of **poststructuralism**, deconstruction derives from the efforts of Jacques Derrida to undermine the foundations of Western philosophy, but as a literary critical practice it often emerges as a kind of close-reading that reveals irreconcilable linguistic contradictions in a text that prevents the text from having a single stable meaning or message.

Denotation The basic meaning of a word; its dictionary definition(s).

Denouement Literally, "unknotting." The end of a play or other literary work, in which all elements of the **plot** are brought to their conclusion.

Description Language that presents specific features of a character, object, or setting; or the details of an action or event. The first paragraph of Franz Kafka's "The Metamorphosis" describes Gregor's startling new appearance.

Deus ex machina Literally, "god out of the machine," referring to the mechanized system used to lower an actor playing a god onto the stage in classical Greek drama. Today the term is generally used disparagingly to indicate careless plotting and an unbelievable **resolution** in a play.

Dialogue Words spoken by characters, often in the form of a conversation between two or more characters. In stories and other forms of prose, dialogue is commonly enclosed between quotation marks. Dialogue is an important element in **characterization** and **plot**: much of the characterization and action in Ernest Hemingway's "Hills Like White Elephants" is presented through its characters' dialogue.

Diction A writer's selection of words; the kind of words, phrases, and figurative language used to make up a work of literature. In fiction, particular patterns or arrangements of words in sentences and paragraphs constitute prose style. Hemingway's diction is said to be precise, concrete, and economical. Aristotle identified diction as one of the six **elements of drama**. See also **poetic diction**.

Dimeter A line of verse consisting of two metrical feet.

Double rhyme A rhyme in which an accented, rhyming syllable is followed by one or more identical, unstressed syllables: *thrilling* and *killing*, *marry* and *tarry*. Formerly known as "feminine rhyme."

Downstage The part of the stage closest to the audience.

Dramatic irony A situation in which a reader or an audience knows more than the speakers or characters, about either the outcome of events or a discrepancy between a meaning intended by a speaker or character and that recognized by the reader or audience.

Dramatic monologue A poem with only one speaker, overheard in a dramatic moment (usually addressing another character or characters who do not speak), whose words reveal what is going on in the scene and expose significant depths of the speaker's temperament, attitudes, and values. See Robert Browning's "My Last Duchess" (p. 60) and T. S. Eliot's "The Love Song of J. Alfred Prufrock" (p. 102).

Elegy In Greek and Roman literature, a serious, meditative poem written in "elegiac meter" (alternating hexameter and pentameter lines); since the 1600s, a sustained and formal poem lamenting the death of a particular person, usually ending with a consolation, or one setting forth meditations on death or another solemn theme. See Thomas Gray's "Elegy Written in a Country Churchyard." The adjective *elegiac* is also used to describe a general tone of sadness or a worldview that emphasizes suffering and loss. It is most often applied to Anglo-Saxon poems like *Beowulf* or *The Seafarer* but can also be used for modern poems, such as A. E. Housman's in *A Shropshire Lad*.

Elements of drama The six features identified by Aristotle in *Poetics* as descriptive of and necessary to drama. They are, in order of the importance assigned to them by Aristotle, **plot, characterization, theme, diction, melody,** and **spectacle.**

Elements of fiction Major elements of fiction are **plot, characters, setting, point of view, style,** and **theme.** Skillful employment of these entities is essential in effective novels and stories. From beginning to end, each element is active and relates to the others dynamically.

Elements of poetry Verbal, aural, and structural features of poetry, including **diction, tone, images, figures of speech, symbols, rhythm, rhyme,** and poetic **form,** which are combined to create poems.

Elision See **compression.**

Empathy The ability of the audience to relate to, even experience, the emotions of characters onstage or in a text.

End-rhyme Rhyme occurring at the ends of lines in a poem.

End-stopped line A line of poetry whose grammatical structure and thought reach completion by its end. Cf. **run-on line.**

English sonnet A sonnet consisting of three quatrains (three four-line units, typically rhyming *abab cdcd efef*) and a couplet (two rhyming lines). Usually, the subject is introduced in the first quatrain, expanded in the second, and expanded still further in the third; the couplet adds a logical, pithy conclusion or introduces a surprising twist. Also called the Shakespearean sonnet. Cf. **Spenserian sonnet.**

Enjambment See **run-on line.**

Epic A long narrative poem that celebrates the achievements of great heroes and heroines, often determining the fate of a tribe or nation, written in formal language and an elevated style. Examples include Homer's *Iliad* and *Odyssey*, Virgil's *Aeneid*, and John Milton's *Paradise Lost*.

Epic theater   The name given by Bertolt Brecht to a theatrical style emphasizing the relationship between form and ideology. It is characterized by brief scenes, narrative breaks, political and historical themes, an analytical (rather than emotional) tone, and characters with whom it is difficult to feel empathy. Though considered **alternative theater** when it was new, many of its **conventions** have since been adopted by mainstream dramatists.

Epigram   Originally, an inscription, especially an epitaph; in modern usage, a short poem, usually polished and witty with a surprising twist at the end. (Its other dictionary definition, "any terse, witty, pointed statement," generally does not apply in poetry.)

Epigraph   In literature, a quotation at the beginning of a poem or on the title page or the beginning of a chapter in a book. See the epigraph from Dante's *Inferno* at the beginning of T. S. Eliot's poem "The Love Song of J. Alfred Prufrock" (p. 102).

Epilogue   A final speech or scene occurring after the main action of the play has ended. An epilogue generally sums up or comments on the meaning of the play.

Epiphany   An appearance or manifestation, especially of a divine being; in literature, since James Joyce adapted the term to secular use in 1944, a sudden sense of radiance and revelation one may feel while perceiving a commonplace object; a moment or event in which the essential nature of a person, a situation, or an object is suddenly perceived, as at the end of Joyce's story "Araby."

Episode   In Greek drama, the scenes of dialogue that occur between the choral **odes**. Now the term is used to mean any small unit of drama that has its own completeness and internal unity.

Euphony   Language that strikes the ear as smooth, musical, and agreeable. An example can be found in Alexander Pope's poem "An Essay on Criticism," lines: "Soft is the strain when Zephyr gently blows, / And the smooth stream in smoother numbers flows." Cf. **cacophony**.

Exact rhyme   Rhyme in which all sounds following the vowel sound are the same: *spite* and *night*, *art* and *heart*, *ache* and *fake*, *card* and *barred*.

Exaggeration   See **hyperbole**.

Explication   The process of making clear that which is implicit or subtle in a work of literature. This is achieved by performing a close-reading—reading a piece of literature with an eye toward such sentence-level elements as sentence structure, style, imagery, word choice, and figurative language—and then explaining the larger purpose and effect of those elements.

Exposition   A means of filling in the audience on events that occurred offstage or before the play's beginning. Clumsily handled exposition, in which characters talk at length about things they normally would not, is characteristic of much bad drama.

Expressionism   Nonrealistic playmaking style using exaggerated or otherwise unreal gestures, light, and sound. Expressionistic techniques are often used to convey a sense of memory, dream, or fantasy.

Extension   Pronunciation that adds a syllable for the sake of the meter. See, for example, the third line of the fifth stanza in John Donne's poem "A Valediction: Forbidding Mourning": "Interassurèd of the mind."

Falling action   The action after the **climax** in a traditionally structured play whereby the tension lessens and the play moves toward the **catastrophe** or **denouement**.

Falling meter   Meter using a **foot** (usually a trochee or a dactyl) in which the first syllable is accented and those that follow are unaccented, giving a sense of stepping down. Cf. **rising meter**.

Farce   Comedy that relies on exaggerated characters, extreme situations, fast and accelerating pacing, and, often, sexual innuendo.

Feminine   rhyme   See   **double rhyme**.

Feminist criticism   A school of literary criticism that examines the roles of women in literature and culture as well as the relationships between men and women. Contemporary feminist criticism rose to prominence in the 1970s, when the modern feminist movement began to explore the patriarchal structures in which many women felt trapped. Some feminist critics seek to show the ways in which literary texts demonstrate the repression and powerlessness of women—or, alternately, to

show how female literary characters could overcome sexist power structures. Still others seek to rediscover and promote writing by women whose works have been excluded from the mostly male **canon** of "great" literature.

Feminist theater   Any play or theater whose primary object is to shine light on the issues of women's rights and sexism.

Fiction   Generally speaking, any imaginative, usually prose, work of literature. More narrowly, narratives—**short stories**, **novellas**, or **novels**—whose plots, characters, and settings are constructions of its writer's imagination, which draws on the writer's experiences and reflections.

Figurative language   Uses of language—employing **metaphor** or **simile** or other figures of speech—that depart from standard or literal usage in order to achieve a special effect or meaning. Figurative language is often employed in poetry; although less often seen in plays and stories, it can be used powerfully in those forms. Alice Walker's story "Everyday Use" opens with a figurative description of the family's yard.

First-person narrator   In a story told by one person, the "I" who tells the story. Sometimes the first-person narrator is purely an observer; more often he or she is directly or indirectly involved in the action of the story. Montresor is the first-person narrator of, and one of two characters in, Edgar Allan Poe's "The Cask of Amontillado." As a first-person narrator, he reveals much about his own emotions and motivations.

Fixed form   Poetry written in definite, repeating patterns of line, rhyme scheme, or stanza.

Flashback   A writer's way of introducing important earlier material. As a narrator tells a story, he or she may stop the flow of events and direct the reader to an earlier time. Sometimes the narrator may return to the present, sometimes remain in the past. The narrator in William Faulkner's story "A Rose for Emily" uses flashbacks to depict the events leading up to Emily Grierson's death.

Foil   A character who exists chiefly to set off or display, usually by opposition, the important character traits of the **protagonist** or another important person.

Foot   The basic unit in metrical verse, comprising (usually) one stressed syllable and one or more unstressed syllables. See also **anapest**, **dactyl**, **iamb**, **spondee**, and **trochee**.

Foreshadowing   Words, gestures, or other actions that suggest future events or outcomes. The opening of Nathaniel Hawthorne's "Young Goodman Brown" foreshadows serious trouble ahead when Faith, Brown's wife, begs him to stay home with her "this night, dear husband, of all nights in the year."

Form   (1) Genre or literary type (e.g., the lyric form); (2) patterns of meter, lines, and rhymes (stanzaic form); (3) the organization of the parts of a literary work in relation to its total effect (e.g., "The form [structure] of this poem is very effective").

Formalism   A broad term for the various types of literary theory that advocate focusing attention on the text itself and not on extratextual factors. Formalist critics are interested in the formal elements of a literary text— structure, tone, characters, setting, symbols, linguistic features—and seek to create meaning by examining the relationships between these different parts of a text.

Fourth wall   The theatrical convention, dating from the nineteenth century, whereby an audience seems to be looking and listening through an invisible fourth wall, usually into a room in a private residence. The fourth wall is primarily associated with **realism** and domestic dramas.

Free verse   See **open form**.

Gender criticism   A broad term for literary criticism that highlights gender roles or relationships between the sexes. In this expansive sense, **feminist criticism** is a kind of gender criticism, although the latter term is most often applied to gay and lesbian approaches to literature that explore the construction of sexual identity.

Genre   A type or form of literature. While the major literary genres are **fiction**, **drama**, **poetry**, and exposition, many other subcategories of genres are recognized, including **comedy**, **tragedy**, **tragicomedy**, **romance**, **melodrama**, **epic**, **lyric**, **pastoral**, **novel**, **short story**, and so on.

Haiku   A lyric form, originating in Japan, of seventeen syllables in three lines, the first and third having five syllables and the second seven, presenting an image of a natural object or scene that expresses a distinct emotion or spiritual insight.

Half rhyme See **slant rhyme.**

Hamartia Sometimes translated as "tragic flaw" but more properly understood as an error or general character trait that leads to the downfall of a character in **tragedy.**

Heptameter A poetic line with seven metrical feet.

Hero, heroine Sometimes used to refer to any **protagonist,** the term more properly applies only to a great figure from legend or history or to a character who performs in a remarkably honorable and selfless manner.

Heroic couplets Couplets in **iambic pentameter** that usually end in a period. See Alexander Pope's poem "An Essay on Criticism." Also called *closed couplets.*

Hexameter A poetic line with six metrical feet. See also **alexandrine.**

Historical criticism A kind of literary criticism based on the notion that history and literature are often interrelated. For example, literary critics might read history books and various sorts of historical documents in order to gain insights into the composition and significance of a literary work.

Hubris An arrogance or inflated sense of self that can lead to a character's downfall. The **protagonists** of **tragedy** often suffer from hubris.

Hyperbole Exaggeration; a figure of speech in which something is stated more strongly than is logically warranted. Hyperbole is often used to make a point emphatically, as when Hamlet protests that he loves Ophelia

much more than her brother does: "Forty thousand brothers / Could not with all their quantity of love / Make up my sum" (5.1.239–41). See also Robert Burns's "A Red, Red Rose."

Iamb A metrical **foot** consisting of two syllables, an unaccented one followed by an accented one (˘´). In iambic meter (the most widely used of English metrical forms), iambs are the predominant foot in a line or poem. The following line from Thomas Gray's "Elegy Written in a Country Churchyard" is in **iambic pentameter:** "Thĕ cúr | fĕw tólls | thĕ knéll | ŏf párt | ĭng dáy." See **pentameter.**

Image (1) Sometimes called a "word-picture," an image is a word or group of words that refers to a sensory experience or to an object that can be known by one or more of the senses. **Imagery** signifies all such language in a poem or other literary work collectively and can involve any of the senses; see, for example, the first two stanzas of T. S. Eliot's poem "Preludes" or the narrator's description of the girl he loves in James Joyce's story "Araby": "The light from the lamp opposite our door caught the white curve of her neck, lit up her hair that rested there and, falling, lit up the hand upon the railing." See also **synesthesia.** (2) A metaphor or other comparison. **Imagery** in this sense refers to the characteristic that several images in a poem may have in common, as for example, the Christian imagery in William Blake's "The Lamb."

Imitation Since Aristotle, drama has been differentiated from fiction because it is said to rely on an imitation (in Greek, *mimesis*) of human actions rather than on a narration of them.

Implied metaphor Metaphor in which the *to be* verb is omitted and one aspect of the comparison is implied rather than stated directly. Whereas "a car thief is a dirty dog" is a direct metaphor, "some dirty dog stole my car" contains an implied metaphor.

Interlude A brief, usually comic, performance inserted between the **acts** of a play or between courses at a formal banquet. Interludes were most popular during the Renaissance.

Internal rhyme Rhyme that occurs with words within a line, words within lines near each other, or a word within a line and one at the end of the same or a nearby line. Edgar Allan Poe's poem "Annabel Lee" offers many examples: "chilling / And killing," "Can ever dissever," "And the stars never rise but I see the bright eyes."

Intertextuality The implied presence of previous texts within a literary work or as context, usually conveyed through allusion or choice of genre. An intertextual approach assumes that interpretation of a text is incomplete until the relation of the work to its predecessors—response, opposition, and development—has been considered.

Irony A feeling, tone, mood, or attitude arising from the awareness that what *is* (reality) is opposite from, and usually worse than, what *seems* to be (appearance). What a person says may be ironic (see **verbal irony**), and a discrepancy between what a character knows or means and what a reader or an audience knows can be ironic (see **dramatic irony**). A general situation also can be seen as ironic (see **situational irony**). Irony should not be confused with mere coincidence. See also **Socratic irony**.

Italian sonnet Generally speaking, a sonnet composed of an octave (an eight-line unit), rhyming *abbaabba*, and a sestet (a six-line unit), often rhyming *cdecde* or *cdcdcd*. The octave usually develops an idea, question, or problem; then the poem pauses, or "turns," and the sestet completes the idea, answers the question, or resolves the difficulty. Sometimes called a Petrarchan sonnet. See Gerard Manley Hopkins's "God's Grandeur."

Juxtaposition Placement of things side by side or close together for comparison or contrast, or to create something new from the union. See Alexander Pope's poem "An Essay on Criticism": "Now his fierce eyes with sparking fury glow, / Now sighs steal out, and tears begin to flow."

Line A sequence of words printed as a separate entity on a page; the basic structural unit in poetry (except in **prose poems**).

Lineation The arrangement of lines in a poem.

Literal In accordance with the primary or strict meaning of a word or words; not figurative or metaphorical.

Litotes See **understatement**.

Lyric Originally, a poem sung to the accompaniment of a lyre; now a short poem expressing the personal emotion and ideas of a single speaker.

Marxist criticism Deriving from Karl Marx's theories of economics and class struggle, Marxist criticism sees literature as a material product of work, one that reflects or contests the ideologies that generated its production and consumption.

Masculine rhyme   See **single rhyme**.

Melodrama   A type of play employing broadly drawn heroes and villains, suspenseful plots, music, and a triumph of good over evil. Melodrama thrived throughout the nineteenth century and remained popular into the twentieth.

Melody   One of the six **elements of drama** identified by Aristotle. Since the Greek **chorus** communicated through song and dance, melody was an important part of even the most serious play, though it is now largely confined to musical comedy.

Metaphor   A figure of speech in which two things usually thought to be dissimilar are treated as if they were alike and have characteristics in common: "Whose *palms are bulls* in china" (John Frederick Nims's "Love Poem"). See also **implied metaphor**.

Metaphysical poetry   The work of a number of seventeenth-century poets that was characterized by philosophical subtlety and intellectual rigor; subtle, often outrageous logic; an imitation of actual speech sometimes resulting in a "rough" meter and style; and far-fetched analogies. John Donne's "A Valediction: Forbidding Mourning" exemplifies the type. See also **conceit**.

Meter   A steady beat, or measured pulse, created by a repeating pattern of accents or syllables, or both.

Metonymy   A figure of speech in which the name of one thing is sub-stituted for something closely associated with it, as in "The *White House* announced today . . . ," a phrase in which the name of a building is substituted for the president or the staff members who issued the announcement; "He's got *a Constable* on his wall"; "The *trains* are on strike"; or *"Wall Street* is in a panic." In the last line of John Frederick Nims's "Love Poem," "All the toys of the world would break," *toys* is substituted for "things that give happiness" (as toys do to a child). See also **synecdoche**.

Mock epic   A literary form that imitates the grand style and conventions of the epic genre—the opening statement of a theme, an address to the muse, long formal speeches, and epic similes—but applies them to a subject unworthy of such exalted treatment. Also called *mock heroic*. See also **epic**.

Monometer   A poetic line with one metrical **foot**.

Motivation   What drives a character to act in a particular way. To be convincing to an audience, an actor must understand and make clear to the audience the character's motivation.

Narrative   A story in prose or verse; an account of events involving characters and a sequence of events told by a storyteller (narrator). A poem such as John Keats's "La Belle Dame sans Merci" tells a story and is thus a **narrative poem**. Usually, the characters can be analyzed and generally understood; the events unfold in a cause-and-effect sequence; and some unity can be found among the characters, plot, point of view, style, and theme. Novels as well as stories are most often narratives, and journalism commonly employs narrative form.

Narrative poem   See **narrative.**

Narrator   The storyteller, usually an observer who is narrating from a third-person point of view or a participant in the story's action speaking in the first person. Style and tone are important clues to the nature of a narrator and the validity and objectivity of the story he or she is telling. Montresor, the narrator of Edgar Allan Poe's "The Cask of Amontillado," creates his own self-portrait as he relates what has happened.

Naturalism, naturalistic   A style of writing or acting meant to mimic closely the patterns of ordinary life.

Near rhyme   See **slant rhyme.**

New comedy   An ancient form of **comedy** that told of initially forbidden but ultimately successful love and that employed **stock characters.** New comedy is particularly associated with the Greek playwright Menander (342–292 B.C.E.).

New Criticism   A kind of **formalism** that dominated Anglo-American literary criticism in the middle decades of the twentieth century. It emphasized close-reading, particularly of poetry, to discover how a work of literature functioned as a self-contained, self-referential aesthetic object.

New Historicism   A school of **historical criticism** that takes account of both what history has to teach us about literature *and* what literature has to teach us about history. New Historicists examine many different types of texts—government records, periodicals, private diaries, bills of sale—in order to re-create, as much as possible, the rich cultural context that surrounded

both an author and that author's original audience.

Novel   An extended prose narrative or work of prose fiction, usually published alone. Nathaniel Hawthorne's *The Scarlet Letter* is a fairly short novel, Herman Melville's *Moby-Dick, or, The Whale* a very long one. The length of a novel enables its author to develop characters, plot, and settings in greater detail than a short-story writer can.

Novella   Between the short story and the novel in size and complexity. Like them, the novella is a work of prose fiction. Sometimes it is called a long short story. Herman Melville's "Bartleby, the Scrivener" and Franz Kafka's "The Metamorphosis" are novellas.

Octameter   A poetic line with eight metrical feet.

Octave   The first eight lines of an **Italian sonnet.**

Ode   (1) A multipart song sung by the **chorus** of Greek drama. A classical ode consists of a **strophe** followed by an **antistrophe** and sometimes by a final section called the *epode.* (2) A long **lyric** poem, serious (often intellectual) in tone, elevated and dignified in style, dealing with a single theme. The ode is generally more complicated in form than other lyric poems. Some odes retain a formal division into strophe, antistrophe, and epode, which reflects the form's origins in Greek tragedy. See William Wordsworth's "Ode: Intimations of Immortality."

Old comedy   Comedy, such as that of Aristophanes, employing raucous (sometimes coarse) humor, elements of satire and farce, and often a critique of contemporary persons or political and social norms.

Omniscient narrator A narrator who seems to know everything about a story's events and characters, even their inner feelings. Usually, an omniscient narrator maintains emotional distance from the characters.

One act A short play that is complete in one **act**.

Onomatopoeia The use of words whose sounds supposedly resemble the sounds they denote (such as *thump, rattle, growl, hiss*), or a group of words whose sounds help to convey what is being described; for example, Emily Dickinson's poem "I heard a Fly buzz— when I died."

Open form A form free of any predetermined metrical and stanzaic patterns. Cf. **closed form**.

Orchestra In Greek theater, the area in front of the stage proper where the chorus performed its songs and dances. Later, a pit for musicians in front of the stage.

Organic form The idea, grounded in Plato and strong since the nineteenth century, that subject, **theme**, and **form** are essentially one, that a work "grows" from a central concept. A contrary idea, that literary works are unstable and irregular because of changes in linguistic meanings and literary conventions, has led to a critical approach called **deconstruction**.

Ottava rima An eight-line stanza in **iambic pentameter** rhyming *abab-abcc*.

Overstatement See **hyperbole**.

Oxymoron A figure of speech combining in one phrase (usually an adjective and a noun) two seemingly contradictory elements, such as "loving hate" or "feather of lead, bright smoke, cold fire, sick health" (from Shakespeare's *Romeo and Juliet*, 1.1.176–80). Oxymoron is a type of **paradox**.

Pantoum A poem composed of **quatrains** rhyming *abab* in which the second and fourth lines of each stanza serve as the first and third lines of the next, continuing through the last stanza, which repeats the first and third lines of the first stanza in reverse order.

Paradox A figure of speech in which a statement initially seeming self-contradictory or absurd turns out, seen in another light, to make good sense. The closing line of John Donne's sonnet "Death, be not proud" contains a paradox: "Death, thou shalt die." See also **oxymoron**.

Parallelism (1) A verbal arrangement in which elements of equal weight within phrases, sentences, or paragraphs are expressed in a similar grammatical order and structure. It can appear within a line or pair of lines ("And he was always quietly arrayed, / And he was always human when he talked"—Edwin Arlington Robinson, "Richard Cory") or, more noticeably, as a series of parallel items, as found in Langston Hughes's poem "Harlem." (2) A principle of poetic structure in which consecutive lines in **open form** are related by a line's repeating, expanding on, or contrasting with the idea of the line or lines before it, as in the poems of Walt Whitman.

Paraphrase   To restate a passage of literature or criticism in your own words, particularly useful as a method for taking research notes, or for interpreting a text. Generally, a paraphrase will be about equal in length to the passage being paraphrased, while a **summary** will be much shorter.

Parody   Now, a humorous or satirical imitation of a serious piece of literature or writing. In the sixteenth and seventeenth centuries, poets such as George Herbert practiced "sacred parody" by adapting secular lyrics to devotional themes.

Partial rhyme   See **slant rhyme**.

Pastoral   A poem (also called an *eclogue*, a *bucolic*, or an *idyll*) that expresses a city poet's nostalgic image of the simple, peaceful life of shepherds and other country folk in an idealized natural setting. Christopher Marlowe's "The Passionate Shepherd to His Love" uses some pastoral conventions, as do certain elegies.

Pause   See **caesura**.

Pentameter   A poetic line with five metrical feet.

Performance art   Loose term for a variety of performances that defy traditional categories of play, monologue, musical act, and so on. The term arose in the late twentieth century as a catch-all to name the growing number of nontraditional performances, many of which addressed controversial subjects and themes.

Peripeteia   A reversal or change of fortune for a character, for better or worse.

Persona   Literally, the mask through which actors spoke in Greek plays. In some critical approaches of recent decades, *persona* refers to the "character" projected by an author, the "I" of a narrative poem or novel, or the speaker whose voice is heard in a lyric poem. In this view, a poem is an artificial construct distanced from a poet's autobiographical self. Cf. **voice**.

Personification   A figure of speech in which something nonhuman is treated as if it had human characteristics or performed human actions. Sometimes it involves abstractions, as in Thomas Gray's phrase "Fair Science frowned" ("Elegy Written in a Country Churchyard"); science cannot literally frown. In other cases, concrete things are given human characteristics, as in the phrase "Wearing white for Eastertide" from A. E. Housman's poem "Loveliest of trees, the cherry now." Cherry trees do not actually wear clothes—but here they are being given, briefly, a human attribute. Difficulty can arise when personification is incorrectly defined as treating something nonhuman in terms of anything alive rather than what is specifically human; "the mouth of time," for instance, in Nancy Willard's poem "Questions My Son Asked Me, Answers I Never Gave Him" is metaphor, not personification, since animals as well as humans have mouths. See also **apostrophe**.

Petrarchan sonnet   See **Italian sonnet**.

Plagiarism   The act of closely imitating or outright adopting the language or ideas of another author and presenting them as one's own work without giving credit to the original author. This includes copying and pasting from any Web source. Most colleges and universities have codes of academic honesty forbidding such practices and imposing severe penalties—including expulsion from the institution in some cases—on students who are caught breaking them.

Plot (1) The sequence of major events in a story, usually related by cause and effect. **Plot development** refers to how the sequence evolves or is shaped. Plot and character are intimately related, since characters carry out the plot's action. Plots may be described as simple or complex, depending on their degree of complication. "Traditional" writers, such as Edgar Allan Poe and Guy de Maupassant, usually plot their stories tightly; modernist writers such as James Joyce employ looser, often ambiguous plots. (2) The action that takes place within the play. Of the six **elements of drama**, Aristotle considered plot to be the most important. Typical elements of plot include a **prologue** or **exposition**, **rising action**, **complication**, **climax**, **falling action**, and **catastrophe** or **denouement**.

Plot development See **plot**.

Poem A term whose meaning exceeds all attempts at definition. Here is a slightly modified version of the definition of William Harmon and C. Hugh Holman in *A Handbook to Literature* (1996): A poem is a literary composition, written or oral, typically characterized by imagination, emotion, sense impressions, and concrete language that invites attention to its own physical features, such as sound or appearance on the page.

Poetic diction In general, specialized language used in or considered

appropriate to poetry. In the late seventeenth and the eighteenth centuries, a refined use of language that excluded "common" speech from poetry as indecorous and substituted elevated circumlocutions, archaic synonyms, or such forms as *ope* and *e'er*.

Point of view One of the elements of fiction, point of view is the perspective, or angle of vision, from which a narrator presents a story. Point of view tells us about the **narrator** as well as about the characters, setting, and theme of a story. Two common points of view are *first-person narration* and *third-person narration*. If a narrator speaks of himself or herself as "I," the narration is in the first person; if the narrator's self is not apparent and the story is told about others from some distance, using "he," "she," "it," and "they," then third-person narration is likely in force. The point of view may be omniscient (all-knowing) or limited, objective or subjective. When determining a story's point of view, it is helpful to decide whether the narrator is reporting events as they are happening or as they happened in the past; is observing or participating in the action; and is or is not emotionally involved. Eudora Welty's story "A Worn Path" is told from the third-person objective point of view, since its narrator observes what the character is doing, thinking, and feeling, yet seems emotionally distant. Stories like Edgar Allan Poe's "The Cask of Amontillado" and James Joyce's "Araby" are told in the first-person subjective and limited point of view, since their narrators are very much involved in the action. In Kate Chopin's story "The Story of an Hour" (p. 89), shifting points of view enable us to see Mrs. Mallard from the outside, as her family does (third-person objective); learn about her most private emotional responses and secrets (third-person subjective); and hear her thoughts directly as if we were inside her mind (first-person subjective).

Postcolonial criticism   A branch of cultural studies that focuses on writing from former British (and other, mostly European) colonies around the world. Postcolonial criticism seeks to recover literary history that was ignored or suppressed during the colonial period, and to celebrate indigenous cultures of storytelling, drama, and poetry. At the same time, it attempts to understand how occupation by a more powerful colonizing nation disrupted and changed the course of history in a particular place.

Poststructuralism   Positing that no text can have a fixed or real meaning because no meaning can exist outside the network of other meanings to which it is connected, poststructuralism carries the insights of **structuralism** one step further. If, as structuralists claim, we can understand things only in terms of other things, then perhaps there is no center point of understanding, but only an endlessly interconnected web of ideas leading to other ideas leading to still other ideas. Meaning, then, is forever shifting and altering as our understanding of the world changes.

Primary source   Term used in writing about literature to refer to the literature itself—the poem, story, or play on which the writing is based. Cf. **secondary source**.

Prologue   A speech or scene that occurs before the beginning of the **plot** proper.

Properties, props   Any movable objects, beyond scenery and costumes, used in the performance of a play. Early drama was performed with few props, but as theater moved toward **realism**, props took on greater importance.

Proscenium arch   An arch across the front of a stage, sometimes with a curtain. The proscenium frames the action and provides a degree of separation between the actors and the audience.

Prose poem   A poem printed as prose, with lines wrapping at the right margin rather than being divided through predetermined line breaks. See Carolyn Forché's "The Colonel."

Prosody   The principles of versification, especially of meter, rhythm, rhyme, and stanza forms.

Protagonist   The lead character of a play, though not necessarily a **hero** in the classic sense.

Psychological literary criticism   A broad term for the various types of literary theory that focus on the inner workings of the human psyche and the ways in which they manifest themselves in literature. Psychological critics often interpret literature as a psychologist might interpret a dream or a wish, often paying special attention to unstated motives and to the unconscious states of mind in characters, authors, or readers.

Pun   A play on words based on the similarity in sound between two words having very different meanings. Also called *paronomasia*. See the puns on "heart" and "kindly" in Sir Thomas Wyatt's poem "They flee from me."

Quantitative verse Verse whose meter is based on the length of syllables. (Phonetic length was a distinguishing feature of ancient Greek and Latin, whereas English is an accentual language.) Classical poetry exhibits a great variety of meters, and some English poets in the late 1500s attempted to fashion English verse on this principle. In *Evangeline*, Henry Wadsworth Longfellow used dactylic hexameter in imitation of Virgil's *Aeneid*, but defined it by accent, not quantity. Cf. **accentual-syllabic verse**.

Quatrain A **stanza** of four lines or other four-line unit within a larger form, such as a **sonnet**.

Queer theory One of the more recent and more challenging critical schools to emerge out of critical interest in gender. Queer theorists, like all literary critics, differ substantially in their focus: Some queer theorists are interested in studying literary texts written by authors known or suspected to be gay, lesbian, bisexual, or transgender. Other queer theorists are interested in portrayals of gay or lesbian characters in literature. Still others seek a "queer subtext" in canonical works of literature that have long been considered heteronormative.

Reader-response criticism The various theories of reader-response criticism hold that a text is an interaction between author and reader, and a text can never be complete unless readers bring to it their own unique insights. Reading, then, is not a passive attempt to understand a text but is itself an act of creation, no less than writing.

Realism Any drama (or other art) that seeks to closely mimic real life.

Realism more specifically refers to a sort of drama that rose in opposition to **melodrama** in the late-nineteenth and early-twentieth centuries and that attempted to avoid some of the more artificial **conventions** of theater and present the problems of ordinary people living their everyday lives.

Recognition See **anagnorsis**.

Refrain One or more identical or deliberately similar lines repeated throughout a poem, such as the final line of a stanza or a block of lines between stanzas or sections.

Resolution A satisfying outcome that effectively ends the conflict of a play.

Rhyme The repetition of the accented vowel sound of a word and all succeeding consonant sounds. See also **exact rhyme; slant rhyme**.

Rhyme royal An alternative term for **Chaucerian stanza** coined by King James I of Scotland in his poem *The Kingis Quair* ("The King's Book"), written about 1424.

Rhyme scheme The pattern of end-rhymes in a poem or stanza usually represented by a letter assigned to each word-sound, the same word-sounds having the same letter (e.g., a **quatrain's** rhyme scheme might be described as *abcb*).

Rhythm The patterned "movement" of language created by the choice of words and their arrangement, usually described through such metaphors as fast or slow, smooth or halting, graceful or rough, deliberate or frenzied, syncopated or disjointed.

Rhythm in poetry is affected by, in addition to meter, such factors as line length; line endings; pauses (or lack of them) within lines; spaces within, at the beginning or end of, or between lines; word choice; and combinations of sounds.

Rising action The increasingly tense and complicated action leading up to the **climax** in a traditionally structured play.

Rising meter A foot (usually an iamb or an anapest) in which the final, accented syllable is preceded by one or two unaccented syllables, thus giving a sense of stepping up. Cf. **falling meter**.

Romance A play neither wholly comic nor wholly tragic, often containing elements of the supernatural. The best-known examples are Shakespeare's late plays, such as *The Winter's Tale* and *The Tempest*, which have a generally comic structure but are more ruminative in theme and spirit than traditional **comedy**.

Run-on line A line whose sense and grammatical structure continue into the next line. In the following lines by William Stafford ("Traveling through the Dark"), the first line is run-on, the second end-stopped: "Traveling through the dark I found a deer / dead on the edge of the Wilson River road." Also called *enjambment*. Cf. **end-stopped line**.

Sarcasm A harsh and cutting form of **verbal irony**, often involving apparent praise that is obviously not meant: "Oh, no, these are fine. I *prefer* my eggs thoroughly charred."

Satire A work, or manner within a work, employing **comedy** and **irony** to mock a particular human characteristic or social institution. Generally, a satirist wants the audience not only to laugh but also to change its opinions or actions.

Scansion The division of metrical verse into feet in order to determine and label its meter. Scanning a poem involves marking its stressed syllables with an accent mark (´) and its unstressed syllables with a curved line (˘), and using a vertical line to indicate the way a line divides into feet, then describing (or labeling) the type of foot used most often and the line length— that is, the number of feet in each line. See also **foot** and **line**.

Scene One of the secondary divisions within an **act** of a play.

Secondary source Outside source used in writing about literature: biographical, historical, or critical writing that discusses the literature but is not the literature itself. (The literature itself is considered a **primary source**.)

Sestet The last six lines of an **Italian sonnet**.

Sestina A lyric poem consisting of six six-line **stanzas** and a three-line concluding stanza (or "envoy"). The last words of the lines of the first stanza must be used as the last words of the lines of the other five stanzas in a specified pattern (the first line ends with the last word of the last line of the previous stanza, the second line with that of the first line of the previous stanza, the third line with that of the previous fifth line, the fourth line with that of the previous second line, the fifth line with that of the previous fourth line, the sixth line with that of the previous third line). The three-line envoy must use the end-words of lines 5, 3, and 1 from the first stanza, in that order, as its last words and must include the first stanza's other three end-words within its lines.

Set   The stage dressing for a play, consisting of backdrops, furniture, and similar large items.

Setting   One of the elements of fiction, setting is the context for the action: the time, place, culture, and atmosphere in which it occurs. A work may have several settings; the relation among them may be significant to the meaning of the work. In Nathaniel Hawthorne's short story "Young Goodman Brown," for example, the larger setting is seventeenth-century Puritan Salem, Massachusetts, but Brown's mysterious journey is set in a forest, and its prelude and melancholy aftermath are set in the village.

Shakespearean sonnet   See **English sonnet**.

Shaped poem   See **concrete poem**.

Short story   A short work of narrative fiction whose plot, characters, settings, point of view, style, and theme reinforce one another, often in subtle ways, creating an overall unity.

Simile   Expression of a direct similarity, using such words as *like, as,* or *than,* between two things usually regarded as dissimilar, as in "Shrinking from far *headlights pale as a dime*" (John Frederick Nims's "Love Poem"). It is important to distinguish *simile* from *comparison,* in which the two things joined by "like" or "as" are *not* dissimilar.

Single rhyme   A rhyme in which the stressed, rhyming syllable is the final syllable: *west* and *vest, away* and *today.* Formerly called "masculine rhyme."

Situational irony   The mood evoked when an action intended to have a certain effect turns out to have a different and more sinister effect. See Thomas Hardy's poem "The Convergence of the Twain."

Slant rhyme   Consonance at the ends of lines; for example, *Room* and *Storm, firm* and *Room,* and *be* and *Fly* in Emily Dickinson's "I heard a Fly buzz—when I died." It can also be internal, if repeated enough to form a discernible pattern.

Socratic irony   A pose of self-deprecation, or of belittling oneself, in order to tease the reader into deeper insight.

Soliloquy   A speech delivered by a character who is alone onstage or otherwise out of hearing of the other characters. Since the character is effectively speaking to himself or herself, a soliloquy often serves as a window into the character's mind and heart.

Sonnet   A fourteen-line poem usually written in **iambic pentameter;** originally lyrical love poems, sonnets came to be used also for meditations on religious themes, death, and nature and are now open to all subjects. Some variations in form have been tried: Sir Philip Sidney's "Loving in truth, and fain in verse my love to show" (1591) is written in hexameters; George Meredith wrote sixteen-line sonnets; John Milton's "On the New Forcers of

Conscience under the Long Parliament," written around 1646, is a "caudate" (tailed) sonnet with a six-line coda appended; and Gerard Manley Hopkins designed "Pied Beauty" as a "curtal" (abbreviated) sonnet (six lines in place of the octave, then four lines, and a half-line ending in place of a sestet). See **English sonnet** and **Italian sonnet**.

Sonnet sequence   A group of sonnets arranged so as to imply a narrative progression in the speaker's experience or attitudes; used especially in the sixteenth century. Also called a *sonnet cycle*.

Speaker   The persona(e) voicing the poem. The speaker is sometimes the poet, though other times a poem may speak from a different perspective.

Spectacle   The purely visual elements of a play, including the **sets**, costumes, **props**, lighting, and special effects. Of the six **elements of drama** he identified, Aristotle considered spectacle to be the least important.

Spenserian sonnet   A variation of the **English sonnet** that employs the structure of three quatrains followed by a couplet but joins the quatrains by linking rhymes: *abab bcbc cdcd ee*.

Spenserian stanza   A stanza of nine iambic lines, the first eight in pentameter and the ninth in hexameter, rhyming *ababbcbcc*. They are used in Edmund Spenser's *The Faerie Queene* (1590, 1596) and in such romantic narrative poems as John Keats's *The Eve of St. Agnes* (1820) and Percy Bysshe Shelley's *Adonais* (1824).

Spondee   A metrical **foot** made up of two stressed syllables (´´), with no unstressed syllables. Spondees could not, of course, be the predominant foot in a poem; they are usually substituted for iambic or trochaic feet as a way of increasing emphasis, as in this line from John Donne's "Batter my heart, three-personed God" (1633): "As yet | but knock, | breathe, shine, | and seek | to mend."

Sprung rhythm   See **accentual meter**.

Stage business   Minor physical activity performed by actors on stage, often involving **props**, intended to strengthen **characterization** or modulate tension in a play.

Stage directions   Written instructions in the script telling actors how to move on the stage or how to deliver a particular line. To facilitate the reading of scripts and to distinguish them from simple dialogue, stage directions are interspersed throughout the text, typically placed in parentheses and set in italics.

Stage left, stage right   Areas of the stage seen from the point of view of an actor facing an audience. Stage left, therefore, is on the audience's right-hand side, and vice versa.

Stanza   A grouping of poetic lines into a section, either according to form—each section having the same number of lines and the same prosody (see Sir Thomas Wyatt's "They flee from me")—or according to thought, creating irregular units comparable to paragraphs in prose (see William Wordsworth's "Ode: Intimations of Immortality").

Stichomythia Short lines of dialogue quickly alternating between two characters.

Stock character Any of a number of traditional characters easily identified by a single, stereotypical characteristic. Stock characters include innocent young women, rakish young men, clever servants, and so forth.

Stress See **accent.**

Strophe The first part of a choral ode in Greek drama. The strophe was traditionally sung as the **chorus** moved from **stage right** to **stage left.**

Structuralism Based on the work of anthropologists, linguists, and philosophers of the mid-twentieth century who sought to understand how humans think and communicate, structuralism is concerned with the cognitive and cultural structures that help us understand and interpret literary texts. The basic insight at the heart of the movement is the realization that we understand nothing in isolation, but rather that every piece of knowledge is part of a network of associations.

Structure (1) The framework— the general plan, outline, or organizational pattern—of a literary work; (2) narrower patterns within the overall framework. Cf. **form.**

Style One of the elements of fiction, style refers to the diction (choice of words), syntax (arrangement of words), and other linguistic features of a literary work. Just as no two people have identical fingerprints or voices, so no two writers use words in exactly the same way. Style distinguishes one writer's language from another's. William Faulkner and Ernest Hemingway, two major modern writers, had very different styles.

Subplot A secondary **plot** that exists in addition to the main plot and involves the minor characters. In **tragedy,** particularly, a subplot might provide **comic relief.**

Substitution The use of a different kind of foot in place of the one normally demanded by the predominant meter of a poem, as a way of adding variety, emphasizing the dominant foot by deviating from it, speeding up or slowing down the pace, or signaling a switch in meaning.

Subtext The unspoken meaning, sense, or **motivation** of a scene or character.

Summary A brief recap of the most important points in a work of literature, such as plot, character, setting, etc.

Surrealism An artistic movement that attempted to portray or interpret the workings of the unconscious mind, especially as realized in dreams, by an irrational, noncontextual choice and arrangement of images or objects. Now more often used to refer to anything defying the normal sense of reality.

Syllabic verse A metrical pattern in which all lines in a poem have the same number of **syllables** (as in Sylvia Plath's "Metaphors") or all the first lines of its stanzas have the same number, all second lines the same, and so on (see Dylan Thomas's "Fern Hill")—while the stressed syllables are random in number and placement.

Syllable A unit of language consisting of one uninterrupted sound.

"Ferry" (feh/ree) has two syllables, for example.

Symbol Something that is itself and also stands for something else; a literary symbol is a prominent or repeated image or action that is present in a story, poem, or play and can be seen, touched, smelled, heard, tasted, or experienced imaginatively, but also conveys a cluster of abstract meanings beyond itself. Most critics agree that the wallpaper in Charlotte Perkins Gilman's short story "The Yellow Wallpaper," the tiger in William Blake's poem "The Tyger," and the glass animals in Tennessee Williams's play *The Glass Menagerie*, for example, carry symbolic meaning. See also **archetype**.

Symbolism The use of objects or events to suggest meaning beyond their immediate, physical presence. Symbolism exists in all genres of literature, but in drama it might include visual or sound elements as well as language.

Synecdoche A special kind of **metonymy** in which a part of a thing is substituted for the whole, as in the commonly used phrases "give me a hand," "lend me your ears," or "many mouths to feed." See, for example, "whose *hands* shipwreck vases" and "For should your *hands* drop white and empty" (John Frederick Nims's "Love Poem").

Synesthesia Description of one kind of sense experience in relation to another, such as attribution of color to sounds ("blue notes") and vice versa ("a loud tie") or of taste to sounds ("sweet music"). See, for example, "With Blue — uncertain stumbling Buzz—" (Emily Dickinson's "I heard a Fly buzz—when I died").

Tercet A **stanza** of three lines, each usually ending with the same rhyme; but see **terza rima**. Cf. **triplet**.

Terza rima A poetic form consisting of three-line **stanzas (tercets)** with interlinked rhymes, *aba bcb cdc ded efe*, and so on, made famous by Dante's use of it in *The Divine Comedy*.

Tetrameter A poetic line with four metrical feet. Robert Frost's line "The woods are lovely, dark, and deep" ("Stopping by Woods on a Snowy Evening") is an example of iambic tetrameter.

Text Traditionally, a piece of writing. In recent **reader-response criticism**, "text" has come to mean the words with which the reader interacts; in this view, a story, poem, or play is not an object, not a shape on the page or a spoken performance, but what is apprehended and completed in the reader's mind.

Theater in the round A circular stage completely surrounded by seating for the audience.

Theater of the absurd/of cruelty See **Absurd, theater of the; Cruelty, theater of**.

Theme The central idea embodied by or explored in a literary work; the general concept, explicit or implied, that the work incorporates and makes persuasive to the reader. Other literary elements, including characters, plot, settings, point of view, figurative language, symbols, and style, contribute to a theme's development.

Thesis statement A few sentences, usually located toward the beginning of a paper, declaring the position the author plans to take on the proposed topic.

Third-person narrator The type of narration being used if a storyteller is not identified, does not speak of himself or herself with the pronoun *I*, asserts no connection between the narrator and the characters in the story, and tells the story with some objectivity and distance, using the pronouns *he, she, it,* and *they*—but not *I*. Eudora Welty chose third-person narration to tell the moving story of Old Phoenix in "A Worn Path," because as a writer she wanted distance.

Title The name attached to a work of literature. For poetry, a title in some cases is an integral part of a poem and needs to be considered in interpreting it. In other cases, a title has been added as a means of identifying a poem and is not integral to its interpretation. Sometimes a poem is untitled and the first line is used as a convenient way of referring to it, but should not be thought of as a title and does not follow the capitalization rules for titles.

Tone The implied attitude, or "stance," toward the subject and toward the reader or audience in a literary work; the "tone of voice" it seems to project (serious or playful; exaggerated or understated; formal or informal; ironic or straightforward; or a complex mixture of more than one of these). For example, the tone of Toni Cade Bambara's story "The Lesson" is streetwise and tough, the voice of its first-person narrator.

Tragedy A play in which the **plot** moves from relative stability to death or other serious sorrow for the

protagonist. A traditional tragedy is written in a grand style and shows a **hero** of high social stature brought down by **peripeteia** or by events beyond his or her control.

Tragicomedy A play in which **tragedy** and **comedy** are mingled in roughly equal proportion.

Transferred epithet A figure of speech in which a modifier that ought, strictly, to apply to one word is transferred to another word that it does not strictly fit. In "The drunk clambering on his undulant floor" (in John Frederick Nims's "Love Poem"), the drunk's perception, not the floor, is undulating.

Trimeter A poetic line with three metrical feet.

Triolet A verse form of eight lines with only two rhymes, rhyming *abaaabab*. The first two lines repeat in the last two lines, with the fourth line the same as the first line.

Triplet A group of three consecutive lines with the same rhyme, often used for variation in a long sequence of couplets. Cf. **tercet**.

Trochee A metrical **foot** consisting of two syllables, an accented one followed by an unaccented one (˘ ˘). In trochaic meter, trochees are the predominant foot in a line or poem. The following lines from William Blake's introduction to *Songs of Innocence* (1789) are in trochaic meter (each line lacking the final unaccented syllable): "Píping | dówn thĕ | vállĕys | wíld, / Pípiňg | Sóngs ŏf | pléasănt | glée, / Ońn ă | clóud Ĭ | sáw ă | chíld, / Ańd hĕ | laúghiňg | sáid tŏ| me."

Understatement   A figure of speech expressing something in an unexpectedly restrained way. Paradoxically, understatement can be a way of emphasizing something, of making people think "there must be more to it than that." When Mercutio in Shakespeare's *Romeo and Juliet*, after being stabbed by Tybalt, calls his wound "a scratch, a scratch" (3.1.92), he is understating, for the wound is serious—he calls for a doctor in the next line, and he dies a few minutes later.

Unities   The elements of a play that help an audience understand the play as a unified whole. Aristotle commented on the unities of time (the action of a play usually takes place within approximately one day) and action (the play should have a single, principal plot line). Renaissance critics added a third unity—unity of place (the play has only one main setting). Though Aristotle intended these merely as observations about the most successful dramas he had seen, some later playwrights took them as inflexible laws of drama.

Unity   The oneness of a short story. Generally, each of a story's elements has a unity of its own, and all reinforce one another to create an overall unity. Although a story's unity may be evident on first reading, more often discovering the unity requires rereading, reflection, and analysis. Readers who engage in these actions experience the pleasure of seeing a story come to life.

Upstage   As a noun or an adjective, the part of the stage farthest from the audience, at the back of the playing area. As a verb, to draw the audience's attention away from another actor onstage.

Verbal irony   A figure of speech in which what is said is nearly the opposite of what is meant (such as saying "Lovely day out" when the weather actually is miserable). The name *Arnold Friend*, in Joyce Carol Oates's "Where Are You Going, Where Have You Been?" is an example, for Arnold is anything but a friend to Connie.

Villanelle   A nineteen-line lyric poem divided into five **tercets** and a final four-line stanza, rhyming *aba aba aba aba aba abaa*. Line 1 is repeated to form lines 6, 12, and 18; line 3 is repeated to form lines 9, 15, and 19. See Elizabeth Bishop's "One Art" and Dylan Thomas's "Do not go gentle into that good night."

Voice   The supposed authorial presence in poems that do not obviously employ **persona** as a distancing device.

Well-made play   A type of play that rose to prominence in the nineteenth century and that relied for its effect on clever, causal plotting and a series of startling discoveries or revelations rather than on subtleties of character or language.

Index

abstract, 132
accents, 99
accentual poems, 99
active reading, 8
analysis, 59, 114
annotation, 8
antagonists, 73
archetypes, 174
argument, 22
assonance, 98
attributed quotation, 42
author, 15

ballad, 99
brainstorming, 27

caesuras, 100
canon, 169, 171
character, 48, 72, 96, 111,
  167
  motivation of, 9
characterization, 59
citation, 132, 146
closed-book exam, 67
close reading, 56
commentaries, 138
common knowledge, 143
comparison and contrast, 63, 92
conclusions, 30, 68
consonance, 99
critical reading, 7
cultural context, 16
cultural studies, 170

deconstruction, 177
dialogue, 111
diction, 75, 111
documenting sources, 143
drafting, 29, 139
drama, elements of, 111

editing
  peer, 38

proofreading and, 35,
  140
revising and, 32, 140
elements
  of drama, 111
  of fiction, 72
  of poetry, 96
ellipses, 44
enjambment, 100
epic, 96
essay exams, 66
  closed-book, 67
  open-book, 67, 68
evaluative criticism,
  166
explication, 56, 107

feminist criticism, 168
fiction, elements of, 72
figurative language, 56
final editing, 35
first-person narrator, 73
floating quotations, 42
form, in poetry, 99
formalism, 167
free verse, 100

gender criticism, 168
genre, 14
global revisions, 32

hidden meaning, 7
historical criticism, 172
iambic pentameter, 99
imagery, 9, 97
implied listener, 97
integrated quotations, 42
intellectual property, 141
interlibrary loan, 134
Internet, 134
interpretive criticism, 166
introductions, 30, 68
irony, 59

journal articles, 133
journal keeping, 12
juxtaposition, 14, 98

language, 9, 74, 98
lineation, 100
listener, 97
literary analysis, 59, 114
literary criticism, 166
literary theory, 166
local revisions, 34
lyric poem, 96

magazines, 133, 155
manuscript form, 49
Marxist criticism, 169
melody, 112
meter, 99
MLA format, 49, 143
motivation, 9

narrative poem, 96
narrator, 73
New Criticism, 16, 167
New Historicism, 173
note taking, 11

omniscient narrator, 73
online indexes, 131
open-book exam, 67, 68
outline, 28

paraphrase, 137
peer editing, 38
periodicals, 133, 154
plagiarism, 140
plot, 72, 96, 111
    development of, 59
poetry, elements of, 96
point of view, 73, 96
postcolonial criticism, 171
poststructuralism, 177
primary source, 130
proofreading, 35, 68, 140
protagonists, 73
psychological literary criticism, 173

Queer theory, 169
quotations, 42, 137, 149

reader, 17
reader-response criticism, 160, 174
reading
    active, 8
    critical, 7

note taking and, 20
    rereading, 6
reference materials, 13
research sources, 130
response, 53
revising, 32, 140
    local, 34
rhyme, 98

scansion, 99
scholarly journals, 133,
    154
secondary sources, 130
set, 111
setting, 167
    in drama, 112
    in fiction, 73
    in poetry, 96
short stories, 74
slant rhyme, 99
sonnet, 99, 101
sound and sense, 98
sources
    evaluating, 135
    in research, 130
    working with, 136
speaker, 96, 97
spectacle, 112
stage directions, 111
stanza, 100
structuralism, 176
structure, 14, 167
style, 9, 14, 74
summary, 51, 138
syllabic poems, 99
syllables, 99
symbol, 59, 74, 167
symbolism, 74

text, 132
theme, 74, 111
thesis, 23, 139
third-person narrator, 73
tone, 59, 74, 167
topic, 21
tragedy, 111
transitions, 31

villanelle, 99

works cited list, 149
writing process, 21
    argument, 22
    prewriting, 21
    thesis, 23